The Angel of Yahweh

In Jewish and Christian History

John Owen (1616-1683)
Peter Allix (1641-1717)
Gerard De Gols (1676-1737)

Edited and Compiled
by Douglas Van Dorn

The Angel of Yahweh

In Jewish and Christian History

John Owen (1616-1683)
Peter Allix (1641-1717)
Gerard De Gols (1676-1737)

Edited and Compiled
by Douglas Van Dorn

Waters of Creation Publishing
Dacono, Colorado

John Owen. First published in 1668 as an exercitation in *Exercitations on the Epistle to the Hebrews, I* (London: Printed by Robert White for Nathaniel Ponder). More recently in *An Exposition of the Epistle to the Hebrews*, ed. W. H. Goold, vol. 18, Works of John Owen (Edinburgh: Johnstone and Hunter, 1854), reprinted by The Banner of Truth.

Peter Allix. First Published in 1689 as an appendix in *The Judgment of the Ancient Jewish Church, Against the Unitarians*. 1699 edition published by R. Chiswell, London.

Gerard De Gols. First Published in 1726 as an *A Vindication of the Worship of the Lord Jesus Christ as the Supreme God, in all the Dispensations, Patriarchal, Mosaick and Christian: Demonstrating, that Christ was so Known and Worship'd in all Ages, from Adam to this Day*, published by J. Darby and T. Browne, London.

Cover Design: Doug, Breanna, and Alesha Van Dorn

ISBN-13: 978-0-9862376-8-3 (Waters of Creation Publishing)

Contents

EDITOR'S INTRODUCTION.. 1

JOHN OWEN 19

   PROMISES OF THE MESSIAH VINDICATED................. 21

PETER ALLIX... 57

   A DISSERTATION CONCERNING THE ANGEL
   WHO IS CALLED THE REDEEMER............................... 59

   EXCERPTS FROM "JUDGMENTS OF THE JEWISH
   CHURCH" 97

      CHAP. VIII: APOCRYPHAL AUTHORS KNEW A TRINITY........................ 97
      CHAP. XII: THE JEWS IN THE OT A PERSON CALLED THE WORD ... 117
      CHAP. XIII: THE ANGEL OF THE LORD IS THE WORD OF GOD 139
      CHAP. XIV: THE JEWS CALLED THE ANGEL THE WORD OF GOD ... 155
      CHAP. XV: THE JEWS CALLED THE ANGEL THE WORD (PART II) ... 175

GERARD DE GOLS 199

   EXCERPTS FROM: A VINDICATION OF THE WORSHIP
   OF THE LORD JESUS CHRIST AS THE SUPREME GOD
   201

      CHAP. V: THAT THE FATHER AND SON ARE EQUALLY GOD 201
      CHAP. VI: DUTIES REQUIRED TO GOD REQUIRED TO CHRIST......... 257
      CHAP. VII: CHRIST WORSHIPED AND THE LOGOS EXPLAINED 281
      CHAP. VIII: CHRIST WORSHIPED IN THE AGE OF THE PATRIARCHS . 297
      CHAP. IX: CHRIST WORSHIP AFTER MOSES 331

GLOSSARY OF WORKS & AUTHORS CITED............. 383

AUTHOR INDEX 395

SCRIPTURE INDEX... 399

Other Books by Waters of Creation

Waters of Creation: A Biblical-Theological Study of Baptism (2009)
Galatians: A Supernatural Justification (2012)
Giants: Sons of the Gods (2013)
Covenant Theology: A Reformed Baptist Primer (2014)
From the Shadows to the Savior: Christ in the Old Testament (2015)
The Unseen Realm: Q & A Companion (2016)
Five Solas (2019)

Christ in All Scripture Series

Vol. 1. Appearances of the Son of God Under the Old Testament by John Owen (2019)

Vol. 2. A Dissertation Concerning the Angel who is called the Redeemer and Other Select Passages by Peter Allix (2020)

Vol. 3. The Worship of the Lord Jesus Christ in the Old Testament by Gerard De Gols (2020)

Vol. 4. The Angel of the LORD In Early Jewish, Christian, and Reformation History, a compilation of Allix, Owen, and De Gols (2020)

Vol. 5. Christ in the Old Testament: Promised, Patterned, and Present revised and expanded second edition of the previously titled: *From the Shadows to the Savior: Christ in the Old Testament* by Douglas Van Dorn (2020).

Vol. 6. Jesus: Who, What, Where, When, Why? by Douglas Van Dorn (2020)

For more information, articles, radio shows, and broadcasts go to: dougvandorn.com

Editor's Introduction

Reason for This Series

I am convinced, after studying the topic of Christ in the Old Testament in some depth for the last several years, and having lived in modern conservative Reformed and Evangelical Christian circles for nearly 50 years, that too many Christians (past and present) far too often presuppose and/or superimpose a kind of Unitarian grid upon the OT. This is a very Liberal way of reading the Scripture, out of line with orthodox Christian teaching throughout history.

It isn't that this is done malevolently, for these same Christians often do see Christ in the OT in one way or another. I am not talking about a Christianity that outright denies the deity of Jesus. In fact, I'm talking about a Christianity that loves him as the *Theanthropos*—The God-man. It isn't that this is done deliberately either. At least, not usually. I would say it is more of a subconscious decision. We speak about Christ being there in type and shadow, but to say that he was actually there—*in person?* This is a hard pill for many to swallow. I had more than one professor in my conservative Baptist schooling tell the students that to see Christ or a Trinity actually there, as if any of the human authors could have deliberately written about these things when they wrote the OT books, was reading the NT back into the Old. It was eisegesis, not exegesis.

In this way, too many of us presuppose that the Jewish church did not, indeed *could not* have known the Christ to write about him actually being present in their midst. He simply wasn't there among them. At best, only the Father was. Yet, somehow, we think, they could foresee his coming. But this is a strange oxymoron, because that would seem to itself presuppose that they knew he already existed, if the Messiah they prophesied about was truly God. But if they knew he already existed, why couldn't he have known them or made himself know to them? Nevertheless, at the end of the day when we ask questions like *Job knew his Redeemer* (Job 19:25) *to be Christ?* Or *Solomon comprehended the Son of a Father who has ascended to heaven* (Prov 30:4) *was Christ?* Or *Abraham believed God* (Gen 15:6), *whom he knew to be Christ?* Not possible is a very common answer to hear.

As a case in point, there is an ancient manuscript variant in Jude 5 where one family of texts say "Jesus" lead Israel in the Exodus, while another family reads the "Lord" did it. Apparently, this discussion has been around for a long, long time. Some scribe was asking the same question: *Jude could call the Savior of the Exodus "Jesus?"* Not possible. So he changed "Jesus" to "Lord." The renowned NT scholar Bruce Metzger ran into the same skepticism I have run into in conservative circles on this very same variant when he was working on his *Textual Commentary on the Greek New Testament* in a committee with a bunch of other scholars. He wrote, "A majority of the Committee was of the opinion that the [Jesus] reading was difficult to the point of impossibility."[1]

Why? Because we presuppose it, that's why. Therefore, any OT text you can think of where a Christian has argued that we see the Trinity or Christ ("Holy, Holy, Holy" or "Let us make man in our image") must be dismissed out of hand.

This Work and Its Place in this Series

The work before you a volume in the series: Christ in All Scripture, by Waters of Creation Publishing. At present, this series consists or will consist of the following volumes:

---

[1] Bruce Manning Metzger, United Bible Societies, *A Textual Commentary on the Greek New Testament, Second Edition a Companion Volume to the United Bible Societies' Greek New Testament (4th Rev. Ed.)* (London; New York: United Bible Societies, 1994), 657.

- *A Dissertation Concerning the Angel who is called the Redeemer and Other Select Passages* by Peter Allix
- *Appearances of the Son of God Under the Old Testament* by John Owen
- *The Worship of the Lord Jesus Christ in the Old Testament* by Gerard De Gols
- *The Angel of the LORD in Early Jewish, Christian, and Reformation History*, a compilation of Allix, Owen, and De Gols
- *Christ in the Old Testament: Promised, Patterned, and Present* by Douglas Van Dorn
- *Jesus: Who, What, Where, When, Why?* by Douglas Van Dorn

The works presented here are an *exercitation*, by John Owen; *A Dissertation Concerning the Angel who is called the Redeemer* and excerpts from *The Judgment of the Ancient Jewish Church Against The Unitarians* by Peter Allix; and portions of *A Vindication of the worship of the Lord Jesus Christ as the Supreme God* by Gerard De Gols. Hopefully, having all three of these divines together in one book will make it more convenient to help you read all three works, as indeed all three add things the others are missing and together they reinforce this extremely important topic.

John Owen

John Owen is by far the most famous of the three. He is also the first to write on the topic of the three, and the other two certainly knew of his work. Owen was born in 1616 in Stadhampton, Oxfordshire England. Though of Welsh descent, he became one of the best known of all the English Puritans. He was married to Mary Rooke, who gave him 11 children, 10 of which died in infancy. He became pastor at Coggeshall in Essex but found himself also influencing politics thanks to his friendship with Oliver Cromwell, through whom he eventually found himself dean of Christ Church Cathedral in Oxford. He published the *Exercitations* in 1668 along with his comments on the early parts of Hebrews. Owen died in 1683.[2]

His exercitation is a kind of preliminary practice to understanding the book of Hebrews and the person of Jesus Christ that Owen printed in the first volume of his commentary on that book. He called it "Promises of the Messiah Vindicated." His treatment of the Angel deals with, among other things, significant passages in Scripture, Philo, and the Targums.

I would recommend Owen's *Exercitation* and the attached quotations in this volume for anyone particularly needing or desiring to see the orthodoxy of this understanding of the Angel of the LORD. The antiquity of the view combined with the pedigree of those espousing it should be deeply considered when coming to your own conclusions. As for John Owen, it is

---

[2] Allow me to recommend a new short biography: *John Owen: The Prince of Puritans*, Wrath and Grace Biographies (Columbus, GA: Wrath and Grace Publishing, 2019), by my friend Luke Walker.

difficult to find a more celebrated or respected Puritan. His views are held in great esteem and should carry no little authority as a pastor/scholar of unsurpassed reputation, reverence, and respect.

Peter Allix

Who was Peter Allix? As the *Dictionary of National Biography* tells it, Peter (Pierre) Allix was born in 1641, the son of Pierre Allix, pastor of the Reformed Church of France at Alençon, where he was born. He attended protestant universities in Saumur and Sedan. He was distinguished in Hebrew and Syriac and used it to work on a new translation of the Bible. He became a pastor at St. Agobille in Champagne, France, but was soon moved in 1670 to Paris to preside over the principle Reformed church of the city. By 1685, due to political unrest, he fled France for England, where he quickly learned the language, nationalized, and began publishing. He received a D. D. from Oxford and Cambridge in 1690. His popularity and reputation as a preeminent preacher and scholar soon reached none other than Louis XIV, who wanted him to return to France. Allix staunchly refused. He died in 1717.

Allix's "dissertation" is like a letter. Hywel Clifford calls the work, "A brief conversation about [the Angel's] meaning that he had recently had with an unconvinced listener (addressed as 'Sir', and not only with politesse but also with rigour and detail throughout)."[3] Its contents are a deep historical study of Genesis 48:15-16.

This short passage is a two-verse prayer by Jacob addressed to his son Joseph. It is a crucial text to any study of the Angel of the LORD, but it is often overlooked in modern discussions concerning the identity of this mysterious figure. It reads:

> [15] And he blessed Joseph and said, "The God before whom my fathers Abraham and Isaac walked, the God who has been my shepherd all my life long to this day,
>
> [16] the Angel who has redeemed me from all evil, bless the boys; and in them let my name be carried on, and the name of my fathers Abraham and Isaac; and let them grow into a multitude in the midst of the earth..."

The key to seeing its importance and how the passage answers the question of the Angel's identity is the poetic parallel:

> The God...
> The God...
> The Angel...

---

[3] Hywel Clifford, "The 'Ancient Jewish Church': the anti-Unitarian exegetical polemics of Peter Allix," in *From Zwingli to Amyraut: Exploring the Growth of European Reformed Traditions*, ed. Jon Balserak and Jim West (Göttingen: V&R Academic, 2017).

As Allix demonstrates beyond a shadow of a doubt, not only does the grammar necessitate that "the Angel" and "the God" be the same Person, this has also been the view of most of the ancient Church Fathers and, more curiously to those who do not know the history, the early Jews. This *Dissertation* is clearly one of the most extensive treatments of the Angel of the LORD as the Divine Christ up to this point in history.

In the larger book in which the *Dissertation* is found (*The Judgment of the Ancient Jewish Church Against The Unitarians in the Controversy Upon the Holy Trinity and the Divinity of Our Blessed Savior*), Allix has several chapters dedicated to thinking about the Angel of the LORD from an early Jewish perspective. He uses these chapters to help convince his reader that the early Jews were not all Unitarians. Far from it. As we should expect, if some Jews before Christ worshiped the One True God, they could not be. These chapters add a more robust Old Testament picture of the Angel than is found in the *Dissertation* alone. Thus, I have transcribed several of them for the sake of helping the reader understand more of the history that lies behind the ancient understanding of this mysterious Angel who is to be found throughout the Old Testament. When the totality of his work is read together, Allix can clearly be seen to be a man writing with a depth of scholarship on this topic that has only in the last few decades begun to be duplicated.

In this light, I would recommend Allix' work for anyone skeptical of the contemporary thesis, and now consensus, of modern scholarship that many Jews of the 1ˢᵗ century and before had some conception of a plurality of Persons in the Godhead. This thesis was first brought to light in modern times in 1977 by the late Dr. Alan Segal, a Jewish professor of religion and Judaic studies at several universities, including Princeton. Segal was no fan of what these Rabbi's themselves dubbed "two powers in heaven." But his book of the same title was the first serious modern study to appear on the vital early Rabbinical view that not all strands of ancient Judaism were Unitarian, though neither were they polytheistic. Scholarship that has pursued this has labeled it as "Binatarian," a monotheistic precursor of Christianity but without a full blown systematic Trinitarianism.[4]

---

[4] A bibliography of relevant works in this field is as follows: Margaret Barker, *The Great Angel: A Study of Israel's Second God* (Louisville, KY: Westminster / John Knox Publishers, 1992); Richard Bauckham "The Throne of God and the Worship of Jesus," in *The Jewish Roots of Christological Monotheism: Papers from the St. Andrews Conference on the Historical Origins of the Worship of Jesus,* ed. C. Newman, J. Davila, and G. Lewis (Leiden: E. J. Brill, 1999): 43-69; Bauckham, *God Crucified: Monotheism & Christology in the New Testament* (Grand Rapids, MI: Eerdmans, 1998); Daniel Boyarin, "The Gospel of the Memra: Jewish Binitarianism and the Prologue to John," *Harvard Theological Review* 94:3 (July 2001): 243-284; Boyarin, "Two Powers in Heaven; or, The Making of a Heresy," in *The Idea of Biblical Interpretation: Essays in Honor of James L. Kugel* (Leiden: Brill, 2003): 331-370; Jarl E. Fossum *The Image of the Invisible God: Essays on the Influence of Jewish Mysticism on Early Christology* (Göttingen: Vandenhoeck and Ruprecht, 1995); Fossum, *The Name of God and the Angel of the LORD: Samaritan and Jewish*

Segal, however, shows no familiarity with Allix or his work on the Angel, nor do several of the other prominent names in the field.[5] This alone makes

---

Concepts of Intermediation and the Origin of Gnosticism (Tubingen: J. C. B. Mohr, 1985); Simon Gathercole, *The Pre-Existent Son: Recovering the Christologies of Matthew, Mark, and Luke* (Grand Rapids: Eerdmans, 2006); Darrell D. Hannah, *Michael and Christ: Michael Traditions and Angel Christology in Early Christianity*, Wissenschaftliche Untersuchungen zum Neuen Testament 109 (Tübingen: Mohr-Siebeck, 1999); Michael S. Heiser, "The Divine Council in Late Canonical and Non-Canonical Second Temple Jewish Literature." A Dissertation at the University of Wisconsin-Madison (2004); Heiser, *The Unseen Realm: Rediscovering the Supernatural Worldview of the Bible* (Bellingham, WA: Lexham Press, 2015); Larry W. Hurtado, "What Do We Mean by 'First-Century Jewish Monotheism'?" in *Society of Biblical Literature 1993 Seminar Papers*, ed. E. H. Lovering Jr. (Atlanta: Scholars Press, 1993): 348-368; Hurtado, *One God, One Lord: Early Christian Devotion and Ancient Jewish Monotheism* (Philadelphia: Fortress, 1988); Hurtado, *Lord Jesus Christ: Devotion to Jesus in Earliest Christianity* (Grand Rapids: Eerdmans, 2003); Hurtado, "First-Century Jewish Monotheism," *Journal for the Study of the New Testament* 71 (1998): 3-26; Hurtado, "The Binitarian Shape of Early Christian Worship," in *The Jewish Roots of Christological Monotheism, Papers from the St. Andrews Conference on the Historical Origins of the Worship of Jesus*, ed. by Carey C. Newman, James R. Davila and Gladys S. Lewis, Supplements to the Journal for the Study of Judaism, ed. John J. Collins (Leiden: E. J. Brill, 1999): 187-213; Hurtado, *How on Earth Did Jesus Become a God?: Historical Questions about Earliest Devotion to Jesus* (Grand Rapids: Eerdmans, 2005); Aquila H. I. Lee, *From Messiah to Pre-existent Son*, Wissenschaftliche Untersuchungen zum Neuen Testament 192 (Tübingen: Mohr-Siebeck, 2005; reprinted Wipf and Stock, 2009); Alan F. Segal, *Two Powers in Heaven: Early Rabbinic Reports about Christianity and Gnosticism* (Leiden: E. J. Brill, 1977); Loren T. Stuckenbruck and Wendy E. S. North, eds., *Early Jewish and Christian Monotheism*, Journal for the Study of the New Testament, Supplement Series 263, Early Christianity in Context Series (New York: T&T Clark International, 2004).
[5] These include Michael Heiser, Larry Hurtado, Margaret Barker, Richard Bauckham, Daniel Boyarin, Jarl Fossum, Simon Gathercole, and others. There are a few exceptions such as Loren Stuckenbruck, but this is a minority.

republication indispensable. Given the newness of this field of study in modern times, Allix was surely centuries ahead of his time. The title of his work is to prove this very point made so persuasively by Segal and those who have followed him. He is even familiar with the concept of "two powers," though I have not transcribed this portion of his book here (they are in chs. 8-9 in his book), as it wasn't as germane to my purposes as were other parts. I do, however, take it up in my *Promised, Patterned, and Present: Christ in the Old Testament* book in this same series.

Allix' *Dissertation* is brilliantly argued and overwhelming in its citations of ancient material in support of the view that the Angel of the LORD is the Second Person of the Trinity. It covers an astonishing breadth of writers, both contemporary to Allix and ancient. These include ancient and medieval Jews, Church Fathers, medieval Roman Catholics, Reformers, and other commentators contemporary to his time. His familiarity of the history is masterful. His knowledge of the issues is astonishing. Indeed, it is difficult to fathom how anyone could even gain access to so many obscure works, let alone read them all in their original languages (Hebrew, Greek, Latin, Spanish, French, and English), and then cull the relevant material into a single decisive book. Therefore, I present Peter Allix on the Angel of the LORD so that the modern reader might become acquainted with this brilliant Christ-centered conservative Reformed theologian so long out of print.

Gerard De Gols

Gerard De Gols is virtually unknown. Perhaps this is due in part because very little is known about him. He was born in Amsterdam around 1676. His father's name was Philip. He was admitted to the Trinity College at Cambridge at the age of 17 in 1693 and two years later he was admitted to the school of St. Paul's. At some point he seems to have gone to Leyden to study in the Netherlands. De Gols became the Rector of St. Peter's Anglican church in Sandwich, England where he presided for 24 years (1713-37), though one source says he began his work here in 1706. He was also a minister to the Dutch congregation at St. Clement's in Sandwich. One of the only remaining facts that we know about him is that he was so well respected by his fellow-townsmen that he was one of the persons selected by the corporation to support the canopies at the coronation of George II and Queen Caroline. He wrote and published *Sermons* (1711-26), a poem called *Samson, or the Unhappy Lover* (London, 1696), as well as the present book which was published in London in 1726. He died on Feb. 22, 1737 at the age of 61 and is buried at St. Clement's.

I am reprinting a significant portion of a powerful, persuasive, and pastoral work titled (in good

Puritanical tradition), *A Vindication of the worship of the Lord Jesus Christ as the Supreme God, in all the dispensations, patriarchal, mosaick and Christian : demonstrating, that Christ was so known and worship'd in all ages, from Adam to this day*, by Gerard De Gols.

The book was is written to Peter Lord King (1669-1734), cousin of John Locke and Baron of Ockham who became Lord High Chancellor of Great Britain, although it is clear that De Gols did not know King, but did reply that unlike his cousin, King "understands the matters" and "believes the Scripture" which is "the great honor of any magistrate to therefore honor and adore God before me." He begins the work with over 120 contemporary names that are all in agreement with its contents. What we will concern ourselves with is the 5th-9th chapters.

We begin at De Gol's unfolding the divinity of Christ in many parallel texts with his Father. He looks especially at the incommunicable attributes of God, which God and God alone can have. Yet, Christ has them too. This lengthy chapter, which can be challenging to read especially at the beginning, is nevertheless of powerful apologetic value for anyone seeking to defend the deity of Christ and his oneness with the Father against skeptics or cults. In this, it also serves as a tool to strengthen one's own faith.

This then lays the foundation for seeing Christ worshiped throughout the OT as the Angel of the

LORD, the Memra, Word, or Logos with a special attention given to a great many OT saints (Adam, Cain and Abel, Enoch, Noah, Melchizedek, Abraham, Hagar, Lot, Isaac, Jacob, Joseph, Moses, Job, Israel in the wilderness, Joshua, Gideon, Manoah, the prophets, David, Solomon, and more) whom De Gols powerfully demonstrates "worshiped Christ as God." This latter section is highly valuable for pastoral care, especially as it relates to helping people see that yes, indeed, those in the OT explicitly knew and worshiped Jesus Christ.

It is almost completely unheard of today that anyone would be so bold as to say that the saints of the OT worshiped Christ as God. Thus, I cannot recommend De Gols highly enough for anyone struggling with or knows someone who struggles with the deity of Christ, for it is his deity, his eternality that allows him to even be present in OT times in order to be worshiped. It is one of the greatest books I can imagine being written to confirm our trust that the New Testament authors knew what they were talking about when they, in every single chapter, returned to the Old Testament to demonstrate the divinity of Jesus Christ. De Gols wants you to believe that Jesus was there, present in the OT, known, and worshiped by all the OT saints. For anyone who desires to have a better grasp of these things, this is the book for you.

A Note on Editing

I have completely revised the English as it is found in Owen's *Works* (most recently published by The Banner of Truth). I have taken some liberties in order to shorten and make the work more accessible to people who might not ordinarily be drawn to this man whose works are unusually difficult to read (both for the depth of content and the often-convoluted English). All original margin notes have been retained as footnotes, but I have added several notes to help in understanding.

I have updated typos and mistakes in citations, as well as antiquated terms and phrases from Allix's 1821 Clarendon Press edition (though I also had to consult the 1699 edition). I have transliterated all Greek and Hebrew and translated some of the foreign languages that were left alone previously. In many cases I have used the ESV for the biblical citation, though any time I felt the original (often the KJV or Geneva Bible) made the point more strongly, I have retained it or made my own translation as close to the original, but with modern language.

Whenever I could track down a modern English translation of a work in a footnote, I have changed the older citations to fit the modern. In other cases, I have left the citation and its reference unchanged. It is up to the reader to track those down. Most of the Scripture passages quoted were originally italicized. I have retained this and italicized the Targum quotations as well. Capitalization was a bit of a subjective decision. Old English capitalized many more words than we do. If I feel a word in any way applied to an attribute or name of God, it remains capitalized.

I have updated antiquated terms and phrases in De Gols. In many cases, I have used the ESV for the biblical citation, though any time I felt the original (often the KJV or Geneva Bible) made the point more strongly, I have retained it or made my own translation as close to the original, but with modern language, as I could.

Whenever I could find a modern English translation of a work in a footnote, I have changed the citations to fit the modern English text. In other cases, I have left the citation and its reference unchanged. It is up to the reader to track those down. Many of the Scripture passages quoted were originally italicized. I have retained this and italicized the Targum quotations as well. Capitalization was a bit of a subjective decision. Old English capitalized many more words than we do. If I felt a word in any way applied to an attribute or name of God, it remains capitalized, though sometimes this may seem inconsistent because of the context.

My hope is that being confronted by these three divines of old, it will help settle the reader into a sure and certain confidence as to the much questioned fact that the OT church did in fact know and worship the

Lord Jesus Christ, especially when he came to them as the Angel of the LORD, who is, in fact, the Second Person of the Holy Trinity, the Son pre-incarnate, the Redeemer whom those people before Messiah came knew, trusted in, and worshiped as Yahweh-God.

A more important topic is difficult to discern, especially in days like ours when the OT has fallen on such hard times. Reading others who have gone before us talk about him in such clear, profound, and direct ways should be a balm to the soul of any Christian and a powerful apologetic against unbelief.

Doug Van Dorn
January 2020

———— ——— ———

John Owen

Promises of the Messiah Vindicated

JOHN OWEN

EXERCITATION X
APPEARANCES OF THE SON OF GOD
UNDER THE OLD TESTAMENT

Overview:

Ends of the promises and prophecies concerning the Messiah—Other ways of his revelation; of his offering, by sacrifices; of his divine person, by visions. 2. What is meant in the Targums by Memra Debar, the Word of God—The expression qol Yahweh, first used in Gen 3:8. Apprehensions of the ancient Jews about the Word of God; of the philosophers—Application of the expression "the Logos of God" to the Son, by John—Expressions of Philo—Among the Mohammedans Christ called the Word of God—Intention of the Targumists vindicated. 3. How the Voice walked—Aben Ezra refuted, and R. Jona—The appearance of the second Person unto our first parents. 4. Gen 18:1–3—God's appearance, and the Suddenness of it. 5. Who appeared. 6. The occasion of it. 7. Reflection of Aben Ezra on some Christian expositors countered—A trinity of persons not proved from this place—Distinct persons proved—No created angel representing the person of God called Jehovah—Gen 19:24, "From the LORD"—Exceptions of Aben Ezra and Jarchi removed—Appearance of the second Person. 8. Gen 32:24, 26–30. 9. Occasion of this vision. 10. The Person; in appearance a man; 11. In office, an angel, Gen 48:16; 12, 13. In nature, God, Gen 32:26, 30, Hos 12:5, who it was that appeared. 14. Ex 3:1–6, 14—God appeared. 15. Ex 19:18–20—Who gave the law—Not a created angel—The ministry of angels, how used therein. 16, 17. Ex 23:20–23—Different angels promised—The Angel of God's presence, who. 18, 19. Josh 5:13–15—Captain of the Lord's host described. 20. Sense of the ancient church concerning these appearances; 21. Of the Jews. 22. Opinion of Nachmanides. 23. Tanchuma—Talmud—Fiction of the angel rejected by Moses, accepted by Joshua—Sense of it. 24. Metatron, who—Derivation of the name.

1. We have seen how often God instructed the church of old by his prophets in the knowledge of the person, office, and work of the Messiah. He did this, partly, so that nothing might be lacking in the faith and comfort of believers, according to a fitting quantity that equaled the amount of light and grace that it was his good pleasure to give them before his actual coming in human flesh. It was also partly so that his righteous judgments that came from the rejection and ruin of those who obstinately refused him, might,

because of their conviction, be justified and rendered glorious. These promises and predictions were not the only means by which God would manifest and reveal him to their faith.

There are two things about the Messiah which are the pillars and foundation of the church. The one is his *divine nature*; and the other, his work of mediation in the *atonement* for sin, which he made by his suffering and sacrifice of himself.

He declared these two things to those whom, according to the promise, looked forward to his coming. He did this in two special ways or means that were graciously designed by God. The second of these was that the *worship* which he instituted, and the various *sacrifices* which he appointed to be observed in the church, would be types and representations of the one perfect sacrifice which he would offer in the fullness of time. The explanation and application of this means of instruction is the main purpose and reason the apostle Paul wrote his Epistle to the Hebrews.

The other way, which concerns his divine person, was through those *visions* and *appearances* of the Son of God (who is the head of the church) which were graciously given to the fathers under the Old Testament. These, as they are directly suited to our purpose, in our inquiry after the prophecies of the advent of the Messiah, are also eminently useful for the conviction of the Jews. For in them we shall demonstrate that a revelation was made of a *distinct person* in the Godhead, who in a peculiar manner managed all the matters of importance in the church after the entrance of sin. Here, also, according to our proposed method, we will inquire into what light was given regarding this truth that was then received by any of the Jewish masters, who also aptly demonstrate what confusion they are driven to, when they seek to evade the evidence that is in their own ancient writings.

2. There is frequent mention in the Targumists[6] of the *Memra Debar*, "The Word of the Lord." It first occurs in them at the first appearance of a divine person after the sin and fall of Adam (Gen 3:8). The words of the original text are, "*And they heard the voice of the LORD God walking in the garden.*" The participle "walking" may be linked as much to the "the voice," as to "the LORD God." And although "the voice" most commonly signifies the outward voice and sound of something, yet when applied to God, it frequently denotes "his almighty power." It is through this power that he affects whatever he pleases. Thus, in Psalm 29:3–9, those things are ascribed to this "*voice of the LORD,*" which elsewhere are assigned to "*the word of his power*" (Heb 1:3).

---

[6] A Targum is essentially a Jewish paraphrase of an OT book like Genesis. In some ways they can be comparable to anything from the NIV to The Message Bible. Some Targums are little more than good translations. Others will add substantial oral tradition to help illuminate a particular passage. The Targums are found in the language of Aramaic.

Now, all these mighty works of creation or providence, which are assigned to this "voice of the LORD," or to "the word of his power," or "his powerful word" are immediately brought to pass by the essential Word of God (John 1:3, Col 1:16), which was with God "*in the beginning*," or at the creation of all things (John 1:1, 2) as his eternal wisdom (Pro 8:22–26) and power. This expression, therefore, of "the voice of the LORD" may also denote the Word of God that is God, the essential Word of God, the Person of the Son: for here our first parents heard this "Word walking in the garden" before they heard the outward sound of any voice or words whatsoever. For God did not speak to them until after this (Gen 3:9) when, "*The LORD God called unto Adam, and said to him…*"

Some of the Jews take notice of this change of the appearance of God. So, the author of *Tseror Hammor*, Sect. *Bereshith*,[7] "Before they sinned, they saw the glory of the blessed God speaking with them; but after their sin they only heard his voice walking." God now dealt differently with them than he did before. And the Chaldee paraphrast [that is the Targum], observing that some special presence of God is expressed in the words, renders them, "And they heard the voice *of the Word* of the Lord God walking in the garden." All the Targums read this way. The Jerusalem

---

[7] Owen refers here to a commentary on the Pentateuch written by Abraham Saba in 1523. See the Glossary and Works Cited at the end of the book for this and other references in this exercitation.

Targum begins the next verse by saying, "And *the Word of* the Lord God called to Adam." And this expression they afterwards make use of in too many places to count,[8] and this in such a way as to plainly denote a distinct person in a Godhead. That this also was their intent is plain, because about the time of the writing of the first of those Targums, it was usual among them to express their conceptions of the Son of God by the name of "the Word of God," which is what *Memra Debar* means.

Thus, Philo express it in *The Confusion of Languages*, "If anyone is not yet worthy to be called the son of God, yet strives to be conformed to his first-begotten Word, the most ancient angel, the archangel with many names; for he is called the Beginning, the Name of God, the Man according to the image of God, the Seer of Israel." How perfectly these things speak to the mysteries revealed in the Gospel is a thing we will discuss elsewhere. Here I only observe how he calls that Angel who appeared to the fathers, and that sometimes in human form, the Word—"The first-begotten Word."

He expresses himself again in the same way to the same end: "For if we are not yet able to be called the sons of God, let us become like his eternal image, the

---

[8] For the curious reader, both Peter Allix and Gerard De Gols go to great lengths to uncover many more references here than Owen did. We are publishing both of their works on Christ in the Old Testament in this same series as Owen's Exercitation.

most sacred Word; for that most ancient Word is the image of God." How these things fit in with our apostle concerning Jesus Christ (Col 1:15–18, Heb 1:3) is easily discerned. This conception of theirs was so well approved by the Holy Ghost as being a thing fitting to the mind of God, that John in the beginning of his Gospel declares the eternal deity of Christ by using this name of The *Logos* ("the Word"), that is *Memra Debar*, "the Word of God." "*The Word was with God, and the Word was God*" (John 1:1). He alludes here to the story of the first creation, where God is described as making all things by his word; for he said of everything, "*Let it be*," and it was made (as the psalmist says it, "*He spoke, and it was done; he commanded, and it stood fast.*" Ps 33:9). This, the Psalmist fully declares in verse 6, "*By the word of the LORD were the heavens made, and all the host of them by the breath of his mouth.*" John thus teaches that all things were made by this Word of God (John 1:3). In the Chaldee, this is elsewhere also assigned to this Word. Where "the Word" is not mentioned in the original Hebrew (such as in Isa 45:12 or 48:13), it is in the Targums, just as it is discussed by Peter himself (2Pe 3:5), for the very reason that he might ascribe the work of the redemption of the church to this Word of the Lord, which was admitted in the church of the Jews. That place, among others, is straight to the point. Consider Hosea 1:7 where the prophet says, "*I will save them by the LORD their God*," the Targumist reads, "I will save (or redeem) them *by the Word* of the LORD their God;" the Word, the Redeemer.

It is not unworthy of consideration that the wisest and most contemplative of the philosophers of old had many notions about "the eternal Word," which was to them "the formative or creative power of the universe." To this end, many sayings have been observed and might be reported out of Plato, with his followers Amelius, Chalcidius, Proclus, Plotinus, and others. These expressions are imitated by our own writers, such as Justin Martyr, Clement, Athenagoras, Tatian, and many more. It is even so among the Mohammedans. This is the name that they give to Jesus in their Koran, "*The Word of God.*" This is how prevalent this notion of the Son of God has been in the world.

There are the words of Ezekiel, "*I heard the voice of their wings, as the voice of the Almighty*" (Ezek 1:24). These are rendered by the Targumist, "as the voice *from the face* of the Almighty." Some copies of the LXX[9] render them by "the voice *of the Word*," that is of God, who was represented in that vision, as shall be made clear. Some would put another sense on that expression of the Targumists, as though it intended nothing but God himself. Instances of this use have been observed. For example, Ecclesiastes 8:17, "If a wise man say '*in his word*,'" that is, say in himself, or

---

[9] LXX = The Greek Septuagint. This is the 3rd-2nd cent. B.C. translation of the OT Hebrew Bible into Koine Greek by seventy [hence LXX] Jewish scribes living in Alexandria, Egypt.

Genesis 6:6, "It repented the LORD *in his word.*" Also, Ruth 3:8 makes some think this, "As did Phaltiel the son of Laish, who placed his sword *between his word* and Michal the daughter of Saul, the wife of David."

But there are a couple of things to say about this. 1. The former places do not use the word *mymr* [*memra*] which is peculiar to the sense we are arguing for. 2. The Targums on the Hagiographa are a late post-Talmudical endeavor, made in imitation of those of Onkelos and Ben Uzziel, when the Jews had both lost all sense of their old traditions and use of the Chaldee language, except for what they had learned from those former paraphrases. Nothing, therefore, can be concluded as to the intention of the Targumists in these words. But they can have no other sense in Psalm 110:1, "The LORD said in (or "to") his Word;" which replaces, "*to my Lord,*" as in the original.

3. The Jews discern that "walking" relates in this place immediately to "the voice," and not to "the LORD God." They therefore try to render a reason for that kind of expression. So Aben Ezra on the place gives instances where a voice or sound in its progress is said to walk, such as Exodus 19:19, "*The voice of the trumpet went and waxed strong;*" and Jeremiah 46:22, "*The voice shall go like a serpent.*" But these examples do not touch these under consideration; for although *halak* ("to walk") may sometimes express the progression or increase of a voice, yet it does so only where it

is hinted to have begun before. But here, nothing is spoken by God until after Adam had heard this Word of God walking. And therefore Rabbi (R.) Jona,[10] cited by Aben Ezra, would apply "walking" to Adam, "he heard the voice of God *as he was himself* walking in the garden." The words of the text and context sufficiently verify the absurdity of this fiction. It is therefore most probable that in the great changes that were now coming upon the whole creation, with mankind being cast out of covenant, the serpent and the earth being cursed, and a way of recovery for the elect of God being revealed, he by whom all things were made, and by whom all were to be renewed that were brought back to God, did in a special and glorious way appear to our first parents, as he in whom this whole dispensation centered, and to whom it was committed. After the promise given, he appeared "in a human shape," to instruct the church in the mystery of his future incarnation, and under the name of Angel, to foreshadow his office as he was sent to it and was employed in it by the Father. So here, before the promise, he discovered his distinct glorious person, as the eternal Voice or Word of the Father.

4. Genesis 18:1–3. "*And the* LORD *appeared unto him* (Abraham) *in the plains of Mamre: and he sat in the tent door in the heat of the day; and he lift up his eyes and*

---

[10] Rabbi Jonah (4th century). Palestinian amora who was the leading rabbinical authority in the 4th amoraic generation.

looked, and, lo, three men stood by him: and when he saw them, he ran to meet them from the tent door, and bowed himself toward the ground, and said, 'My Lord, if now I have now found favor in your sight...'" The Jews, in Bereshith Ketanna,[11] say that this appearance of God to Abraham was three days after his circumcision. Because he was still sore and was not yet recovered, he sat in the door of his tent. Thus, God came to visit him in his sickness. But the reason for his sitting in the door of the tent is given in the text, namely, because it was "*as in*" (or "*about*") "*the heat of the day.*" The day growing hot was the very opposite of the time God appeared to Adam, which was "*in the cool air of the day.*" Just as when God comes to curse and nothing can refresh the creature, even though its own nature is suited for the cool of the day, it shall wither nevertheless wither; so also when he comes to bless, nothing shall hinder the influence of that blessing upon his creatures, even if a thing like the heat of the day is found to be troublesome or disconcerting.

5. "*He lift up his eyes and looked, and, behold, three men stood by him.*" The title is, "*The LORD appeared to him;*" and the narrative is, "*Behold, three men stood by him.*" The LORD, therefore, was among them. This seems to be a sudden appearance that was made to him. He saw them suddenly standing by him; he

---

[11] Bereshith Ketanna is one of many ways the midrashim on the Pentateuch are referred to by the Jews.

looked up and saw them, and this satisfied him that it was a heavenly apparition.

6. The business of God with Abraham at this time was to renew to him the promise of the blessing Seed, and to confine it to his posterity by Sarah. This was because he had grown despondent and began to desire that Ishmael might be his heir. Joined to this work of mercy was the declaration of an eminent *vindictive justice*, where God would set forth an example to all coming generations, in the destruction of Sodom and Gomorrah. Both of these are the proper works of him on whom the care of the church was in a special way incumbent. All whose blessedness depended on that promise, and to whom the rule of the world, the present and future judgment thereof, is committed, needed to see the person of the Son. And hence, in the overthrow of those cities, he who will be their judge is said to set forth an example of his future dealings with all the ungodly (2Pe 2:6).

7. Aben Ezra reflects with scorn on the Christians from this place. Because three men are said to appear to Abraham and he calls them, "*My Lord,*" some would prove the tri-personality of God. "Because of the appearance of three men, God is three, and he is one, and they are not separated or divided." How does he answer what they say? "Behold, they forget that two angels came to Sodom" (in other words, two of those who appeared were angels and nothing more). But if

any Christians have taken these three persons to have been the three persons of the Trinity,[12] it is an easy thing to demonstrate their mistake with instances of his own and companions wicked curiosities and errors.

It is true, a Trinity of Persons in the Godhead cannot be proved from this place, seeing that one of them is expressly called Jehovah, and the other two, in distinction from him, are said to be angels (this and no more, Gen 19:1). Yet a distinction of persons in the Deity, although not the precise number of them, is certainly demonstrable. For it is evident that the one of the three who spoke to Abraham, and to whom he made his supplication for the sparing of Sodom, was Jehovah, *the Judge of all the earth*" (18:22–33). And yet all the three were sent for the work, that one being the Prince and Head of the embassy; as he who is Jehovah is said to be sent by Jehovah (Zech 2:8-9).[13]

Neither is there any ground for the late exposition of this and similar places, namely, that a created angel representing the person of God both speaks and acts in his name and is called Jehovah [Yahweh]. This is an invention crafted to evade the appearances of the Son of God in the Old Testament. It is against the

---

[12] This Interpretation became common in in the fourth and fifth century in the Christian Church, though prior to that, the Fathers tended to see only one of the three as God—God the Son.

[13] Modern scholars have noted certain two-powers texts (as the rabbis called them) which seem to show not one but two Yahwehs. This passage in Zechariah is drawing upon that kind of tradition, as will be seen below when Owen cites Genesis 19:24.

interpretation of all antiquity. And it is contrary to any reason or instance produced to make it good. The Jews, indeed, say that they were three angels, because of the threefold work they were employed in; for they say, "No more than one angel is at any time sent about to the same work." So, one of these was to renew the promise to Abraham; another, to deliver Lot; and the third, to destroy Sodom. But this is a rule of their own making, and evidently false. This is easily proven from places like Genesis 32:1-2 or 2 Kings 6:17. Besides, in the story itself it is obvious that they were all engaged in the same work, one as Lord and Prince, the other two as his ministering servants.

This is further clarified in that expression of Moses, "*The LORD rained upon Sodom and upon Gomorrah brimstone and fire from the LORD out of heaven*" (Gen 19:24). Here, the Targum reads, "from before the Lord," or "the face of the Lord." Aben Ezra answers that this is the elegance of the language, but the sense of it is, "from himself;" and this gloss some of the late critics embrace. There are instances collected by Solomon Jarchi to confirm this sense:

- The words of Lamech (Gen 4:23): "*Hear my voice, you wives of Lamech*," not "my wives."
- The words of David (1 Kings 1:33): "*Take with you the servants of your lord*," not "my servants."
- The words of Ahasuerus to Mordecai (Esther 8:8): "*Write for the Jews in the king's name*," not "in my name."

But the difference of these from the words under consideration is wide and evident. In all these places the persons are introduced speaking of themselves and describe themselves either by their names or offices. But in this place, it is Moses who speaks of the Lord, and he had no reason or purpose to repeat "from the Lord," except to hint at the distinct persons to whom that name, denoting the nature and self-existence of God, was proper. One appeared on the earth; the other manifested his glorious presence in heaven.

Rashi, observing somewhat more in this expression, does not content himself with his supposed parallel places; but adds, that the "house of judgment" is to be understood. He then gives this as a rule, "Every place where it is said, '*And the LORD,*' he and his house of judgment are intended"! as if God had a Sanhedrin in heaven, an imagination which they have invented to avoid the expressions which testify to a plurality of persons in the Deity. There is therefore in this place an appearance of God in a human shape, where one distinct person in the Godhead, who now represented himself to Abraham in the form and shape where later he would dwell among men, would be "*made flesh*" from Abraham's seed. This was the chief way that Abraham "*saw his day and rejoiced;*" which proves his *pre-existence* before his incarnation, more than just the promise of his coming (John 8:56, 58). This was a solemn introduction to his taking of flesh, a revelation of his divine nature and person, and a pledge of his coming in human nature to converse with men.

8. Genesis 32:24, 26–30. "*And Jacob was left alone. And a man wrestled with him until the breaking of the day … Then he said, 'Let me go, for the day has broken.' But Jacob said, 'I will not let you go unless you bless me.' And he said to him, 'What is your name?' And he said, 'Jacob.' Then he said, 'Your name shall no longer be called Jacob, but Israel, for you have striven with God and with men, and have prevailed.' Then Jacob asked him, 'Please tell me your name.' But he said, 'Why is it that you ask my name?' And there he blessed him. So Jacob called the name of the place Peniel, saying, 'For I have seen God face to face, and yet my life has been delivered.'*"

This story is twice reflected upon in the Scripture after the fact. Once is by Jacob himself, "*And he blessed Joseph and said, 'The God before whom my fathers Abraham and Isaac walked, the God who has been my shepherd all my life long to this day, the angel who has redeemed me from all evil, bless the boys'*" (Genesis 48:15-16). The other is by the prophet Hosea, "*In the womb he took his brother by the heel, and in his manhood he strove with God. He strove with the angel and prevailed; he wept and sought his favor. He met God at Bethel, and there God spoke with us—the LORD, the God of hosts, the LORD is his memorial name*" (Hos 12:3–5). In the first place he is called a "man" ("a man wrestled with him," Gen 32:24). In the second,

Jacob calls him an "Angel" ("The Angel which re-deemed me," 48:16). In the third, he is expressly said to be "God, the LORD God of hosts" (Hos 12:3, 5).

9. Jacob was now passing with his whole family into the land of Canaan, to take possession of it by virtue of the promise on the behalf of his posterity. At the entrance of it he is met by his greatest adversary, with whom he had a severe contest about the promise and the inheritance itself. This was his brother Esau, who was coming against him with a power which he was in no way able to withstand. He feared that he would utterly destroy both he himself and his children (Gen 32:11). In the promise which brought about that dreadful contest, the blessed Seed, with the whole church-state and worship of the Old Testament, was included. This made it the greatest controversy, and had the utmost weight depending on it, of any contest that ever was among the sons of men. Thereupon, to settle Jacob's right, to preserve him with his title and interest, he who was principally concerned in the whole matter did here appear to him; some special facts of this manifestation of himself may be observed.

10. First, he appeared in the form of "a man." "*A man wrestled with him.*" He is called a man because of his shape and his actions. He "wrestled." R. Menachem in Rashi says literally, "he dusted." This, he says, is the sense of *'abaq*, for "*they stirred up the dust with their feet,*" as men do when they wrestle; or, as he

would have it in allusion to another word to signify *"the closing with their arms,"* to cast one another down, as is the manner of wrestlers. A great contention is denoted, and an appearance in the form of a man, further manifested by his *"touching the socket of Jacob's thigh."*

11. Second, he is called an *"Angel"* by Jacob himself. *"The Angel that redeemed me"* (Gen 48:16). This was the greatest danger that Jacob was ever in, and this he remembers in his blessing of Joseph's children, praying that they may have the presence of this Angel with them, who preserved him all his life, and delivered him from that imminent danger from his brother Esau. And he calls him, *"The Angel the Redeemer;"* which is the name of the promised Messiah, as the Jews grant, *"And the Goël* (the 'Redeemer') *shall come to Zion"* (Isa 59:20). He is also expressly called *"The Angel"* in Hosea 12:4.

12. Third, this man in appearance, this angel in office, was in name and nature God over all, blessed forever. For, in the first place, Jacob prays solemnly to him for his blessing (Gen 32:26), and refuses to let him go, or to cease his appeals, until he had blessed him. He does so, he blesses him, and gives him a double pledge or token of it, in the touch of his thigh and change of his name; giving him a name to denote his prevailing with God—that is, with himself. From this, Jacob concludes that he had *"seen God,"* and calls the name of the place, *"The face of God."* In the second

place, Genesis 48:16, besides that he invokes this Angel for his presence with and blessing on the children of Joseph,—which cannot regard any but God himself without gross idolatry—it is evident that "the Angel who redeemed him" (16) is the same with *"the God who fed him,"* that is, the God of his fathers.

And this is all the more evident in the prophet. For with regard to this story of his power over the Angel, he says, *"He had power with God;"* and proves it, because *"he had power over the Angel, and prevailed."* And he shows exactly how he prevailed. It was by *"weeping and making supplication to him;"* which he neither did nor lawfully might do to a created angel. And therefore some of the Jews apply these words, *"He wept and made supplication,"* to the Angel's desire for Jacob to let him go!—foolishly enough; and yet they are also followed by some late critics, who too often please themselves in their curiosities. Again, this Angel was he whom he found, or *"who found him, in Bethel;"* an account that we have in Genesis 28:10–22 and 35:1. Now, this was none other than he to whom Jacob made his vow, and entered into solemn covenant so that he should be his God. And therefore, the prophet adds expressly in the last place that it was *"the LORD God of hosts"* (Hos 12:5) whom he intended.

13. From what has been spoken, it is obvious that he who appeared to Jacob, with whom he earnestly wrestled, by tears and supplications, was God; and

because he was sent as the angel of God, it must be some distinct person in the Godhead condescending to that office. Appearing in the form of a man, he represented his future assumption of our human nature. And in all this God instructed the church in the mystery of the person of the Messiah, who it was that they were to look for in the blessing of the promised Seed.

14. Exodus 3:1–6. "*Now Moses was keeping the flock of his father-in-law, Jethro, the priest of Midian, and he led his flock to the west side of the wilderness and came to Horeb, the mountain of God. And the angel of the LORD appeared to him in a flame of fire out of the midst of a bush. He looked, and behold, the bush was burning, yet it was not consumed. And Moses said, 'I will turn aside to see this great sight, why the bush is not burned.' When the LORD saw that he turned aside to see, God called to him out of the bush, 'Moses, Moses!' And he said, 'Here I am.' Then he said, 'Do not come near; take your sandals off your feet, for the place on which you are standing is holy ground.' And he said, 'I am the God of your father, the God of Abraham, the God of Isaac, and the God of Jacob.' And Moses hid his face, for he was afraid to look at God.*"

Here also have we expressed another glorious appearance of the Son of God. He who is revealed here is called "*Jehovah*" (4); and he affirms of himself that he is "*the God of Abraham*" (6); who also describes himself by the glorious name of "*I AM THAT I AM*" (14); in whose name and authority Moses dealt with

Pharaoh in the deliverance of the people, and whom they were to serve on that mountain upon their coming out of Egypt; he whose *"merciful good-will"* Moses prays for (Dt 33:16). And yet he is expressly called an "Angel" (Ex 3:2), namely, the Angel of the covenant, the great Angel of the presence of God, in whom was the name and nature of God. He thus appeared so that the church might know and consider who it was that was to work out their spiritual and eternal salvation, that deliverance which he then would affect was a type and pledge. Aben Ezra would have the Angel mentioned in vs. 2 to be another from him who is called "God" (6). But the text will not tolerate any such distinction, but speaks of one and the same person throughout, without any alteration; and this was none other but the Son of God.

15. Exodus 19:18–20. *"Now Mount Sinai was wrapped in smoke because the LORD had descended on it in fire. The smoke of it went up like the smoke of a kiln, and the whole mountain trembled greatly. And as the sound of the trumpet grew louder and louder, Moses spoke, and God answered him in thunder. The LORD came down on Mount Sinai, to the top of the mountain. And the LORD called Moses to the top of the mountain, and Moses went up."*

The Jews do well interpreting these words to be about the descent of God by way of the manifestation of his glory, rather than a change of place. Hence Aben Ezra interprets that expression, *"You have seen that I have talked with you from heaven*" (20:22). God was still in heaven when his glory was on the mount. Yet these words, "from heaven" refer to his descent, described earlier, rather than denote the place from which he spoke. For in giving the law, God "*spoke on earth*" (Heb 12:25). God did, in the glorious manifestation of his presence on mount Sinai, make use of the ministry of angels. The nature of the thing declares it, and the Scripture testifies to it (Ps 68:17). The voices, fire, trembling of the mountain, smoke, and noise of the trumpet, were all effected by them. So also was the forming of the words of the law conveyed to the ears of Moses and the people. Hence, the law is not only said to be received by them "*by the disposition* (or "*orderly ministries*") *of angels*" (Acts 7:53), and to be placed by them into the hand of Moses (Gal 3:19); but is also called "*the word spoken* (or "*pronounced*") *by angels*," that is, outwardly and audibly.

As to him who presided and ruled the whole action, some Christians think it was a *created angel*, representing God and speaking in his name. But if this is so, we have no certainty of anything that is affirmed in the Scripture. It may refer directly and immediately to God, yet we may, when we so please, substitute a *delegated angel* whenever we want; for in no place, not even in that concerning the creation of the world, is God himself more expressly spoken of than here in Exodus. Besides, the psalmist in the place mentioned affirms that when those chariots of God were on mount Sinai, Jehovah himself was in the midst of them. The Hebrews call this presence of God the *Kavod*, and the *Shekinah*, and the *Yeqar*; by which they understand a majestic and sanctifying presence. Indeed, it certainly fits him who is the *"brightness of the Father's glory, and the express image of his person,"* who was delegated to this work as the great Angel of the covenant, giving the law *"in the strength of the LORD, in the majesty of the name of the LORD his God."*

16. Exodus 23:20–22. *"Behold, I send an angel before you to guard you on the way and to bring you to the place that I have prepared. Pay careful attention to him and obey his voice; do not rebel against him, for he will not pardon your transgression, for my name is in him. But if you carefully obey his voice and do all that I say, then I will be an enemy to your enemies and an adversary to your adversaries."*

The Angel here promised is he who went in the midst of the people in the wilderness, whose glory appeared and was manifested among them. Moreover, another angel is promised to them in vs. 23, *"For my angel shall go before you, and bring you in to the Amorites ... and I will cut them off."* It is a ministering angel, to execute the judgment and vengeance of God upon the enemies of his people. That this angel of verse 23 is different from that of verse 20 appears from Exodus 33:2-3 compared with verses 13–16 of the same chapter. Verse 2, *"I will send an angel before you, and I will drive out the Canaanites, the Amorites…*"; which is the promise and the angel of 23:23. But he says, "*I will not go up among you*" (33:3), which he had promised to do in and by the Angel of 23:20-21, in whom his name was. From this the people feared evil tidings and mourned because of it (33:4). Now, God had not promised to go in their midst in any way other than by the Angel mentioned; with which both Moses and the people were abundantly satisfied. But whereas here he renews his promise of the ministry and assistance of the angel of 23:23, yet he denies them his own presence in the Angel of verse 20, for which Moses renews his request (33:13). To this God replies, "*My presence will go with you*" (14): concerning which presence, or face of God, or which Angel of his presence we must look at just a little bit more.

17. (1.) It is said to the people concerning him, "*Beware of him*," or rather, "*Take heed to yourself before him*,"—before his face, in his presence (23:21). This is the caution that is usually given the people whenever reverence and awe is to be paid to the holiness of the presence of God. (2.) "*And obey his voice.*" This is the great command that is solemnly given and so often reiterated in the law with reference to God himself. (3.) "*Do not provoke him*" or "*Do not rebel against him.*" This is the usual word whereby God expresses the transgression of his covenant—a rebellion that can be committed only against God. (4.) The reason for these

commands is twofold. The first is taken from the sovereign authority of this Angel. "*For he will not pardon your transgressions.*" That is, as Joshua afterwards tells the same people, "*He is a holy God; he is a jealous God; he will not forgive your transgressions nor your sins*" (Josh 24:19)—namely, sins of rebellion that break and annul his covenant. "*Who can forgive sins but God?*" To suppose here a created angel is to open a door to gross idolatry; for the one who has absolute power to pardon and punish sin, this one may certainly be worshipped with religious adoration.

The second reason is taken from his name: "*For my name is in him.*" This is "*a more excellent name*" (Heb 1:4) than any of the angels enjoy. He is God, Jehovah, that is his name; and he answers to it. Hence, Exodus 23:22 adds, "*If you will truly obey his voice and do all that I say...*" His voice is the voice of God, and when he speaks God speaks. Thus, the people's obedience depends on the accomplishment of the promise. Moreover, in Exodus 33:14, God says concerning this Angel, "*My presence ("my face"; panim) shall go with you.*" Moses calls this presence the "glory" (18). This essential glory was manifested to him (34:6), though it was obscure in comparison to what was shown to them who, in his human nature said, "*In him the whole fullness of deity dwells bodily*" (Col 2:9) and "*we have seen his glory, glory as of the only Son from the Father*" (John 1:14).

This face of God is the face of the one of whom it says, *"Whoever has seen me has seen the Father"* (John 14:9). This is because he is *"the radiance of the glory of God and the exact imprint of his nature"* (Heb 1:3). He accompanied the people in the wilderness (1Co 10:4). Moses prayed for his merciful good pleasure towards them (Dt 33:16)—that is, *"Every good gift and every perfect gift that comes down from the Father of lights"* (Jam 1:17). These things evidently express God, and no one else; and yet he is said to be an angel sent of God, in his name, and to his work. Thus, he can be none other than a certain person of the Godhead who accepted the task and was thus revealed to the church, as the one who was to take upon him the seed of Abraham, in order to be their eternal Redeemer.

18. Josh 5:13–15, *"When Joshua was by Jericho, he lifted up his eyes and looked, and behold, a man was standing before him with his drawn sword in his hand. And Joshua went to him and said to him, 'Are you for us, or for our adversaries?' And he said, 'No; but I am the commander of the army of the LORD. Now I have come.' And Joshua fell on his face to the earth and worshiped and said to him, 'What does my lord say to his servant?' And the commander of the LORD's army said to Joshua, 'Take off your sandals from your feet, for the place where you are standing is holy.' And Joshua did so."*

The appearance here is of a man, *"a man of war"* (13), just as God is called Exodus 15:3, armed, with his sword drawn in his hand, as a sign of the business he came to do. At first sight, Joshua apprehends him to be only a man; which prompted his question, "*Are you for us, or for our adversaries?*" This question displays his courage and undaunted magnanimity; for doubtless the appearance was imposing and glorious. But he answers his question *lo*, "I am not." That is, a man neither of your party nor of his enemy's, but quite another person, "*the Prince of the LORD'S host.*" And this was another renowned manifestation of the Son of God to the church of old, accompanied with many instructive circumstances.

1. From the *shape* in which he appeared, namely, that of a man, as a pledge of his future incarnation.
2. From the *title* that he assumes to himself, "*The Captain of the LORD'S host,*" he to whom the guidance and conduct of them towards sabbath rest, not only temporal but eternal, was committed. Hence the apostle, in allusion to this place and title, calls him "*The Captain of our salvation*" (Heb 2:10).
3. The *person* to whom he spoke when he gave himself this title was the captain of the people at that time; teaching both him and them that there was another, supreme Captain of their eternal deliverance.
4. From the *time and place* of his appearance, which was upon the entrance of he and his

family into Canaan, and the first opposition which he immediately met with Esau. Thus, he engages his presence with his church in all things which oppose them in their way to eternal rest.

5. From the *adoration and worship* which Joshua gave to him; which he accepted, contrary to the duty and practice of created angels (Rev 19:10; 22:8, 9).

6. From the *prescription of the ceremonies* expressing religious reverence, "*Take off your shoes;*" with the reason added, "*For the place where you stand 'is holy,*" made so by, of course, by the presence of God; the same command that was given to Moses by the God of Abraham, Isaac, and Jacob (Ex 3:5).

By all these things the church was instructed in the person, nature, and office of the Son of God, even in the mystery of his eternal distinct subsistence in the Godhead, his future incarnation and condescension to the office of being the Head and Savior of his church.

19. These manifestations of the Son of God to the church of old, as the Angel or Messenger of the Father, existing in his own divine person, are each of them *revelations* of the promised Seed, the great and only Savior and Deliverer of the church, in his eternal pre-existence prior to his incarnation; and *pledges* of his future taking our flesh for the accomplishment of all the word committed to him by the Father. Many

other instances of this similar nature could be added from the early and later prophets; which, because in the most important circumstances they are coextensive with these, but we do not need to talk about them here.

20. Some late interpreters would apply all these appearances to a created delegated angel. The conceit of this is irreconcilable with the sacred text, as we have already shown, and it is contrary to the sense of the ancient writers of the Christian church. A large collection of testimonies from them is not suited to our present design and purpose. I shall therefore only mention two of the most ancient of them, one of the Latin Fathers, the other of the Greek.

The first is Tertullian, who tells us, "*Christ always dealt (with men) in the name of God the Father; and so he himself conversed with the patriarchs and prophets from the very beginning*" (*Against Marcion, lib. ii*). And again, "*It was Christ who descended into communion with men, from Adam to the patriarchs and prophets, in visions, dreams, and appearances, or representations of himself, instructing them in his future condition from the beginning; and God who conversed with men on earth was no other but the Word who was to be made flesh*" (*Against Praxeas*). The other is Justin Martyr, whose words need not be produced, seeing it is known how he contends for this very thing in his *Dialogue with Trypho*.

21. That which is more direct to our purpose is to inquire into the apprehensions of the Jewish masters concerning the *divine appearances* that were given to the patriarchs and church of old, with what may thus be collected for their conviction concerning the person of the Messiah. Most of their expositors do, I confess, pass over the difficulties of the places mentioned (I mean those which need to further their present infidelity) without taking the least notice of them. Some would have the angel mentioned to be Michael, to whom they assign a privilege above all the other angels, angels who preside over other countries. But who that Michael is, and what that privilege consists of, they do not know. Some say that Michael is the high priest of heaven, who offers up the prayers of the righteous. So R. Menachem. "*He is the priest above, who offers or presents the souls of the righteous,*" says another, more agreeably to the truth than they are even aware.

One chief example of this, in the words of Moses Nachmanides Gerundensis,[14] on Exodus 23, which has been taken notice of by many, shall suffice. His words are, "This Angel, if we speak exactly, is the Angel Redeemer, concerning whom it is written, '*My name is in*

---

[14] Moses ben Nahman (1194-1270), was commonly called Nachmanides or Ramban. He was a leading medieval Jewish scholar, rabbi, philosopher, physician, kabbalist, and biblical commentator who lived in Spain but was an important figure in the reestablishment of the Jewish community in Jerusalem after the crusaders destroyed it in 1099.

him' (Ex 23:21); that Angel who said to Jacob, '*I am the God of Bethel*' (Gen 31:13); he of whom it is said, '*And God called unto Moses out of the bush*' (Ex 3:4). And he is called an Angel because he governs the world: for it is written (Dt 6:21), '*The LORD brought us out of Egypt;*' and elsewhere (Num 20:16), '*He sent his Angel, and brought us out of Egypt.*' Moreover, it is written (Isa 63:9), '*And the Angel of his face (presence) saved them,*'— namely, that Angel who is the face of God; of whom it is said (Ex 33:14), '*My face shall go before you, and I will cause you to rest.*' Lastly, it is that Angel of whom the prophet speaks (Mal 3:1), '*And the Lord, whom you seek, shall suddenly come to his temple, the Angel of the covenant, in whom you delight.*'" His following words are to the same purpose: "Mark diligently what the meaning is of these words, '*My face shall go before you;*' for Moses and the Israelites always desired the chief Angel, but who that was they could not truly understand, for neither could they learn it of any others nor obtain it by prophecy. But the '*face of God*' signifies God himself, as all interpreters acknowledge. But no man can have the least knowledge of this unless he is skilled in the mysteries of the law." He adds moreover: "'*My face shall go before you,*' that is, '*the Angel of the covenant, whom you desire, in whom my face shall be seen;*' of whom it is said, '*In an acceptable time have I heard you; my name is in him; I will cause you to rest, or cause that he shall be gentle or kind to you, nor shall lead you with rigor, but qui-etly and mercifully.'"*

22. R. Moses Bar Nachman wrote around the year of the Lord 1220, in Spain, and died at Jerusalem in 1260, and he is one of the chief masters of the Jews. There are many things occurring in his writings that are beyond the common present understanding of the Jews. We see this especially in the places cited where he plainly exposes one of the principal foundations of their present infidelity. For he not only grants, but contends and proves, that the Angel spoken of was God; and being sent of God as his angel, he must be a *distinct person* in the Godhead, just as we have proved.

The reason why he says he is called an Angel is, *"because he governs the world."* Although the thing in it-self is true, it is not so proper. He is called this because of his eternal designation and actual delegation by the Father to the work of saving the church, in all conditions from first to last. As he acknowledged that his being called *"The face of God"* proves him to be God, it also no less evidently reveals his personal distinction from him whose face he is—that is, *"the brightness of his glory, and the express image of his person."* The language he adds about the mercy and kindliness of God which comes by the appointment of God, is implemented towards his people, and is a fitting symbol of the tenderness and mercy which the great Captain of our salvation exercises by God's appointment towards all those whom he leads and brings to glory.

23. It is also beneficial to consider what some of them write in *Tanchuma*, an ancient comment on the five books of Moses. Speaking of the Angel that went before them from Exodus 23:20, "God," they say, "said to Moses, *'Behold, I send my Angel before you face.'* But Moses answered, *'I will not have an angel, I will only have yourself.'* But when Joshua the son of Nun first saw the angel, he said, *'Are you for us, or for our adversaries?'* Then the angel answered, *'I am the Captain of the LORD'S host, and now I come.'* As if he had said, 'I have come a second time, that I may lead the Israelites into their possession. I came when Moses your master was the ruler; but when he saw me, he would not have me to go with him, but refused me.' As soon as Joshua heard this, he fell on his face and worshipped, saying, *'What does my Lord say to his servant?'"*

An answer to this in the Talmud[15] comes from a gloss on these words, *"He will not pardon your transgressions"* (Ex 23:21). It says, *"'He cannot spare or pardon your transgressions;'* what then does he do, or could he do? Thus, he said to him (to God), 'We believe that he cannot pardon our transgressions, and therefore we refuse him, and will not accept him; certainly not as a leader to go in and out before us.'" They greatly mistake in supposing that the angel who Moses refused

---

[15] *Tractat. Sanhed.*, cap. iv., Echad dine Mamonoth.

was the same who afterwards appeared to Joshua; for the angel appearing to Joshua was the same with him in whom was the "name of God," and who was promised to them under the name of the face or presence of God. But they were right enough on one thing, not that Moses, but their *church* under the law refused the "Angel of God's presence," who was to conduct all who obey him into everlasting rest. And the church of believers under Joshua, which was a type of the church of the New Testament, when they conformed themselves to him, found rest for their souls.

24. This Angel of whom we have spoken is the one whom the Talmudists call "Metatron." Ben Uzziel,[16] in his Targum on Genesis 5, ascribes this name to Enoch. He ascended, he says, into heaven, by the word of the Lord, "and his name was called Metatron, the great scribe." But this opinion is rejected and confuted in the Talmud. There they tell us that "Metatron" is "the prince of the world," or, as Elijah calls him in Tishbi,[17] "the prince of God's presence." The mention of this name is in Talmud,[18] where they plainly intimate that they meant an uncreated Angel by this name. For they assign such things to him as are impossible to any other. And, as Reuchlin informs us from the Cabbalists, they say, "Metatron was the

---

[16] This is Targum Pseudo-Jonathan.
[17] Elijah Levita (1469-1549). *Tishbi* refers to his dictionary of the Talmud, Midrash, and Targums.
[18] *Tract. Sanhed.*, cap. iv.

master or teacher of Moses himself." "He it is," says Elijah, "who is the angel always appearing in the presence of God; of whom it is said, 'My name is in him.'" The Talmudists add, that he has power to blot out the sins of Israel, which is why they call him "The chancellor of heaven." Bechai, a famous master among them, affirms that his name signifies both a lord, a messenger, and a keeper (on Exodus 23). A *lord*, because he rules all; a *messenger*, because he always stands before God, to do his will; and a *keeper*, because he keeps Israel.

The etymology, I confess, which he gives for this name is weak and foolish; nor is the one Elijah gives any better, when he tells us that "Metatron" is the "one sent." But it is evident that what they intend by these obscure guesses, which are the corrupted relics of ancient traditions, namely, the uncreated Prince of glory, who, being Lord of all, appeared long ago to the patriarchs as the angel or messenger of the Father. As for the word itself, it is either a corrupt expression of the Latin "mediator," such as is usual amongst them, or a made-up word using gematria in order to answer to *Shaddai*, the "Almighty," given that there is numerical significance to their letters.[19]

---

[19] *Metatron*. No one to this day quite knows the origin of this name. Sometimes called "lesser Yahweh," some have suggested the possibility that the "him" in Ex 23:21 ("because my name is within him [the Angel])" refers to Metatron, where the *ttr* in the word comes from *tetra*, the word for "four" in Greek, and a shorthand for the Tetragrammaton—YHWH. See Andrei A. Orlov, *The Etymology of*

This was another way in which God instructed the church of old in the mystery of the person of the Messiah who was promised to them.[20]

the Name 'Metatron," in *The Enoch-Metatron Tradition* (TSAJ, 107; Tuebiingen: Mohr-Sieback, 2005). An excerpt is here (http://www.marquette.edu/maqom/meta-tronname.html#_ftnref24).
[20] You can read the Banner of Truth version of this work in John Owen, *An Exposition of the Epistle to the Hebrews*, ed. W. H. Goold, vol. 18, Works of John Owen (Edinburgh: Johnstone and Hunter, 1854), 215–233.

Peter Allix

A Dissertation Concerning the Angel Who is called the Redeemer

SIR,

YOU DO VERY TRULY observe, that the subject of our last but short conversation is a matter of the greatest moment and deserving the utmost care in the discussion of it. When mention was made there of the Angel, whose blessing Jacob prayed might descend on the sons of Joseph, I asserted he was none other than the *Logos*, or Word. You were not then very inclined to embrace this notion, being carried away with the authority of some great names, especially of Grotius,[21] who understands this Angel in Jacob's prayer to be only a created angel.

But having not the time to hear the grounds of my assertion, you were desirous I should put them with whatever clarity I could into writing, in hopes that the same arguments, if they should prove cogent to bring you over to my opinion, might be of use to others who were in the same sentiments with yourself. So with this good end being proposed, I set myself without delay to your commands; and having digested my thoughts in this paper, I now send them to you, entreating you to judge of them, as you are inclined of the labors of your friend, with all impartiality and humanity, still remembering that I made it my only care to express my thoughts clearly, and to find out the truth, and to deliver it naturally, according to the best of my understanding. And so, I come to the question in hand.

SECT. I.

MOSES HAVING RELATED how Joseph took his two sons along with him to Jacob his father that lay sick, in order to obtain his blessing on them before he died,

---

[21] Hugo Grotius (1583-1645). Dutch Jurist and Arminian theologian, he is noted for his "governmental" or "moral government" theory of the atonement and for being imprisoned for his views.

goes on to give us the form in which he blessed them, Gen 48:15-16:

> 15 And he blessed Joseph and said, "The God before whom my fathers Abraham and Isaac walked, the God who has been my shepherd all my life long to this day,
> 16 the angel who has redeemed me from all evil, bless the boys; and in them let my name be carried on, and the name of my fathers Abraham and Isaac; and let them grow into a multitude in the midst of the earth."

These words are thus rendered by the Greek Interpreters, commonly called the Septuagint:

> 15 And he blessed them and said, "The God, whom my fathers Abraham and Isaac were pleasing before him, the Lord who nourishes me from youth to day, this
> 16 the angel who rescues me from all evils, may he bless these children, and in them my name and the name of my fathers Abraham and Isaac will be invoked, and may they be multiplied into a great multitude upon the earth.[22]

And in the Latin version;

---

[22] Rick Brannan et al., eds., *The Lexham English Septuagint* (Bellingham, WA: Lexham Press, 2012), Ge 48:15–16.

¹⁵ And Jacob blessed the sons of Joseph, and said: God, in whose sight my fathers Abraham and Isaac walked, God that feeds me from my youth until this day:

¹⁶ The angel that delivers me from all evils, bless these boys: and let my name be called upon them, and the names of my fathers Abraham and Isaac; and may they grow into a multitude upon the earth.[23]

You see there is little or no difference between these versions and the Hebrew, with which also agrees the Spanish version of Athias and Usquez, which was printed in the last age at Ferrara,[24] and which is of great authority with the Jews and serves in the place of the Hebrew text to those who cannot read it. It renders indeed, *The God who fed me*, by *El dio governan a mi*, and the word *goel who has redeemed me*, by *El redimien a mi*, or, *my Redeemer*; but the sense is not altered at all.

Drusius[25] notes in his fragments of the ancient interpreters of the Old Testament that the participle *goel* here attributed to the Angel, is rendered *agchisteus* by

---

[23] *The Holy Bible, Translated from the Latin Vulgate* (Bellingham, WA: Logos Bible Software, 2009), Ge 48:15–16. Language slightly modernized.

[24] Allix refers here to The Ferrara Bible of 1553, which was paid for and made by Yom-Tov Ben Levi Athias (the typographer) and Abraham ben Salomon Usque the translator) and dedicated to the Duke of Ferrara. It was a translation of an older circulating Spanish translation.

[25] Johannes van den Driesche (1550-1616). Flemish Protestant divine who was an Orientalist, Christian Hebraist, and exegete.

the Greek translators in Ruth 4:8, which imports the next of kin to whom the right of inheritance belongs and with it the relict of his deceased relation. From this translation of the word, St. Jerome, and after him many other divines, taking this Angel to be the Messiah, have collected a relation peculiar of this Angel to the family of Jacob, of which the Messiah was to be born.[26] Christ, he says, shall come and redeem us with his blood; who, as the Hebrew has it, is of kin to Zion, and is descended from the stock of Israel; for so the word *goel* or *agchisteus* signifies.

But there is another sense of the words, *g'l* and *goel* and according to which the Greek interpreters do more commonly render them, I mean that of *lutroun* and *lutrōtēs*, which confirms the use of the like word in the Spanish version. If you would see the places, you may consult Kircher's Concordance.[27]

The whole difficulty therefore of the place may be reduced to three heads, which I shall propose by way of question:

I.   Whether the *elohim* spoken of in vs. 15 is the very YHWH [or YHVH or Yahweh or LORD] whom the Jews acknowledge for their God?

---

[26] Jerome on Isaiah 59.
[27] Nearly 300 years before Strong would publish his famous concordance (in 1890), the Lutheran Conrad Kircher published a concordance of the Greek Septuagint in 1607.

II.   Whether the mentioned in vs. 16 is the same as the *elohim* in vs. 15 or differs from him as a creature does from its Creator?

III. Whether the prayer contained in Jacob's blessing is made to God alone, or to the redeeming Angel together with him?

SECT. II.

IN ANSWER TO THE FIRST QUESTION we do not need to look far: for Onkelos[28] in his Chaldee [i.e. Aramaic] paraphrase expounds the word *elohim* by *YHVH*. Jonathan has done the same in his version. Nor do I know any Christian who ever blamed them for it. Why should they? Since it is evident for those who consider this text carefully, as the Christians generally do the holy Scriptures, that these Targumists have faithfully expressed the mind of Jacob.

Jacob had been remembering that appearance where God had blessed him at Luz, in these words,

---

[28] This is the Aramaic Targum Onkelos. A Targum is a paraphrastic rendition of the Hebrew Scripture into Aramaic for Jews who did not speak Hebrew. They were probably written down around the first century by Jews. Genesis has three main Targums: Onkelos, Neofiti, and Pseudo-Jonathan (which he cites next). To help with their differences, think of them like the *NIV*, *The Living Bible*, and *The Message*, in that order. They can be mostly literal like Onkelos, or more adventuresome like Pseudo-Jonathan.

"God Almighty appeared to me at Luz in the land of Canaan, and blessed me, and said to me, 'Behold, I will make you fruitful, and multiply you, and I will make of you a multitude of people; and give this land to your descendants [seed] *after you as an everlasting possession'"* (Gen 48:3-4).[29] Now what can be more absurd than to imagine that Jacob, when he blesses Joseph's sons and prays for the increase of his posterity by them, would direct his prayers to anyone other than the one whose kindnesses he had so abundantly experienced, and whose promises for the multiplication of his seed were even now fresh in his memory?

This I thought fit to observe against those of the Jews that doubt of it, following as they think the author of the book of Genesis Rabbah[30] who notes that a lesser title is given to the Angel than to him who is called *Elohim*; as if he had a mind thereby to tell us that by the angel here mentioned, Jacob meant a mere angel and not God.

If the author of Genesis Rabbah had understood this of a created angel, he certainly made a very great mistake. For, besides the absurdity of this opinion, it is a blasphemy to suppose that Abraham and Isaac are

[29] The 1821 edition does not quite read like the KJV, but it is close. So, I have used the NKJV for better readability here and in many places.
[30] Written between 300-500 A.D., *Genesis Rabbah* is a midrash (interpretation) of ancient rabbinical sermons interpreting the book of Genesis. The reference in the margin is *Mattenot Kehun* [*Matnoth Kehunah*], f. 23. Col. 4. And f. 108. Col. 3.

commended for walking before the angel as Jacob asserts they did before God. "*God*," he says, "*before whom my fathers Abraham and Isaac walked*" (Gen 48:15). For the word "to walk" in this place comprehends all the acts of their religion throughout their whole lives, and so Moses uses the word to describe the entire obedience of Enoch (Gen 5:22). A modern Jew, R. Salomon Aben Melek,[31] acknowledges in his *The Perfection of Beauty* on this place, that the word *to walk* denotes the worship of the heart which a creature owes to God.

But that the author of the Rabbah understood it of an uncreated Angel, who is often called in the Old Testament *Elohim* and *Jehovah* and *Jehovah Elohim*, I little doubt, because he quotes the same authority in this place, which we meet with in *Bab. Talm. Pesachim*[32] (cap. x. fol. 118. col. 1). And which makes this Angel to be God.[33]

---

[31] The "R." refers to Rabbi. Solomon ben Melek was from Fez, in modern Morocco. Little is known of him. He published his Bible commentary *Michlol Jophi* (*Perfection of Beauty*) in 1549 through a press in Constantinople. It was later published in 1660 and 1685 in Amsterdam by Jacob Abendana.

[32] The Talmud is the long, written oral traditions of the Jews written down in the centuries after the destruction of the temple in 70 A.D. "Pesachim," in the Babylonian Talmud, is mostly taken up with the laws of Passover and the lamb offering.

[33] The Talmud can be difficult to figure out what is original and what is not. This reference is a good case-study. For instance, in Neusner's English edition, the Hebrew reads that R. Yohanan said, "Providing food for a person is more difficult than redemption, for with respect to redemption, it is written, 'The angel who has redeemed me from all evil' (Gen. 48:16) ... of food: 'the God who has fed me' (Gen. 48:15)." This seems to support Allix' point. But when you add the Aramaic you get, "Providing food for a person is more

But if he was of another mind, we might have other Jews, and of no less authority, to oppose to him. These understand it as we do. Particularly, we have the prayers of the Jewish Church. Many of them allude to this and places like it in Genesis as saying they refer only to God exclusively, and not from a created angel, for he has the title of Redeemer, who delivers from all evil (see *Talm. Hier. tr. Berac.* cap. 4. fol. 8. col. 1. and their Liturgies).

I know Cyril of Alexandria[34] would have Jacob to understand God the Father by *Elohim* (vs. 15), and the eternal Son of God by the redeeming Angel. He confirms this explication with Ephesians 1:2, "*Grace be to*

---

difficult than redemption, for with respect to redemption, it is written, 'The angel who has redeemed me from all evil' (Gen. 48:16) *thus an everyday angel was enough*; of food: 'the God who has fed me' (Gen. 48:15)." (Jacob Neusner, *The Babylonian Talmud: A Translation and Commentary*, vol. 4 [Peabody, MA: Hendrickson Publishers, 2011], 546). This obviously makes his point null and void. But, again, it is not in the original Hebrew and it is clear that Allix is not reading any edition that merges both languages into a single text.

Another edition reads very much like the Aramaic addition. "R. Johanan said again: The earning of a man's daily bread is beset with more difficulty than the redemption; for concerning the redemption it is written [Gen. 48:16]: 'The angel who redeemed me from all evil,' while concerning a man's daily bread it is written [ibid. 15]: 'The God who fed me from my first being unto this day,' whence we see that for redemption it only required an angel, while for the sustenance of a man it required God's providence." (Michael L. Rodkinson, tran., *The Babylonian Talmud: Original Text, Edited, Corrected, Formulated, and Translated into English*, vol. 5 (Boston, MA: The Talmud Society, 1918), 250–251). Curiously, many online editions do not have this section at all!

[34] Lib. vi. in Gen. p. 210. This is found in Cyril's *Glaphyrorum in Genesim* (*Elegant Comments on Genesis*) in *Patrologia Graeca (PG)*, vol. 69.

you, and peace from God our Father, and the Lord Jesus Christ," because grace is nothing but the blessing of God communicated to the Church by the Father and the Son. But St. Chrysostom's[35] opinion is much more probable to me, who asserts *Elohim* to be the eternal Son of God, that is described in both the fifteenth and sixteenth verses by different titles.

In this he followed all the ancient Christians, who used to ascribe to the Son all the appearances of God or of the Angel of Jehovah that are mentioned by Moses; and who teach in particular, that the blessing of the *Logos* was prayed for by Jacob in this place.

I have no misgivings in asserting that the ancient Christians ascribed all the appearances of God in Moses' writings to the eternal *Logos*, having the following authorities for my assertion. Justin Martyr, *Against Trypho*; Clement of Alexandria, *The Instructor* 1.7; Tertullian, *Against the Jews* 9; Origen, *On Isaiah* 6; Cyprian, *Against the Jews* 2.5; *Apostolic Constitutions* 5.20; Eusebius, *Church History* 1.3; Cyril, *Catechetical Lectures* 12.16; *The Council of Sirmium* (351), Canon 13;[36]

---

[35] Homily 66. In Gen. p. 7.

[36] The original reference appears to be slightly off. Variously numbered 15 or 14, the first reads, "If anyone says that the Son did not appear to Abraham, but the unbegotten God, or a part of Him, let him be anathema." The next reads, "If anyone says that the Son did not wrestle with Jacob as a man, but the unbegotten God, or a part of Him, let him be anathema." The next, "If anyone understands the words, 'Then the Lord rained fire from the Lord' (Gen 19:24), not as referring to the Father and the Son, but says that He (the Father) sent rain from Himself, let him be anathema. For the Lord the Son sent rain from the Lord the Father. See Charles Joseph

Gregory of Elvira, *On Faith*; Theodoret of Cyrus, *Questions on Exodus* 5; Leo, *Letter 31 to Pulcheria*, and many others. In like manner, they refer to the Word, those appearances of God, which he promised to Abraham, Isaac, and Jacob himself, as you may see in Justin Martyr, *Apology*, for those to Abraham and Isaac; and for those to Jacob, in Clement of Alexandria, *The Instructor* 1.7; Novatian, *On the Trinity* 26, 27; Procopius of Gaza in h. 1.

In this, the ancient Christians did no more than the even older Jews did before them, who by *Elohim* in this place did not understand a created angel, but the *Logos*, whom the Targumists and the strictest followers of their fathers' traditions are wont to express by the *Shekinah* (Glory) and the *Memra* (Word).

Philo makes all the appearances which we meet with in the books of Moses to belong to the Word, and the latter Cabalists (since Christ's time) not only do the same, but deny that the Father ever appeared, saying, it was the *Logos* only that manifested himself to their fathers, whose proper name is *Elohim*. For this consult R. Menachem de Rekanati,[37] from *Genesis Rabbah* on the *Parasch* (see *Bresch.* f. 14. c. 3. *Ed. Ven.* and on *Par.* לד לד, f. 30. c. 1).

Hefele, "72. New Synod and First Formula of Sirmium in 351," in *A History of the councils of the Church from the Original Documents*, vol. 2 A.D. 326 to 429, (Edinburgh: T&T Clark, 1896), 196.
[37] Menahem ben Benjamin Recanati (1223-1290). Italian rabbi who wrote a commentary on the Torah.

I have often wondered how it came to pass, that most of the Divines of the Church of Rome, who would seem to have the greatest veneration for antiquity, would so much despise it in this question, while the ancient Jewish and Christian Church agree. Sanctius[38] in his notes on Acts 7 says it is a difficult question among Divines, whether God's appearances in Scripture were performed immediately by God himself, or by his angels. And then having cited several ancient Fathers who thought it was the *Logos* that appeared, he adds, "But currently, the theologians prefer that judgment which states that in the ministry of angels a divine form was presented to ancient people; this is the judgment of Dionysius, etc."[39] Lorinus,[40] another Jesuit, says something similar in Acts 7:31.

But this is not the worst of it, that they forsake the judgment of the ancients; for they also make bold to contradict the plain words of Christ himself in John 1:18. Christ says, *"No man has seen God at any time, the only-begotten who is in the bosom of the Father he has declared him."* And parallel to this text is John 6:46. Certainly he must be very blind who does not see that Christ in

---

[38] Gaspar Sanchez (1553-1628). Spanish Jesuit. Taught at Oropesa in Madrid. Spent thirteen years writing commentaries on Scripture.
[39] Thanks to Arjen Vreugdenhil for the translation.
[40] Lorinus of Avignon (1559-1634). *The Cambridge Encyclopedia of the Jesuits* has only one entry for "Lorinus." It reads, "Three other Jesuits are known to have published commentaries on Scripture, but beyond their names and the approximate time in which they lived, not much is known of them."

these words not only denies that the Father had showed himself in those appearances that were made to the ancient patriarchs, but that he also ascribes them to himself and not to the angels.

Away then with such Divines who, setting aside the authority of Christ, choose to theologize in the principal heads of religion according to the sense and prejudices of the modern Jews. We do not desire to be wiser in these matters than the primitive Christians were, among whom it passed for an established truth, that the *Elohim* in Jacob's prayer was the very Jehovah of the Jews, termed by them sometimes as *Shekinah*, and sometimes as *Memra*.

SECT. III.

As to the second question it would be no question at all, but for the obstinacy of some latter Jews. He who reads the Hebrew text without prejudice cannot but see that the Elohim in vs. 15. is called *ha-melek ha-goel 'oti* ("*the angel who has redeemed me*") in the following verse. Thus, it follows that this redeeming Angel is *Jehovah*.

Because this opinion is contradicted by some of the chief modern Jews such as Abarbanel[41] and Alshek[42] on this place, and by most of the Popish Divines, as well as by a few of the Reformed that have not sifted this matter accurately, we will offer some proofs for the conviction of those who are not obstinately bent against the truth.

1. If Jacob had two Persons in his mind as different as God and a created angel are, he would have coupled them together by the particle which is not only conjunctive, but very proper to distinguish the Persons of whom we speak. He would have said, "*God before whom my Fathers walked, God who fed me from my youth; and the Angel that delivered me, bless the lads.*" But Jacob is so far from doing this that on the contrary he puts a ה (*he*) demonstrative before the "Angel," just as he did before "God," without any copulative between. This sufficiently demonstrates that he means the same Person by God and the Angel. Munsterus[43] was well aware of this, and therefore being willing to distinguish the

---

[41] Don Isaac Abravanel (1437-1508). Jewish statemen, religious Jew, scholar, Bible commentator and philosopher of the "Spanish Golden Age."

[42] Moshe Alshich (1508-1593). Prominent rabbi, preacher, commentator. Little is known of him. Legend says his son was kidnapped as a child and became a Muslim and that a special prayer was written for his return.

[43] Sebastian Münster (1488-1552). German cartographer, cosmographer, and Christian Hebraist scholar. Early on he was a Franciscan, then became Lutheran to accept a chair at the University of Basel.

redeeming Angel from God, he translates it with an addition, the Angel also.

2. It cannot be easily supposed that Jacob would, in a prayer, use the singular verb *ybrk* ("to bless") as saying the same thing of two persons so very different in their natures as are the Creator and a creature. He certainly ought to have said, "God and the angel" (*ybrcu*, the plural form) may they bless the lads, if he had spoken of two. But his speaking in the singular, "may he bless," is an argument of his having in his eye one Person alone, whose blessing he asked for his seed. Otherwise it would have been a prayer of a strange composition; for according to Athanasius, nowhere do we find that one prays to God and the angel, or any other created being at the same time for anything. Nor is there any similar instance of such a form as this, "God and an angel give you this."

3. But setting aside those rules with which the contrary opinion can never be reconciled, consider the thing itself in Jacob's prayer, and you will find it absurd to distinguish between the offices of God and those of a created angel toward Jacob. The office ascribed to God is feeding him from his youth; the office ascribed to the angel is delivering him from all evil; which must be very distinct offices, if the Persons are to be distinguished. And so R. Jochanan[44] accounts them (*Gem.*

---

[44] R. Yohanan ben Zeccai (30-90 A.D.). A primary contributor to the core text of the Mishnah.

Pesasch. fol. 118). Though he believes the Angel to be the same with *Elohim*, yet he contends that feeding, the greater work, is attributed to God; and delivering, the lesser work, to an angel. The same thing is said by the author of Jalkut[45] on this place; and R. Samuel[46] on the book Rabboth above mentioned. But in the phrase of these Jewish masters this distinction is very insipid; it is harshly formed, without considering that Jacob in this blessing reflected on the words of the vow which he made at Luz and afterwards called Bethel, because of God's appearing to him there.

Now, these were the words of Jacob's vow, "*If God will be with me, and keep me in the way in which I shall walk: if he will give meat to eat, and clothing to put on, and bring me home in safety to the house of my father, then shall the Lord be my God*" (Gen 28:20-21). Here you see it is from God that Jacob expects to be kept in his way, *i.e.* to be redeemed from all evils that might happen, and that he esteems this to be no less a benefit than sustenance or clothing, which he mentions in the second place. Here is no angel spoken of; and since the redeeming Angel is to be expounded from this place, he cannot be a created angel, for here is no other spoken of but the Lord.

4. By fancying him a created angel who delivered Jacob from all evil, they make Jacob to be a mere

---

[45] R. Shimeon of Frankfurt (13th cent.). Jalkut is a collection of commentaries from various ancient books.
[46] One of the early rabbinical authorities cited in Genesis Rabbah.

idolater, as ascribing to a creature that which belongs only to the Lord of the creation. The Scripture appropriates to God the title of Redeemer, *kat exochen*; nor do godly men ever say of a creature that it delivers them from all evil. David, I am sure, never does; but when he speaks of *"the tribulations of the righteous"* he adds, *"but the Lord delivers him out of all"* (Ps 34:19). And Jacob on another occasion directs his prayer to the Lord that appeared to him at Luz, saying, *"Save me from the hand of my brother Esau, for I fear him much"* (Gen 32:9, 10, 11).

5. God, as I said, has so appropriated the name of Redeemer to himself, so that Jacob could not without sacrilege communicate this title to any creature, no matter how excellent. We cannot be ignorant that David makes this the proper name of God (Ps 19:14), as does Isa 23:14 and 47:4. And this Jonathan confesses on Isa 63:16 in these words, *"You are our Redeemer, your name is from everlasting,"*[47] *i.e.* this is the name that was designed for God from the beginning; which yet cannot hold true, if in Gen 48:16 Jacob is talking about a created angel.

6. It appears plainly from Genesis 49 that Jacob neither desired nor expected any blessing from a created angel, but only from God. Thus he prays, *"The*

---

[47] "Jonathan" appears to be a reference to the Targum by Jonathan ben Uziel. But while this targum does have these words, so does the Scripture itself. The Targum does reference Abraham here, but not Jacob.

God of your father shall be your helper, and the Almighty shall bless you with the blessings of heaven above..." (Gen 49:25). Not a word of a mere angel that redeemed him from all evil; so far was the Patriarch in his former blessing from begging of an angel the multiplication of his seed, which was the only thing which he could now expect of God, as the Jews own (see *Bechai Prof, in Pent.* fol. 1. c. 1).

7. The same conclusion may be drawn from the very order of Jacob's prayer. Had Jacob intended a created angel by the one he says redeemed him from evil, and whose intercession with God he signifies on behalf of his children, would he not have prayed to the angel in the first place? It was most rational to do so. He who wants the interest of a great man to introduce him to the king does not in the first place direct his petition to the king immediately, but first to the great man, and afterwards by him to the king. Let the Papists therefore look to the absurdity of their proceeding, while they pray first to God, and then to saints and angels. Let those Jews who are of the mind of Isaac Abarbanel and Franco Serrano,[48] in his Spanish notes on this place, and contend for angel-worship, see how they can clear themselves of this difficulty, as well as reconcile

---

[48] Joseph Franco Serrano (1652-1695). Rabbi, teacher of Hebrew at the Portuguese synagogue in Amsterdam. He provided a Spanish translation of the books of Moses with marginal notes from the Talmud and the Rabbis who commented on them.

themselves with those ancienter Jews who abhorred this sort of idolatry (Maimonides, *Per, Misna ad tit. Sank.* c. xi).

SECT. IV.

HOW FIRM THESE REASONS ARE that the angel we are speaking about is uncreated and not a created angel is, I hope, evident to everyone. Something, however, of great importance may be still added to illustrate this weighty argument, and that is the judgment of the ancient synagogue. The most ancient Jewish writers, and those who received the traditional doctrine from them, though mortal enemies of the Christian religion, still agree with the Christians in the sense of this text. For, God be thanked, such truths were not renounced all at once by these enemies of our faith. Rather, they began to conceal or discard them by degrees, as they found those arguments turning against themselves in their disputes with the Christians.

To begin with the writings of the Jews before Christ, we find it is *God* the Word, ver. 12. who is described as he that delivers from all evil, in the Book of Wisdom (Wis 16:8, 12),[49] no doubt with respect to this

---

[49] "And in this you made your enemies confess, that it is you who delivers from all evil ... For neither herb nor poultice cured them, but it was your Word, O Lord, that helps all people."

place, where he takes the angel that delivered Jacob from all evil, to be God.

The same doctrine can be found in Philo the Jew, who lived both before and during the life of Christ (20 B.C. – 50 A.D.). He expressly affirms of the Angel that delivered Jacob from all evil, that he was the *Logos*.[50] And so does Onkelos in his Chaldee paraphrase, translating the words of Jacob naturally, as they lie in the text, without any addition.

Jonathan[51] indeed seems to be of another mind in his paraphrase which runs thus, "*God before whom my fathers Abraham and Isaac worshipped, the Lord that fed me from the time I began to be till this day, may be pleased that the Angel may bless the lads, whom you have ordained to deliver me from all evil.*" Here he distinguishes the Angel from God; but that he did not mean a creature by this Angel is clear, for in other places he translates this Angel by the Word, or *mmr' dvvy* (or *mymr' dyy*, that is "Word of the Lord, cf. Gen 15:6), and especially in that remarkable place where the same Angel is treated in Isa 63:8-10, he says it was the *Word* that redeemed Israel out of all their afflictions.

---

[50] The margin note has Allegor. Ii. P. 71. D. In *Allegorical Interpretation* III 177 we read, "But these men pray to be nourished by the Word (*Logos*) of God: But Jacob, raising his head above the Word, says that he is nourished by God himself, and his words are as follows ... and he speaks of the angel, which is the word, as the physician of his evils, in this speaking most naturally."

[51] Targum Pseudo-Jonathan.

Let us pass on to the Jews after Christ's time, and show that they did not immediately renounce the doctrine of their forefathers.

The author of the book of Zohar[52] (Par. ויהי Fol. 123) has these words, which he repeats often afterwards, "*Come, see the Angel that redeemed me*" is the Shekinah that went along with him.

This is sufficiently intimated by the ancient author Tanchuma,[53] in his book Jelammedenu,[54] who notes on Exodus 33 that the Jews would not have a created angel to go before them, but God himself, in these words, "*Moses answered, I will not have an angel, but your own self.*" Now the Jewish commentators on this place of Exodus 33 explain of the *Shekinah*, the words, "*your own self*," and always distinguish the *Shekinah* from all created beings.

R. Solomon in his notes on this text has these words, "*The Angel that delivered me,*" i.e. The Angel who was accustomed to be sent to me in my affliction (Gen 31) as it is said, "*And the Angel of God spoke to me in a dream, saying, Jacob, I am the God of Bethel,*" etc.

The note of R. Moses Ben Nachman[55] on Genesis 48:16 is very remarkable. "'*The redeeming Angel,*' he

---

[52] The foundational text of the Kabbalah.
[53] Tanchuma bar Abba. Jewish Rabbi (fl. 350-71).
[54] A popular Homily-Midrash originating in Israel after the 8th century. It bears Tanchuma's name but was not written by him.
[55] Moses ben Nahman (1194-1270). Leading medieval Jewish scholar, rabbi, philosopher, physician, kabbalist, and biblical commentator. He lived most of his life in Girona, Catalonia (Spain).

says, is he who answered him in the time of his affliction, and who said to him, '*I am the God of Bethel,*' etc.
'*he,*' of whom it is said, that '*my name* is in him.'" He
says the same thing on Exodus 3 where the appearance
in the bush is mentioned: "'*This is he of whom it is said,
and God called Moses out of the bush.*' He is called an Angel, because he governs the world; for it is written in
one place, And '*Jehovah,*' that is, the '*Lord God, brought
us out of Egypt;*' and in another place, '*He sent his Angel
and brought as out of Egypt.*' And again, '*The Angel of his
presence saved them,*' viz. that Angel who is the face of
God, of whom it is said, '*My face shall go before you.*'
Lastly, that Angel of whom the prophet Malachi mentions, '*And the Lord whom you seek shall suddenly come to
his temple, even the Angel of the covenant, whom you desire.*'"
At length he adds, "The face of God is God himself, as
all interpreters do acknowledge; but none can rightly
understand this without being instructed in the mysteries of the Law."

R. Menachem of Rekan on Genesis 48:16, is the
same who later commented on the whole Pentateuch,
was no stranger to this notion. "He means the Shekinah, says he, when he speaks of the redeeming Angel"
(f. 52. See also f. 55).

Similarly, R. Bechai,[56] the famous Jewish writer,
whose comments are constantly in the hands of the

---

[56] Bahya ben Asher ibn Halawa (1255-1340). Distinguished Spanish
rabbi who wrote a commentary on the Hebrew Bible.

Jewish Doctors. He proves that this blessing is not different from that which is afterwards repeated in Genesis 49 where no angel is mentioned. Thus, it follows that the three terms in Gen 48, "*God ... God that fed me ... the Angel that redeemed me,*" are synonymous to the Mighty One of Jacob (Gen 49:25), the title the Jews in their prayers frequently ascribe to God (*Bech.* f. 71. c. 4. ed. *Rivæ di Trento*). He also teaches there that this Angel was the *Shekinah*. As does R. Joseph Gekatilia[57] in his book called *Saare Ora* (*Gates of Light*), according to Menasseh Ben Israel[58] (q. 64. in Gen. p. 118). Aben Sueb[59] on this place, a man of name among his party, writes much to the same purpose here as well.

These are followed by two eminent authors of the Cabalists. The one in his notes on the Zohar (f. 122) toward the end says, "*The Angel that delivered me from all evil is the Shekinah,*" is the one of whom it had said, "'*And the Angel of the Lord, who went before the camp of Israel, removed and went behind them;*'" and may God bless us in the age to come" (Ex 14:19). The other is he who contracted the Zohar on Genesis and is called R. David

---

[57] Joseph ben Abraham Gikatilla (1248-1305). Spanish kabbalist.
[58] Born Manoel Dias Soeiro (1604-1657). Portuguese rabbi, kabbalist, writer, diplomat, and founded the first Hebrew printing press in Amsterdam in 1626. The book cited seems to be *Primo Questionum in Genesis*, previously published as *The Conciliator*.
[59] Joel ibn Shu'aib (15th cent). Spanish rabbi, preaching, commentator.

the Less.[60] In that book (*ed. Thessalonic.* f. 174), he professes to follow the opinion of R. Gekatalia in his *Saare Ora*.

Nor does Menasseh Ben Israel himself dissent much from these in the above-mentioned place. For though he attempts to reconcile Gen 48:16[61] with the First Commandment, "*You shall have no other gods before me*" (Ex 20:3), by saying it was the opinion of several of their masters that there was no contradiction between them. Yet he produces the opinion of the Cabalists at length, for the satisfaction of his readers, who possibly would not agree in former reasons drawn only from modern authorities.

I did not mention R. Levi ben Gersom's[62] opinion, who denies the Angel here spoken of to be a creature, but calls him the *Intellectus Agens*, because he seems to have borrowed this notion from the Arabian philosophers; nor is it commonly received by those of his religion. Many others might be added to these Jewish testimonies; but what I have already produced is, I think, very sufficient.

---

[60] Probably David ben Yom Tov ibn Bilia (c. 1300-1361). Portuguese Hebrew scholar, translator, philosopher, exegete, and poet who wrote *Me'or Enayim*, a commentary on the Pentateuch.
[61] The original reads 28:16. This is surely a typo, though a difficult one (xxviii vs. xlviii). See comments on R. Menasseh below.
[62] Better known as Gersonides or Magister Leo Hebraeus (1288-1344). French Jewish philosopher, Talmudist, Mathematician, physician, astronomer. Wrote several commentaries on Scripture.

SECT. V.

HAVING THUS SHOWED the opinions of the ancient Jews concerning Jacob's Angel, and that to this day the tradition is not quite worn out that exalts him above a created angel; I now proceed to the third question, the clearing of which will fully justify that opinion of the ancient Jews concerning this text.

And that is, whether this form of blessing is also a prayer? The soundest and most popular view of Jews and Christians agree, that we cannot worship angels without idolatry. This Maimonides[63] affirms, as I quoted him above; and the Protestants, as all men know, abhor this idolatry in the Roman Church.

I do therefore positively assert that these words contain a prayer to the Angel, as well as to God, for a blessing on his children. This the Jews cannot oppose, since Jonathan their paraphrast, and other writers after him, do commonly term this blessing *tephillah* or a *prayer*. For this reason, R. Menasseh thought it necessary to endeavor to reconcile this section of the prayer of Jacob with the First Commandment; which forbids angel-worship according to the Jews' interpretation (R. *Menach. de Reh. in Pent.* f. 97. c. 4).

It is true that Jacob's form of blessing does seem to proceed from him either as a wish or a prophecy: a

---

[63] Moses ben Maimon (1135-1204). Spanish born rabbi who become one of the most influential of all medieval Torah scholars.

wish, as if he had said, "Would to the Lord, God and his Angel would bless the lads." A prophecy, as if he had foretold that God and his Angel would in after-times fulfil what he now wished. But it might be both a wish and a prophecy, and notwithstanding be a direct prayer to God and the redeeming Angel. It is well known how the Jews commonly delivered their petitions to God in this form. And yet I cannot refrain from giving one instance to confirm it. You may read it in Numbers 6:22ff. *"And the Lord said to Moses, saying, Speak to Aaron and his sons, Thus shall you bless the children of Israel, and say, 'The Lord bless[64] you, and keep you: The Lord make his face shine upon you, and be gracious to you: The Lord lift up his countenance upon you, and give you peace.' And they shall invoke my name for the children of Israel* [so our translation is to be mended] *and I will bless them."* So that in plain terms the form of blessing here prescribed by God is called *invocation*.

I cannot therefore see what should hinder, but that we, after Jacob's example, may offer up our prayers to a created angel, supposing, as some do, that Jacob prayed for a blessing to such a kind of an angel. It is a necessary consequence that Bellarmine[65] and others of

---

[64] The margin has *ybrk* here. This word was seen earlier and is from Gen 48:16. It means "to bless," thus linking the two passages in the author's mind.

[65] Robert Bellarmine (1542 –1621). Italian Jesuit and Cardinal. He was an important figure in the Counter-Reformation and a proponent of the Council of Trent. Margin has the reference: De Sanct. Beat. 1.i.c.29. Corn. A. Lap. On Gen. xlviii.

his communion draw from this instance: holy Jacob invoked an angel, therefore it is not unlawful for the Protestants to do the like; therefore, one may worship others besides God; these things, he says, cannot be denied, unless you reckon prayer to be no act of worship, and not to be peculiar to God alone.

But let those who believe Jacob's Angel was a mere creature, as they do in that Church, rid themselves of these difficulties as well as they can. Let them try how to convince a Socinian[66] from Ephesians 1:2 and other places of Scripture, where worship is ascribed to Christ. The Socinian has his answer ready; he may wish and pray to Christ for grace, though he is not God, since he does no more than Jacob did, when he prayed for a blessing on his children to a mere angel.

I am more concerned for these Divines of the Reformed Church, who have given the same interpretation of Jacob's Angel with as the Papists, though they cannot be ignorant they therefore dissent from the divinity of the ancient Jews, and the Fathers of the Christian Church, and even the more learned and candid Romanists, such as Masius[67] was; I might add, (which perhaps they have not considered) though they therein

---

[66] Socinianism. Named for Italian theologian Fausto Sozzini (Lat: Faustus Socinus). It is nontrinitarian in its view of Christ and precursor to many forms of Unitarianism within Protestantism.

[67] Andreas Masius (1514-73). Catholic priest, humanist, and one of the first Europeans to specialize in the Syriac language.

contradict the whole strain of the New Testament (See *Mercerus ad Pagnini* Lexicon, p. 1254).

The intended shortness of this treatise will not permit me to enlarge on this subject. However, there is one thing I must not pass over, which ought to be taken into consideration by the less cautious divines. It is very certain that the God who appeared to Jacob in Bethel was the very God who fed Israel in the desert, and against whom the Israelites in the wilderness rebelled. The Apostle is express that he was Christ, whom the Jews tempted in the wilderness, i.e. he was the *Logos*, and not a mere angel (cf. 1Co 10:4). The Apostle takes it for granted; and it was a thing undisputed by the synagogue in his time. And indeed, unless this is allowed, St. Paul's reasoning in this chapter is trifling and groundless.

Well, what can Bellarmine say to this, he who asserts a created angel to be spoken of in Gen 48:16? He has forgotten what he said on that text when he comes to this place. He here strenuously urges it against the Socinians, to prove that Christ was then in being when the Jews tempted him in the wilderness. And since he owns in this place that Christ in his Divine nature was he who led Israel through the wilderness, who is sometimes called God, and sometimes an Angel, he inconsiderately grants what he had denied before, that the Angel who redeemed Jacob from all evil, being the same Angel that conducted Israel, was also God.

SECT. VI.

YOU SEE WHAT CONTRADICTIONS Bellarmine
falls into, out of his zeal to promote the doctrine of *invocation of saints*. I wish there was not something as bad
in our Divines, that carries them into the very same
contradictions. The best I can say for their excuse is
only this, they have not carefully attended to the style
of the holy Scriptures. Two or three things therefore I
will mention, which occur frequently in the Scripture,
that I think would have suggested higher thoughts of
this Angel to one that considered what he read.

He who considers how often our Lord Christ is
called in the New Testament *the Spouse*, or *Husband of
the Church*, and compares it with the same title that God
appropriates to himself under the Old Testament estate, will make little doubt that it was the same Christ
who was then married to Israel. By the same rule one
may infer that our Lord Christ, in calling himself a
Shepherd, had a respect to that title by which he is so
often described in his dealings with Jacob and his posterity. This the older Jews were sensible of; and therefore, in both Genesis 48:15 and 49:24 where God is
mentioned as a Shepherd, they understand it of the
Shekinah or *Logos* (cf. R. Menachem de Rekanah, from
the book *Habbahir in Pent.* f. 84. c. 2). Of this also the
Jews in Christ's time were certainly not ignorant. For
when they heard Christ liken himself in one of his

sermons to *the Good Shepherd* (John 10), they immediately understand that he was claiming to be the Messiah, and therefore they took up stones to stone him. And then in the process of his discourse, to reinforce this claim, he made himself One with the Father.

As Christ called himself a Shepherd to show that he was the God who had fed Jacob and his posterity like sheep; so also is Christ most frequently represented in the New Testament under the notion of a Redeemer; intimating by this that he was the same redeeming Angel of whom Jacob had spoken. It was he who was called the *Angel of his Presence* (Isa 63:9), by whom God redeemed his ancient people; and he is also called the *Angel of the Covenant* (Mal 3:1), in the promise of his coming in the time of the Gospel.

Here I should have put an end to this tract, but there are two objections that lie in my way and seem to require some kind of an answer.

The first is taken from the doctrine of the Jews, who, many of them, expound this redeeming Angel by *Metatron*;[68] and *Metatron*, according to them, is a

---

[68] Metatron (*mttron*). No one quite knows the origin of this name. Sometimes called "lesser Yahweh," some have suggested the possibility that the "him" in Ex 23:21 ("because my name is within *him* [the Angel]" refers to Metatron, where the *ttr* in the word comes from *tetra*, the word for "four" in Greek, and a shorthand for the Tetragrammaton—YHWH (i.e. four letters). See Andrei A. Orlov, *The Etymology of the Name 'Metatron,"* in *The Enoch-Metatron Tradition* (TSAJ, 107; Tuebiingen: Mohr-Sieback, 2005). An excerpt is here (http://www.marquette.edu/maqom/metatronname.html#_ftnref24). See point #7: last accessed 8-30-2019.

created angel, or, as some say, none other than Enoch who was translated. On this there seems to be as many authorities against us as for us.

But let it be observed, 1. Though the Jews have several names of angels which are not mentioned in Scripture, yet they are all formed out of the names of God, according to the rules of their Kabbalah, and that with respect to the ten Sephiroth,[69] as Buxtorf[70] has noted (*Lex. Talm.* p. 828).

2. This is plain from the word *Actariel*, which is at the beginning of the Jewish forms of excommunication. This is derived from כתר (*ktr*)[71] the name of the first of the ten Sephiroth. From this, the Talmudists place Actariel upon the throne (Beracotb, f. 7. c. 1) and distinguish him from the ministering angels that stand before the throne. But I refer the curious reader that would know more of this to the ancient Jewish book entitled *Berith Menucha*, c. 1.[72]

3. This is no less plain of the Angel *Metatron*, who, as they say, was he who discoursed with Moses (Ex 3) and the Angel in whom God placed his name. So that

---

[69] In Kabbalah, Sephiroth are emanations that allow the Creator to create indirectly. Some think of them as intermediary states or stages somewhere between this Creator and all else that exists.

[70] Johannes Bustorf (1564-1629). Hebraist, professor of Hebrew at Basel (Switzerland), known as "Master of the Rabbis."

[71] V. Bartolocci, f. 4. Et 450.

[72] Berit Menuchah (Covenant of Rest) is a work of practical Kabbalah written down in the 14th century by Rabbi Abraham ben Isaac of Granada. It contains a system of theurgy which uses secret names of God and his emanations for spiritual and magical purposes.

they acknowledge that though it is formed from the Latin tongue, yet it expresses the same that the Hebrew word *Shaddai* does, as R. S. Jarchi[73] on Exodus 23 confesses. Now, St. Jerome on Ezekiel 1:24 notes that the Greek interpreters sometimes render God's name *Shaddai* by *Logos*, which leads us into the meaning of those ancient Jews who believed Shaddai and Metatron were the same.

4. The majority of the Jews are so far from believing *Metatron* is Enoch, that they believe him to be the Messiah, the *Logos* before his incarnation (our phrase), or in their words, the soul of the Messiah, which they look on as something between God and the angels, whom nothing separates from the living God (see Reuchlin,[74] 1.i. *de Cabala*, p. 651 where he proves *Metatron* to be the Messiah from their writings or, in short, take the confession of Menasseh ben Israel q. 6. in Gen 2).

Truly, if one would compare all those places of the Old Testament that mention the Angel, whom the later Jews call *Metatron*, he would find such properties belonging to this Angel as are incommunicable to a creature. And this shows that they who have departed in this point from the tradition of their fathers did it on this ground, because they were loath to acknowledge

---

[73] Shlomo Yitzchaki (1040-1105). Also known as Rashi, he was a medieval French rabbi and author of a commentary on the Tanakh.
[74] Johann Reuchlin (1455-1522). German humanist and Greek and Hebrew scholar. He wrote a treatise *On the Art of Kabbalah* (1517).

the Divinity of the Messiah, which seemed to be clear upon allowing *Metatron* to be the Messiah. They were more careful to defend their own prejudices than the opinions of the ancients.

II. Another objection is made from the place in Revelation 1:4. The words are these, "*John to the seven churches that are in Asia, grace be to you, and peace from him that was, and is, and is to come, and from the seven spirits that are before his throne; and from Jesus Christ, who is the faithful witness...*" John here seems to wish and pray for grace, not only from the Father, but also from the seven angels that are before the throne of God, and so Jesus Christ must be reckoned among the ministering spirits.

This place is indeed abused by those of the Romish Church to show that prayers may be lawfully directed to angels. And the Jews themselves have contributed to lead some people of note into this mistake. For, besides the four chief angels, whom they make to preside over the four armies of angels, which they have chiefly grounded on Ezekiel 1, they speak of seven other angels that were created before the rest, and that wait on God before the veil that divides them from the *Shekinah*.[75]

The hearing of these things so often repeated by the Jews has given occasion, I say, to some considerable Divines believing these seven to be proper angels, whom St. John mentions in his Revelation. But then,

---

[75] R. Eliezer, *in capit.* c. 4.

not apprehending how prayers could be offered to them, nor why the priority is given to them before Christ, they would not have John here to have spoken a prayer, but only to have wished grace on the seven churches; and this they thought was consistent enough with the angel-worship forbidden by St. Paul (Col 2:18) and even in this very book (Rev 19:10, 22:9).

But to shorten this matter, I altogether deny that St. John intended here any created angels. What then did he mean by them? Nothing else but the Holy Spirit, for whose most perfect power and grace on the seven churches he here makes supplication. For as Cyril on Zechariah 3:9: "The seven of them are very important." The number seven is always a mark of perfection in the thing to which it is applied. St. John therefore thought of no allusion to the Jewish opinion of seven angels, when he prayed for grace from the seven spirits before the throne; but had in his mind to express the far more plentiful effusion and more powerful efficacy of the Holy Spirit under the Gospel than under the Law, and his never-ceasing ministry for the good of the Church, for which purposes he has received a vicarious authority under God, immediately after Christ, as Tertullian speaks (*Against Praxeas* c. 13), and for this interpretation I have Justin Martyr (*Exhortation to the Greeks*) and St. Augustine on my side.

St. John's way of expressing himself is borrowed from Zechariah 3:9, where God is represented as having seven eyes running through the earth, to signify by this symbol God's perfect knowledge of all things, as Cyril of Alexander notes. Hence, we read of Christ (Rev 3:1), "*The words of him who has the seven spirits of God.*" And in another place seven eyes and seven horns are ascribed to him. But we never read (which is worth our observation) of these seven spirits as we do of the four beasts and twenty-four elders, that they fell down and worshipped God.

But why does St. John put the Holy Spirit before Christ? If I should say St. Paul has done something similar in Galatians 1:1 and Ephesians 5:5 (putting the Son before the Father) to teach us the unity and equality of each Person in the blessed Trinity, or because St. John in the following verses was to speak more at large of Christ, I think I should not answer improperly. But I shall add another reason, which may explain the whole matter.

In a word, I do believe this difficulty must be resolved another way; for that which makes this place so intricate according to the judgment of many interpreters is their referring to the Father the words of Revelation 1:4, "*Grace to you, and peace from him who is and who was and who is to come.*" This ought to be referred particularly to Christ himself, who is described in 4:8 according to the description of the *Logos* in Jonathan's Targum on Deuteronomy 32:39. But then some will say, why is there any mention made of the seven spirits,

if we conceive that the grace which is asked for the
Church, in the first words, is asked from Jesus Christ?
The thing is so clear that Socinus has perceived it.

Seven spirits are here mentioned to denote the
Spirit of God, who was to reside with his sevenfold
gifts in the Messiah, according to the prophecy of
Isaiah 11:2-3. From here it comes that in Rev 5:6, the
Lamb is described having seven horns and seven eyes,
which are the seven spirits of God, sent forth into all
the earth. To Christ there are attributed seven horns,
which denote his empire, in opposition to the empire
of the little horn, which is spoken of (Dan 7:8). So
there are seven eyes, which are the seven spirits of God,
attributed to him; likewise, to denote the gracious
providence of Jesus Christ by the Holy Ghost, and that
in opposition to the little horn, in which there were
eyes, "*like the eyes of man*" (Dan 7:8).

Here then *the grace asked* is from the seven spirits,
that is, from the Holy Ghost, who is united in one with
the Messiah Jesus Christ, and is sent by him; and so it is
said to be asked from Jesus Christ himself, who both
has those spirits as his eyes and does cause the mission
of them to his Church.

St. John therefore does not place the Holy Spirit
before Christ, but mentions him with Christ, because
after Christ's ascension and during the time of Christ's
continuance to God's right hand, he has a more particular hand in the immediate government of the Church,

and is especially watchful to do her good. For this reason, I think it is that the Holy Spirit is placed as it were without the veil, like a ministering angel. Many of the ancients knew this, as Victorinus of Pettau, Ambrose, Bede, Arethas,[76] Autpert Ambrose, Walafrid Strabo, Haymo,[77] Rupertus,[78] from whom Thomas Aquinas, and Cælius of Pannonia,[79] who rebukes those that understand it otherwise, and other elder Divines of the Roman Church learnt it, to say nothing of those of the Reformed Church: but it is time now to be finished.

---

[76] Probably the ninth century Arethas of Caesarea rather than the 6th century martyr.

[77] Probably the 9th century Haymo of Halberstadt rather than the 13th century Haymo of Faversham.

[78] Probably Rupert of Deutz (1075-1129) rather than Rupert of Bingen (712-732) or Rupert of Salzburg (660-710).

[79] Allix may refer here to Gregory Bánffy (d. 1545), also called Caelius Pannonius. He was a Hungarian from the Paulist order who wrote on Revelation and the Song of Songs.

Excerpts from "Judgments of the Jewish Church"

CHAP. VIII.

That the authors of the apocryphal books acknowledged a Plurality and a Trinity in the Divine nature.

HAVING FINISHED OUR general reflections on the traditional sense of the Scriptures, which was received among the Jews before the time of our Lord Jesus Christ, and of the books wherein we can find such a tradition, it is time for us to come now to the chief matter of our purpose. The question is whether the Jews before Christ's time had any notion of a Trinity, or not? For the Socinians would make us believe, that Justin Martyr, having been formerly a Platonist, and then turning Christian, was the first to invent this doctrine, or rather he adopted it out of the Platonic and into the Christian divinity; and that neither the Jewish nor the Christian Church had ever before conceived any notion of a Trinity or of any plurality in the Divine essence.

The doctrine of the Trinity supposes the Divine essence to be common to three Persons, distinguished from one another by incommunicable properties. These Persons are called by St. John: the Father, the Word, and the Spirit (1Jn 5:7). "*There are three,*" he says, "*that bear witness in heaven, the Father, the Word, and the Spirit; and these three are one.*"

This personal distinction supposes the Father is not the Son nor the Holy Ghost, and that the Son is not the Father nor the Holy Spirit. Revelation teaches that the Son is begotten of the Father and that the Holy Spirit proceeds from the Father and the Son, or from the Father by the Son. This distinction is the foundation of their order and of their operations.

For although the unity of the Divine nature makes it necessary that these three Persons should all cooperate in the works of God *ad extra* [external, outward, towards the outside], as we call them, nevertheless there being a certain order among the Persons, and a distinction founded in their personal properties, the Holy Scripture mentions an economy in their operations; so that one work *ad extra* is ascribed to the Father, another to the Son, and a third to the Holy Spirit.

But this distinction of Persons, all partaking of the same common nature and majesty, does not hinder their being equally the object of that worship which religion commands us to pay to God.

I will touch on this matter only very briefly, because my business is only to examine whether the Jews had any notion of this doctrine, or not. Our opinion is this, that though the Gospel has proposed that doctrine more clearly and distinctly, yet there were in the Old Testament sufficient notices of it, so that the Jews before Christ's time did draw from them their notions concerning it.

On the contrary, the Socinians maintain, this doctrine is not only equally foreign to the books of the Old and New Testament, but it was altogether unknown to the Jews before and after Christ, until Justin Martyr first brought it into the Church.

In opposition to this, I affirm the truth as such:

1. That the Jews before Jesus Christ had a notion of a plurality in God, following certain traces of this doctrine that are found in the books of Moses and the Prophets.

2. That the same Jews, following the Scriptures of the
Old Testament, acknowledged a Trinity in the Divine nature.

I begin the examination of this subject by considering the notions of the authors of the apocryphal
books.[80] One cannot expect that these authors should
have explained their mind with relation to the notions
of a plurality and of a Trinity in the Godhead as if they
had been interpreters of the books of the Old Testament. But they express it sufficiently apart from
them, and speak in such a manner that nobody can
deny that they must have had those very notions,
since it appears that their expressions in speaking of
God suppose the notions of a plurality in the Godhead, and of a Trinity in particular. Let us consider
some of those expressions.

---

[80] What we deem as "Apocrypha" usually consists of the following
dozen or so books all in existence at the time of the NT: 1 Esdras
(Vulgate 3 Esdras); 2 Esdras (Vulgate 4 Esdras); Tobit; Judith; Rest
of Esther (Vulgate Esther 10:4 – 16:24); Wisdom; Ecclesiasticus
(also known as Sirach); Baruch and the Epistle of Jeremy ("Jere-
miah" in Geneva) (all part of Vulgate Baruch); Song of the Three
Children (Vulgate Daniel 3:24–90); Story of Susanna (Vulgate
Daniel 13); The Idol Bel and the Dragon (Vulgate Daniel 14);
Prayer of Manasseh; 1 Maccabees; 2 Maccabees. There are NT
Apocrypha, but these are usually not what people have in mind.
There are OT Pseudepigrapha, but the same goes for those. For a
brief explanation see Douglas Van Dorn, "Apocrypha," *Decablog*
(March 13, 2015), https://thedecablog.wordpress.com/tag/apocry-
pha/.

1. They were so full of the notion of a plurality, which is expressed in Gen 1:26, that the author of Tobit has used it as the form of marriage among the Jews of old, "*Let us make for him a helper.*" So, Tobit 8:6, "*You made Adam, and for him you made his wife Eve as a helper and support. From the two of them the human race has sprung. You said, 'It is not good that the man should be alone; let us make a helper for him like himself;*" whereas in the Hebrew it is only, "*I shall make.*"

Secondly. We see that they acknowledge the creation of the world by the Word of God and by the Holy Ghost, as David. "*By the word of the LORD the heavens were made, and by the Spirit of his mouth all their host*" (Ps 33:6). So the Book of Wisdom 9:1, "*O God of my fathers, and Lord of mercy, who has made all things with your Word,*" or more properly "*by your Word,*" as it is explained in the second verse ("*and by your Wisdom have formed man…*"); and vs. 4. he asks Wisdom in these words, "*Give me Wisdom, that sits by your throne;*" and vs. 17, "*Who has learned your counsel, unless you have given Wisdom and Sent your Holy Spirit from on high?*" where he distinguished the *Logos*, or Wisdom, and the Holy Spirit, from God, to whom he directs his prayer. And so the Book of Judith 16:13-14, "*I will sing to the Lord a new song: O Lord, you are great and glorious, wonderful in strength, and invincible. Let all creatures serve you: for you spoke, and they were made, you sent forth your Spirit, and it created them, and there is none that can resist your voice.*"

Thirdly. They speak of the emanation of the Word from God: those are the words of Wisdom 7:25. *"For she is the breath of the power of God, and a pure influence flowing from the glory of the Almighty: therefore no defiled can thing fall into her."* That description of Wisdom deserves to be considered, as we have it in the same place (vv. 22-26). For, *"Wisdom, which is the worker of all things, taught me: for in her is a spirit that is intelligent, holy, unique, manifold, subtle, lively, clear, un-polluted, distinct, invulnerable, loving the good, keen, irre-sistible, beneficent, humane, steadfast, sure, free from anxi-ety, all-powerful, overseeing all things, and penetrating through all spirits that are intelligent and pure and most sub-tle. For Wisdom is more mobile than any motion; because of her pureness she pervades and penetrates all things. For she is the breath of the power of God, the brightness of the glory of the Almighty; and the image of his goodness."* And indeed St. Paul has borrowed from this what we read touch-ing the Son, that he is the brightness of God's glory, and the express image of his person (Heb 1:3). So the Book of Ecclesiasticus says, *"That it is come out of the mouth of the Most High"* (Sirach 24:3).

4thly. There are several names in Scripture which serve to express the second Person: the Son, the Word, the Wisdom, the Angel of the Lord, but who is the Lord indeed. Now those authors use all these names to express a second Person.

For they acknowledge a Father; and a Son, by a natural consequence. Thus the author of Ecclesiasticus, *"I called upon the Lord the Father of my Lord"* (Sir 51:10), in the same way as David speaks of the Messiah (Ps 2 and 110), and as Solomon in his Proverbs (8:25) as of a son in the bosom of his father, and 30:4, *"What is his sons name, if you can tell?"*

They speak of the *Logos* as the Creator of all things; so the author of Wisdom 9:1, *"O God of my fathers, and Lord of mercy, who has made all things with your Word;"* or more properly *by your Word.* And so they call that Wisdom the worker of all things (Wis 7:22).

They speak of the Wisdom in the same words as Solomon does (Prov 3 and 8:22), where he expresses the true notion of eternity. And indeed, they attribute her to have been eternal (Sir 24:18).[81]

They refer constantly to God himself, that is, to the *Logos* of God, as we shall hereafter show at large, what is attributed to the Angel of the Lord in many places of the books of Moses, as to have delivered the Israelites from the Red Sea. So Wisdom 19:9, *"They went at large like horses, and leaped like lambs, praising you, O Lord, who had delivered them."* Again, to have had his throne in a cloudy pillar (Sir 24:4). To have been caused by the Creator of all things to rest and to have his dwelling in Jacob, and to have his inheritance in

---

[81] Some translations do not have vs. 18. But the LXX reads, *"I am the mother of fair love, and fear, and knowledge, and holy hope: I therefore, being eternal, am given to all my children which are named of him."*

Israel (8), and so to have given his memorial to his children, which is the law commanded for a heritage into the congregation of Jews (23).

So they attribute to him to have spoken with Moses, "*He made him to hear his voice, and brought him into the dark cloud, and gave him commandments before his face, even the law of life and knowledge, that he might teach Jacob his covenants, and Israel his judgments*" (Sir 45:5).

Again, to have come down from heaven to fight against the Egyptians, "*Your almighty Word leaped down from heaven, out of your royal throne, as a fierce man of war into the midst of a land of destruction.*" And brought your authentic commandment "*as a sharp sword*," and standing up filled all things with "*death*," and it touched the heaven, but it stood upon the "*earth*" (Wis 18:15-16).[82]

So they maintain that the angel who appeared to Joshua (Josh 5:13-15) was the Lord himself; so the author of Ecclesiasticus, "*He called upon the most high Lord, when the enemies pressed upon him on every side; and the great Lord heard him. And with hailstones of mighty power he made the battle to fall violently upon the nations, and in the descent [of Bethhoron] he destroyed those who resisted, that the nations might know all their strength, because he fought in the sight of the Lord, and he followed the Mighty One*" (Sir 46:5-6). They refer the miracles wrought by Elijah to the *Logos*, as you see in Ecclesiasticus 48:3, 4, 5) . "*By the Word of the Lord he shut up the heavens, and*

---

[82] The original adds vs. 17 to the reference.

also three times brought down fire. O Elijah, how honored you were in your wondrous deeds! And who has the right to boast which you have? You who raised a corpse from death and from Hades, by the word of the Most High."

As there is nothing more common in the Old Testament than to call the *Logos* the Angel of the Lord, because the Father sent him to do all things under the former dispensations, so one can see that there is nothing more ordinary in the apocryphal books, than to speak of an angel in particular, to whom are attributed all the things which could not be performed but by God.

Three things prove clearly that they did not conceive that angel to be a created angel, but an Angel who is God.

First. Because they have this maxim, according to the constant divinity of the Jews, grounded upon Scripture (Deut 32:9) that God took Israel for his portion among all the nations of the world, as if he had left the other nations to the conduct of angels (see Esther 13:15).[83]

Second. Because they refer to the *Logos* some histories of the Old Testament, which the Jews till this

---

[83] There are several recensions of Esther 13:15. One English translation it reads, "*And now, O Lord, O king, O God of Abraham, have mercy on your people, because our enemies resolve to destroy us, and extinguish your inheritance. Despise not your portion, which you have redeemed for yourself out of Egypt. Hear my supplication, and be merciful to your lot and inheritance, and turn our mourning into joy, that we may live and praise your name, O Lord, and shut not the mouths of them that sing to you*" (Est 13:15-17).

day refer to an uncreated Angel, or to the Logos, or Shekinah, or Memra of Jehovah, as I shall prove afterwards. We see it in Wisdom 16:12, "*For it was neither herb, nor poultice cured them, but it was your Word, O Lord, that helps all people.*" Also Wisdom 18:15-16, "*Your Almighty Word leaped down from heaven out of your royal throne, as a fierce man of war into the midst of a land of destruction, and brought your authentic commandment as a sharp sword, and standing up filled all things with death; and it touched the heaven, but it stood upon the earth.*" I thought fit to repeat this here, to make Mr. N. ashamed. For he has exposed those ideas and laughed at them, which I believe he would not have done if he had but considered two things. The first is that this Logos who is spoken of is that very man of war mentioned in Moses' song (Ex 15:3)[84] and in Judith (9:7).[85] The other is that St. Paul has followed the notions of the Book of Wisdom, speaking of a sharp sword, which is to be understood, not of the Gospel, but of the Logos (Heb 4:12).[86] But Mr. N. was in the right to ridicule such an authority, which destroys to the ground the principles of the Unitarians; for nothing can be more clear, than that this author acknowledges a plurality in God; that

---

[84] "*The Lord is a man of war, the Lord is his name.*"
[85] "*Behold now, the Assyrians are increased in their might; they are exalted, with their horses and riders; they glory in the strength of their foot soldiers; they trust in shield and spear, in bow and sling, and now not that you are the Lord who crushes wars; the Lord is your name.*"
[86] "*The Word of God is living and active, sharper than any tow-edged sword…*"

the *Logos* must be a Person, and a Person equal to the Father, since he is set upon the royal throne.

Third. Because they bring such appearances of that Angel, it shows they conceived of him as the God who ruled Israel, and who had taken their temple for the place of his abode. And, on the contrary, they speak of God, whom they considered as dwelling in the temple, with the same words which are used in Scripture, when it is spoken of the name of God (Ex 23:31 and 1Sa 8:16[87]), of the angel of the covenant (Mal 3:1), and such expressions. So you see in the first Book of Esdras, "*If any one of you, therefore, is of his people, may his Lord be with him, and let him go up to Jerusalem, which is in Judea, and build the house of the Lord of Israel—he is the Lord who dwells in Jerusalem*" (1Esd 2:5). And again, "*When the young man went out, he lifted up his face to heaven toward Jerusalem, and praised the king of heaven*" (4:58). And Judith 5:18[88] and 9:8.[89] and 2 Maccabees 1:25, "*The only giver of all things, the only just, almighty and everlasting, you who delivered Israel from all*

---

[87] This reference is rather inexplicable. The citation 1Sa 8:16 has nothing to do with the name of God. The closest I find with these numbers is 2Sa 6:18, "*David ... blessed the people in the name of the LORD of hosts.*" The context does have to do with the temple as well.
[88] This verse does have to do with the temple, but it does not support the point other than calling it "*the temple of their God.*" I cannot figure out the typo here.
[89] "*Break their strength by your might and bring down their power in your anger; for they intend to defile your sanctuary, and to pollute the tabernacle where your glorious name rests, and to cast down the horn of your altar with the sword*" (Jdt 9:8).

trouble, and did choose the fathers and sanctify them." And 2:17, "*We hope also, that the God that delivered all his people, and has returned the inheritance to all, and the kingship and priesthood, and the sanctuary.*" And 14:35, "*O Lord of all things, who has need of nothing, you were pleased that the temple of your habitation should be among us.*"

I can add, fourthly, that they distinguish exactly the Angel of God from the prophets, though they are called by the same name of angels or messengers, and they distinguish him from angels, whom as creatures they exhort to praise God, as in the Prayer of Azariah, "*O you angels of the Lord, bless ye the Lord, praise and exalt him above all forever*" (PrAz 36 LXX). Such a distinction appears in 1 Esdras 1:50-51, "*Nevertheless the God of their fathers sent by his messenger (aggelos) to call them back, because he spared them and his tabernacle also. But they mocked his messengers (aggelos), and, whenever the Lord spoke, they made a sport of his prophets.*" Also in Tobit 5:16 (LXX), "*So they were well pleased. Then said he to Tobias, 'Prepare your for the journey, and God send you a good journey. And when his son had prepared all things for the journey, his father said, Go with this man, and God, who dwells in heaven, prosper your journey, and the Angel of God keep you company.*" This is just like the prayer of Jacob in Genesis 48:16, "*The Angel who redeemed me from all evil, bless the boys.*" And that very Angel is called God by Jacob in the verse before. Then there is Ecclesiasticus (Sirach) 17:17. "*For in the division of the nations of the whole earth he set a ruler over every people; but Israel is the Lord's portion.*" Also in the Epistle of Jeremiah vv. 6, 7, "*But say in your heart, 'O Lord, we must worship you. For my Angel is with you, and I myself am watching for your souls.*" In the Greek, caring for their souls is referred to the same Angel. Again in 2 Maccabees 11:6, "*When Maccabeus and his men got word that Lysias was besieging the strongholds, they and all the people, with lamentations and tears, prayed to the Lord to send a good Angel to deliver Israel.*"

To show that the Jews before Jesus Christ had such a notion of the *Logos* who was to save his people, we must take notice of two things. First, that the author of the books of Maccabees speaks of God at the end of his book in the same terms which are used by Jacob in Genesis 48:15-16 and are to be referred to the *Logos*, not to a created angel, as I have explained it in a particular discussion of that very place of Genesis.

Second, the Greek interpreters of Scripture have used a method of translating some places of the prophets, which shows they understood that the Messiah should be the very Angel of the Lord who is called the Counsellor, and that the Angel of the Lord was the Lord himself. Two examples will show that clearly. The first is in that famous oracle of Isaiah 9:6, they have these words, *hoti paidon egennēthē hēmin uios kai edothē hēmin ou hē arxē egenēthē epi tou ōmou outou kai kaletai to onoma outou megalēs boulēs aggelos*. The end (*megalēs boulēs aggelos*) reads, "*The Angel of the great counsel,*"[90] whereas in the Hebrew it is said, he shall be called the "wonderful"[91] (*pele'*, "*wonderful*") (which is the very word that the Angel of the Lord gives to himself in Judges 13:18) "*the Counsellor of the Mighty God;*" and it is clear that they understood these words to refer to the Messiah, who is spoken of as the son of David (Isa 9:7) in the same words which are used in Psalm 72.

The other example is in this other famous place of Isaiah 63:9 where they have translated, "*... nor an angel, but himself saved them,*" as if they had read *la-'ă'šer* instead of *lō-ṣār*, which we translate as "now." Some of the modern Jews are mightily entangled in explaining that place, but it appears that these interpreters of Isaiah looked upon *the face of God* to have been God himself, which is the reason of their translation, and shows that they understood *the face of the Lord*, which is so often spoken of by Moses, to be the *Logos*, which is *Jehovah*. I can add a reflection concerning their version of the Daniel 3:25. *Species quarti similis filio Dei*

---

[90] This text from the LXX was a vital and very commonly quoted passage by the Church Fathers, used to demonstrate the link between the Angel and Christ. It is usually translated "Angel of the great counsel," but can be translated as "Angel of the great council" (see De Gols in another volume in this series) as in the divine council of the heavenly beings that rule over the affairs of the cosmos (cf. 1Kg 22:19-23, Dan 4:17; 7:9ff. , etc.). In citing "wonderful" and the link to the Angel in Judges 13:18 (cf. Gen 32:29; Ex 15:3, 11), Allix is giving one of the reasons why it may have been translated this way.

[91] Allix' original has "admirable," but the way modern translation render it is "wonderful," which is consistent in other related passages (cf. Ex 15:11; Ps 77:14).

("the fourth is like a/the Son of God"), as Aquila a Jew says,[92] who lived under Hadrian; but the ancient Greeks had translated it *similis Angelo Dei* (like an/the Angel of God)[93] as say an old scholion [notes], related by Drusius (*Fragmentis*, p. 1213), which shows that the ancient Hellenists had the same notion of the Angel of God as of the Son of God. But all those things shall be better understood when we come to the authority of the other Jews, which we will produce later.

Some perhaps may think that the Book of Ecclesiasticus supposes the Wisdom which we maintain to be eternal, to have been created (*ektisthē*), and so says that author (Sir 1:4; 24:9). But I take notice of three things. First. That such an objection may be good in the mouth of an Arian, but not at all in the mouth of a Socinian, and much less in the mouth of an Unitarian of this kingdom, after their writers have owned that the *Logos*, or Word of God, signifies the essential virtue of God.

Second. The author of Ecclesiasticus follows in that expression the very words of the Greek version of Proverbs 8:22 where it answers to the word possessed, which is not *ektisthē* (create) but *ektēthē*.[94]

---

[92] He quotes the Vulgate but refers to the Aquila (fl. 130 A.D.) who translated the OT into Greek and whom Jerome used from liberally in his Latin translation.

[93] The LXX reads "angel of God," while Greek Theodosian reads "Son of God."

[94] His Greek typing here is inexplicable. The LXX actually has *ektisen* (created). Allix clearly has the Hebrew *qanah* ("to possess," "acquire) in mind.

Third. That the word *ektisthē*, although we should suppose it to be the true reading, can mean many things; and indeed Aristobulus, a Jew of Alexandria, who lived about the same age of the authors of those apocryphal books (d. 103 B.C.),[95] and whose words are quoted by Eusebius (*Preparation for the Gospel* 1.7.14. p. 324) declares that the Wisdom which Solomon speaks of in the Book of Proverbs was before heaven and earth, and the very author of Ecclesiasticus calls it positively "*eternal*" (Sir 24:18).

There is another objection which is backed by the authority of Grotius, who by the *Logos*, or Wisdom, understands a created angel; but I shall show afterwards the absurdity of that opinion of Grotius; and his error is so plain, that Mr. N. and the Unitarian authors have been ashamed to follow his authority in this point, daring not to maintain that the *Logos* in the first of St. John signified an angel, which they would have done, if they could have digested the absurdity of Grotius's notions upon that place of Wisdom 18:15.

As for the Holy Ghost, that they acknowledged him for a Person, and for a Divine one, there is as much evidence from the same apocryphal books.

First. I have noted that they attributed to him the creation of the world, as you see in Judith 16:14. "*You*

---

[95] Aristobulus of Alexandria (181-124 B.C.). A Hellenistic Jewish philosopher, was the predecessor of Philo and trued to fuse Hebrew Scriptures with Greek thought.

sent forth your Spirit, and it created them," which is an imitation of David's notions (Psalm 33:6).

Second. They call him the mouth of the Lord. So in the 1 Esdras, *"But Josiah did not turn back his chariot, but tried to fight with him, and did not heed the words of Jeremiah the prophet from the mouth of the Lord"* (1Esd 1:28). *"He also did evil in the sight of the Lord and cared not for the words that were spoken to him by the prophet Jeremy from the mouth of the Lord"* (47; also vs. 57).

Third. They speak of the Bina, or *"understanding,"* by which is to be understood the Holy Spirit, from Proverbs 3 and 8. So in Ecclesiasticus, *"Wisdom has been created before all things, and the understanding of prudence from everlasting"* (Sir 1:4). Also the Book of Wisdom, *"Because wisdom will not enter a deceitful soul, nor dwell in a body enslaved to sin. For the Holy Spirit of discipline will flee from deceit, and will rise and depart from foolish thoughts, and will be ashamed at the approach of unrighteousness. For Wisdom is a loving spirit, and will not acquit a blasphemer of his words; because God is witness of his inmost feelings, and a true observer of his heart, and a hearer of his tongue. Because the Spirit of the Lord has filled the world, and that which holds all things together has knowledge of the voice"* (Wis 1:4-7).

Fourth. They acknowledge him to be the Counsellor of God who knew all his counsels. So you read in the Book of Wisdom, *"Who has learned your counsel, unless you have given Wisdom and sent your Holy Spirit from above?"* (Wis 9:17).

Fifth. They speak of him as of him who discovers the secrets of God, *"He will reveal instruction in his teaching, and will glory in the law of the Lord's covenant"* (Sir 39:8). And again, *"By the spirit of might he saw the last things and comforted those who mourned in Zion. He revealed what was to occur to the end of time, and the hidden things before they came to pass"* (Sir 48:24).

Sixth. They acknowledge him to be sent from God, *"Who has learned your counsel, unless you have given wisdom and sent your Holy Spirit from on high?"* (Wis 9:17).

After all, if we consider what notions they had of the Messiah who was promised to them, we will find that they had much nobler ideas than those which are now entertained by the latter Jews, and more like to them which we find among the Prophets.

First. It is clear that they looked upon him as the Person who was to sit upon the throne of God; the title of my Lord which is given by the author of Ecclesiasticus (51:10) shows beyond exception by a clear allusion to the Psalm 110:1 which speak both of the Messiah.[96]

---

[96] *"I appealed to the Lord, the Father of my Lord, not to forsake me in the days of affliction, at the time when there is no help against the proud"* (Sir 51:10). Psalm 110:1, *"The LORD [Yahweh] said to my Lord [Adonai]: 'Sit at my right hand, until I make your enemies your footstool.'"* This verse is used many times by the NT to prove that Jesus is the Son of the Father.

Second. They did not look upon it as an absurd thing to suppose that God is to appear in the earth, as you see in Baruch 3:37. *"Afterward he appeared upon the earth and lived among men."* Here it refers either to his appearance upon Sinai or to the incarnation of the *Logos.*

Third. They suppose another coming of the Messiah, and then *"the saints are to judge the nations, and have dominion over the people, and their Lord shall reign forever"* (Wisdom 3:8). These words have been borrowed by St. Paul (1Co 6:2).[97]

Fourth. They acknowledge such appearances of God, as we have an example in 2 Maccabees 11:6, *"When Maccabeus and his men got word that Lysias was besieging the strongholds, they and all the people, with lamentations and tears, prayed to the Lord to send a good Angel to deliver Israel"* (cf. 15:22-23).[98]

Fifth. They speak of the appearances of God as an *epiphaneia*, which is the very word used by St. Paul for the first and second "appearance" of Jesus Christ. *"So every man praised toward the heaven the glorious Lord, saying, 'Blessed be he that hath kept his own place undefiled. So that fighting with their hands, and praying to God with their hearts, they slew no less than thirty and five thousand men;*

---

[97] *"Do you not know that the saints will judge the world?"*

[98] *"And he called upon him in these words: 'O Lord, you sent your angel in the time of Hezekiah king of Judea, and he slew fully a hundred and eighty-five thousand in the camp of Sennacherib. So now, O Sovereign of the heavens, send a good angel to carry terror and trembling before us."*

for through the appearance of God they were greatly cheered" (2Ma 15:34, 27).

Sixth. They expected at the second coming of the Messiah such a manifestation of his glory as in the consecration of the temple. *"And then the Lord will disclose these things, and the glory of the lord and the cloud will appear, as they were shown in the case of Moses, as Solomon asked that the place should be specially consecrated"* (2Ma 2:8).

I believe these proofs are sufficient to demonstrate, 1. That there was before Jesus Christ's time a notion of plurality in the Godhead. 2. That they believed that such a plurality was a Trinity. 3. That they looked upon the Son or the Logos and the Holy Ghost not as created beings, but as beings of the same Divine Nature with the Father, by an eternal emanation from him, as having the same power and the same majesty.

But these ideas of the apocryphal books will appear clearer when we take them in conjunction with the explication of the same notions among other Hebrew writers, which I shall now consider more particularly, and in addition to those places of Scripture on which they ground their explications.

CHAP. XII.

That the Jews had a distinct notion of the Word as of a Person and of a Divine Person at that.

THE GREAT PART OF THE DISPUTE we have with the Socinians depends on the true meaning of the first chapter of St. John's Gospel, where the *Logos* is spoken of as having created the world, was in time made flesh, and whom we Christians look upon as the promised Messiah. I do not think I can do the truth a greater service than by clarifying this notion of the *Logos* and showing what thoughts the ancient Jews had concerning it.

Socinus confesses that the *Logos* is a Person; for he owns that St. John did describe the man Christ Jesus by the *Logos* and attributed to him the creation of the Church, which is, according to him, the new world. But here in England, the followers of Socinus will not stand by this exposition but understand by the *Logos* that virtue by which God created heaven and earth, as Moses relates in Genesis 1. They obstinately deny this virtue to be a person, i. e. an intelligent subsistence, and rather look upon it as a Divine attribute, which, they say, was particularly discovered in the mission of Jesus Christ for the salvation of mankind.

It cannot be denied by them that St. John, being one of the circumcision, wrote with a special respect to the Jews, so that they might understand him, and receive benefit by it; and therefore it cannot be doubted, but that when he called Jesus Christ the *Logos*, he used a word that was commonly known among the Jews of those times in which he lived.

Otherwise, if he had used this word in a sense not commonly known to the Jews, he would have signified to them the new idea he alone had fastened to it. But he gives not the least intimation of anything new in it, though he uses the word so many times in the very beginning of his Gospel. It is certain therefore, that he used it in the sense that it was then commonly understood by the Jews.

Now the idea the Jews had of the *Logos* was the same they had of a real and proper person, that is, a living, intelligent, free principle of action. That this was their notion of the *Logos*, or Word, we shall prove by the works of Philo and the Chaldee paraphrases [i.e. the Targums].

I'll begin with Philo. He conceives the Word to be a true and proper cause: for he declares, in about a hundred places, that God created the world by his Word. He conceived the Word to be an intelligent cause; because in him, according to Philo, are the original ideas of all things that are expressed in the works of the creation.[99]

He makes the Word a cooperator with God in the creation of man, and says that God spoke those words to him, "*Let us make man*" (Gen 1:26). It may be added that he calls the Word "the image of God," and makes man the image of this image.[100]

These are some of the characters that represent the Word as a true Person. But there are others no less demonstrative of this truth. 1. Philo asserts that the *Logos* is begotten of God (*Allegorical Interpretation* 2) which can agree only to a person. 2. He proves that the Word acted and spoke in all the Divine appearances that are mentioned in the Old Testament; which certainly supposes a person. 3. He describes the Word as presiding over the empires of the world and determining the changes that befall them.[101] Where he brings in the Word for a mediator between God and men[102] that renders God propitious to his creatures,[103] that is, the instructor of men[104] and their shepherd, alluding to Psalm 23:1.[105]

The Chaldee paraphrases are full of notions and expressions relating to the Word, conformable to

---

[99] Philo, *On the Creation of the World* 8-9.
[100] Philo, *Who Is the Heir of Divine Things* 231.
[101] Philo, *That God is Unchangeable* 176.
[102] Philo, *Who Is the Heir of Divine Things* 205-206.
[103] Philo, *On Dreams* 1.66.
[104] Ibid. 1.68.
[105] Philo, *On the Change of Names* 115-116.

those of Philo when he discusses the *Logos*, so that he must wink hard who does not see that in their sense the Word is truly a Person. We see this in the following ways:

1. They almost always distinguish the Memra, or Word of the Lord, which is the Aramaic equivalent to Philo's Greek *Logos*, from the word *Pithgama*, which signifies a matter or a discourse, as does in Greek.
2. They ascribe the creation of the world to the Word.
3. They make it the Word that appeared to the ancients under the name of the Angel of the Lord.
4. They have the Word that saved Noah in the time of the Flood and made a covenant with him (Onkelos on Gen 6:7, 8:21).
5. They say that Abraham believed in the Word, which thing was imputed to him for righteousness (Onk. on Gen 15:6).
6. They say that the Word brought Abraham out of Chaldea, (Onk. on Gen 15:7) and commanded him to sacrifice (Gen 15:9) and gave him the prophecy related vs. 13.
7. They have Abraham swearing by the Word (Onk. on Gen 21:23).
8. For them the Word succored Ishmael (Gen 21:20) and Joseph in his bondage (Gen 39:2-3).

Targum Onkelos continues these translations in his Targum on Exodus:

1. It is the Word's assistance that God promises to Moses (Ex 3:12; 4:12; 18:19)
2. It is the Word in whom Israel believed, as well as in Moses (Ex 14:32).
3. It is the Word that redeems Israel out of Egypt (Ex 15:2).
4. It is the Word against whom Israel murmured in Sin (Ex 16:8).
5. It is the Word before whom the people marched to receive the Law (Ex 19:17).
6. It is the Word whose presence is promised in the tabernacle (Ex 29:42; 30:6 which is repeated in vs. 36).[106]
7. It is between the Word and Israel the sabbath is made a sign (Ex 31:13, 17).[107]
8. It is the Word whose protection was promised Moses, when he desired to see God (Ex 33:22-23).

Onkelos has the same things on Leviticus and Numbers.

1. It is the Word whose commandments the Israelites were to carefully observe (Lev 8:35; 18:30; 22:9; Num 9:19; 20:24).
2. It is spoken of the Word, that he will not forsake the people, if they continue in their obedience (Lev 26:11).[108]

---

[106] Num 8:29 is an inexplicable typo. This passage does not have the Word in it, nor is he talking about Numbers until the next section. Ex 30:36 does repeat vs. 6 and is in the same chapter.

[107] The original reads, "…and so also Lev 36:46. This is an inexplicable typo to which I can find no resolution.

[108] The original 28:11 should probably be 26:11.

3. By the Word God looks upon his people (Ibid).
4. The majesty of the Word rested among the Israelites (Num 11:20).
5. It is the Word whom Moses exhorts the Jews not to rebel against (Num 14:9; 20:24).
6. They believed in the Word (Num 14:11; 20:12).
7. The Word meets Balaam (Num 23) and opens his eyes (22:31).

Yet again, the same things, or the like, we find in Onkelos on Deuteronomy:

1. The Word brought Israel out of Egypt and fought for them (Dt 1:30; 3:22; 8:2-3; 20:1).
2. The Word led Israel in the pillar of a cloud (1:32-33; cf. 33:3).[109]
3. The Word spoke out of the fire at Horeb (4:33, 36). Moses was mediator between the Word and his people (5:5).
4. Moses exhorts the Jews to obey the Word (13:19; 15:5; 26:14; 28:1, 2, 15, 45, 62; 30:8, 10, 20).
5. The Word conducts Israel under Joshua to the land of Canaan (31:6, 8).
6. The Word created the world (33:27).

You can see how agreeable the notions of Onkelos are with those of Philo, even though the one wrote in Egypt and the other in Palestine, and both before the time of our Lord Jesus Christ.

---

[109] The original reads only 1:32. The "cloud" verse is in the next verse. I have added 33:3 where they are both in the same verse.

But besides Onkelos on the Pentateuch, we have two other paraphrases: the one, which is very diffuse,[110] is said to be Targum Jonathan's; the other, which is called the Jerusalem Targum,[111] and is short, and, as it seems, imperfect. The reader may soon judge by comparing them, whether they differ from Philo and Onkelos, or not:

1. The Jerusalem Targum says that God created the world by his Wisdom, which he grounds on the word *Bereshith* (Gen 1:1). And Philo means the same thing, when he calls the *Logos*, *arche* (the first emanation or firstborn word; *The Confusion of Languages* 146).
2. The same Targum says, the Word made man after his image (Gen 1:27).
3. Jonathan's affirms that the garden of Eden was planted by the Word for the just before the creation of the world (Gen 2:8).
4. Both Jonathan's and the Jerusalem Targum say the Word spoke to Adam in the garden (Gen 3:8-10); and that the Word lifted up Enoch to heaven (Gen 5:24).
5. Jonathan's affirms that the Word protected Noah and shut the door of the ark upon him (Gen 7:16).
6. That the Word threw down the tower at Babel (Gen 11:8).
7. Both have it that God promised Abraham that his Word should protect him (Gen 15:1).

---

[110] Perhaps he means here more than one author.
[111] Sometimes equated with Targum Neofiti.

8. Jonathan's makes it the Word that plagued Pharaoh for Abraham's sake (Gen 12:17).

9. The Jerusalem Targum says it was the Word that appeared to Abraham at the tent door (Gen 18:2); and that the Word rained fire from before the Lord (Gen 19:24).

10. Both this Targum and Jonathan's say that Abraham taught his people to hope in the name of the Word of the Lord (Gen 21:33).

11. The Jerusalem Targum makes Abraham say, The Word of the Lord will prepare a sacrifice (Gen 22:8); and asserts that Abraham invoked the Word and called him Lord in his prayer (Gen 22:14).

12. Jonathan's Targum brings in Abraham swearing by the Word of the Lord (Gen 24:3); and God promising that his Word would succor Isaac (Gen 26:24, 28 repeated in Gen 31:3).[112]

13. The same Targum says that the Word of the Lord made Rachel bear a child (Gen 30:22); which is in agreement with what Philo says, that the *Logos* caused Isaac to be born (*Alleg*. 1. 2. p. 77).

14. According to this Targum, the Word sent Michael to save Tamar (Gen 38:25). The Word went down with Jacob into Egypt (Gen 46:4).

15. The Word succors Joseph (Gen 49:25); which Joseph acknowledges (Gen 50:20).

We may trace the same notions in their Targums on Exodus:

---

[112] Ch. 23 is a typo. 31:5, 42 and 32:9 are inexplicable, so I have deleted them.

1. According to Jonathan's, the Word built houses for the midwives that feared God (Ex 1:21).
2. The Word caused that miraculous heat which disposed Pharaoh's daughter to go and bathe herself in the Nile (Ex 2:5).
3. It was he who spoke and the world was made, according to Jonathan's Targum; or it was the Word of the Lord, according to the Jerusalem Targum, that spoke to Moses (Ex 3), which clearly shows that they made use of the word Memra to express what is so often repeated, "*And God said*" (Gen 1).
4. It is the Word who, as God promised to Moses, was to be his mouth (Ex 4:12, 15).
5. According to the Jerusalem Targum, the Word appeared to Abraham by the name of the God of heaven; and the name of his Word was not declared to the patriarchs (Ex 6:8).
6. The Word of the Lord slew the first-born of Egypt, (Ex 12:29).
7. The Word of the Lord has appeared on three remarkable occasions: first, at the creation of the world; second, to Abraham; third, at Israel's departure out of Egypt. A fourth time he shall appear at the coming of the Messiah (thus Jonathan and Targ. Jerusalem on Ex 12:42).
8. The Word wrought miracles by Moses (Ex 13:8).
9. The Word raised up those Israelites which were killed by the Philistines that left Egypt three years before the departure of their brethren out of Egypt (Ex 13:17).
10. For the neglect of the commands of the Word were the Israelites killed (Ex 13:17).

11. It is the Word that looked on the host of the Egyptians; and to him the Israelites cried (Ex 14:24, 31).

12. It is the Word that gives the law concerning the sabbath (Ex 15:25), and he against whom Israel murmured (vs. 8).

13. The Israelites hear the voice of the Word (Ex 19:5), who speaks (vs. 9), and pronounces the Law (20:1); being the same that redeemed Israel from Egypt (*ibid.* and Lev 1).

14. God promises to send his Word with his people, and Israel is strictly enjoined to obey him (Ex 23:20-22).

15. The Word punishes Israel for the golden calf (Ex 33:35).

16. The Word talks with Moses in the tabernacle, and the people worship him (Ex 33:9, 11; Lev 1).

17. It is the Word whose appearance is promised to Moses (Ex 33:19), and the Word is distinguished from the angels that attend him (Ex 33:23).

18. It is the Word to whom Moses prays, and who is called the name of the Lord (Ex 34:5).

These things continue in their Targums on Leviticus, Numbers, and Deuteronomy:

1. The Word makes statutes (Lev 23:11; Num 22:18) according to the same Jonathan.

2. It is the Word of whom the Jerusalem Targum understands what is spoken by Jonathan of the face of the Lord (Num 9:8).

3. By the order of the Word of the Lord the Israelites encamp (Num 9:19, 23).

4. It is the Word to whom prayer is made upon removing the ark of the covenant (Num 10:35, 36).
5. The Word spoke to all the Prophets before Moses (Num 12:6).
6. The Word gives answer (Num 14:20).
7. The Word sent fiery serpents, and those that were healed were healed by the name of the Word of the Lord (Num 21:6, 8, 9).
8. It is before the Word that the idolatrous Israelites were hanged (Num 25:4).
9. It is the Word that wrought wonders in the desert on behalf of Israel (Dt 1:1; 4:34; 6:22) and whom the Israelites provoked (Dt 1:1).
10. The Word multiplied Israel, and fought for them, yet they did not believe in him (Dt 1:10, 30, 32 and 3:2) both in Jonathan and the Jerusalem Targum.
11. The Word punished Israel for the business of Peor (Dt 4:3).
12. The Word sits on a throne high lifted up, and hears the people's prayers, and speaks from the midst of the fire, and gives the Law (Dt 4:7, 12, 33; vv. 23, 24, 25).
13. Moses is a mediator between the Word and the people (Dt 5).
14. It is by the name of the Word that Israel ought to swear (Dt 6:13).
15. The Word was to drive out the nations before Israel (Dt 11:23).
16. The Word chose the Levites for his service (Dt 21:5) and the whole people of Israel (Dt 26:18).
17. The Word protected Jacob from Laban (Dt 26:5).
18. The Word destroyed Sodom (Dt 29:22).
19. The Word swore to the Patriarchs (Dt 31:7).

20. The Word shall judge the people (Dt 32:36).
21. The Word says of himself, that he was, is, and is to come (Dt 32:39).
22. The Word takes Moses up to Mount Ibraee (the mountain of Nebo); and Moses prays to him for a sight of the land of Canaan (Dt 32:49).
23. The Word shows Moses the generations of the great men of Israel (Dt 34:1).
24. The Word said he had sworn to give Israel the land of Canaan (Dt 34:4).
25. To conclude, Moses dies according to the decree of the Word of the Lord; that is to say, the Word recalls his soul with a kiss, and with a huge train of angels inters his body; being the same Word that had appeared to him, and sent him into Egypt; and by so many miracles redeemed Israel from there (Dt 34:5, 6, 10, 11, 12).

There is no need of making any profound consideration on these many places of Philo and the Chaldee paraphrases, to convince the reader that the Jews before Jesus Christ did look upon the Word as a true and real Person. The consequence is easily drawn by whomever looks them over with but half an eye.

I know the word *Memra* in the Hebrew is sometimes taken in another sense, as well as that of *Logos* is in the Greek. But all the personal characters of action, of commanding, of speaking, of answering, of giving laws, of issuing out decrees, of being prayed to, of receiving worship, and the like, are so expressly given to that Word we now discuss as to render it absurd to take it for anything other than a Person.

Let us next inquire into the nature of this Person, according to the same testimonies of the ancient Jews, whether it be angelic or divine, and consequently whether this Person be truly God.

I propose this, not that I think there is any necessity of proving it after all that I have already observed from the ancient Jews touching the Word; but for the clearer manifestation of the absurdity into which our adversaries fall by their striving to force another sense upon the word, as the more knowing men among them cannot but see, when they consider these proofs with attention.

He who wrote against Vechnerus[113] endeavors in general to persuade us that in those places of the Targums where the *Memra* is spoken of, it is used to express the Divine providence over the faithful of ancient times; or else in particular it signifies the attributes of God, his affections or actions, his miracles, his appearances, his inspirations, and the like. This he repeats in several parts of his dissertation, and at the end of his work he tries to apply it to several texts in the Targum.

One might reasonably doubt whether he himself were satisfied with his own performance in this. I have two great reasons to think he was not. The first is that it seems he never consulted Philo's notions of the

---

[113] Probably Daniel Vechner (1572-1632).

Logos before he made this judgment, notwithstanding that he could not help but see them in Grotius on St. John's Gospel, which he quotes; and he could not but know how much they were insisted upon by those writers whom he pretended to answer. They do indeed so distinctly and clearly establish the personality of the *Logos* that they render useless and unsuitable all the interpretations he has found out for the texts in the Targums.

The second is that he himself, though he fitted his interpretations to divers passages in the Targum, thereby to break the force of them when turned against him, is yet forced to acknowledge that sometimes the word *Memra* signifies a person properly so called, according to our use of it. The several places where the Word is said to create the world give him much trouble, though he tries to elude them. And though he endeavors to rid his hands of them by asserting that the Word does there signify the power of God; nevertheless he lets you understand that if you are not pleased with that solution, you may have his consent to take it in the Arian sense of the word, for a created God by whom, as by a real and instrumental cause, God did truly create the universe.

This is the strangest answer that could be returned to so great an objection. For he must have lost his reason who imagines that God can make a creature capable of creating the universe. Grant this and by what character will you distinguish the creature from the Creator? By what right then could God appropriate, as he does very often in the Old Testament, the work of the world's creation to himself, excluding any other from having to do in it but himself? Why should God upon this result forbid the giving of worship to the creature which is due to the Creator? The Arians, who worship Jesus Christ, though they esteem him a creature, and those Papists who swallow whole the doctrine of transubstantiation; they may teach in their schools that a creature may be enabled by God to become a Creator. But as for us, who deny that anything but God is to be adored, as Philo denied it before us (*On the Decalogue* p. 581; *de Monarch*,[114] p. 628), we reject all such vain conceits of a creature being in any way capable of receiving the infinite power of a Creator.

There are other places which he also found he could not easily evade, so that at length he consents that the *Memra* does in fact quite often denote a person in the language of the Targums; such as where we read the Word spoke and the Word said. But what kind of person? An angel, a created angel in his judgment, who speaks in the name of God. And thus, he thinks the Word is to be understood in those paraphrases when they ascribe to the Word the leading of Israel through the desert.

---

[114] This work is not listed in the *SBL Handbook of Style* on Philo of Alexandria.

The reader may judge how many texts this answer will fit, by reviewing what has been said in the two foregoing chapters. He will find I have there prevented this answer, and showed that Philo and the Targums did not take this for a created angel, but for a Divine Person, who was called an angel in respect of the office he discharged according to the economy between the three Persons of the blessed Trinity; and of whom the Targums generally make express mention in places where the Hebrew text has *Jehovah Elohim*, or the Angel of the Lord; and sometimes where it has simply the name Jehovah.

However, to leave no doubt in this matter, we will undertake to prove further that the Word does not signify a created angel in Philo or in the Targums, but a Person truly Divine.

It is true, that Philo sometimes calls the angels *Logos* in the plural. But elsewhere he speaks of the *Logos* singularly, in terms that express his acknowledgment of him for the Creator of angels, and consequently for God. This he does in his book *On the Sacrifices of Cain* (p. 202)[115] where he declares him to be the Word that appeared to Moses, and separates him from the angels, who are the hosts of God.

Again, he describes the *Logos* under the name of *Epistēmē* as true God, as Creator of the world (*Lib. de*

---

[115] Allix possibly has Philo, *Sacrifices* 8 in mind.

Temulentia,[116] p. 190. D. 194. B); but the angels after another manner (*On Planting*, p. 168. F. G.; *On Giants* p. 221. E; *De Mundo*, p. 391).

It is true, he calls the Word an archangel (*On the Confusion of Tongues* 146), but in the same place he calls him the firstborn of God, the image of God, the Creator of the world; and in another place, the Son of God that conducted Israel through the wilderness (*On Husbandry* 51; *The Heir of All Things* 201-205).

He was so far from taking the Word to be an angel that he affirmed the Word used to appear to men under the form of an angel. Thus, he says, the Word appeared to Jacob (*On Dreams* 1.189-90); and to Hagar (*On Dreams* 1.238-41). We are to observe this carefully, that we may make Philo agree with Philo: for on one hand he says an angel appeared to the patriarchs; and on the other he says the *Logos* appeared to them. His purpose is to acquaint us with the notion that the *Logos* is named an angel because he appeared as an angel in these kinds of manifestations of himself.

Now as to the Targums, they likewise understand by this Angel a Person that is truly God. For:

1. Could they ascribe the creation of the world to the Word, as they do, and yet think him to be a creature? Could they profess him to be the Creator of mankind, without asserting his Divinity? Could they think him

---

[116] This work is not listed in the *SBL Handbook of Style* on Philo of Alexandria.

to be no better than an angel, and yet suppose him to be worshipped by men, whom they know to be little lower than the angels? Could they imagine him to have given the Law on mount Sinai, and not make some considerations upon the preface of the Law; wherein the great Lawgiver says, *"I am Jehovah your God, who brought you out of the land of Egypt?"* The Word is not so often called an angel in the Targums, as he is set forth with these characters of God; as the reader may see especially in Jonathan's Targum, and in that of Jerusalem (Ex 3:14; 12:42) and in many other places.

2. The Targums always distinguish the Word from the angels; representing them as messengers employed by the Word, as the Word himself is often described as God's messenger. Thus, the Targum on 1Kg 19:11, 12;[117] Ps 68:11, 18[118]; 2Chr 32:21.[119]

---

[117] *"And he said: 'Go forth and stand on the mountain before the Lord.' And behold the Lord was revealing himself, and before him were armies of the angels of the wind breaking apart the mountains and shattering the rocks before the Lord; not in the army of the angels of the wind was the Shekinah of the Lord. And after the army of the angels of the wind was the army of the angels of the earthquake; not in the army of the angels of earthquake was the Shekinah of the Lord. And after the army of the angels of the earthquake was the army of the angels of fire; not in the army of the angels of the fire was the Shekinah of the Lord; and after the army of the angels of the fire was the voice of those who were praising softly.*

[118] *"You set your revival in it, you established the hosts of angels to do good to the poor, O God ... The chariots of God are twice ten thousand of blazing fire; two thousand angels lead them; the Shekinah of the LORD dwells among them on Mount Sinai in the sanctuary."*

[119] *"Then the Memra of the Lord sent the angel Gabriel, and during the night of the Passover he destroyed with a molten stream of fire and burnt up their breath within them."*

3. They say the Word was attended with angels, when he gave the Law (Targ. on 1Ch 29:11),[120] and when he assisted at the interment of Moses (Jonathan on Dt 34:6).[121]

4. The Targums represent the Word as sitting on a high throne and hearing the prayers of the people (Jonathan on Dt 4:7).

5. Jonathan says expressly that the Word that spoke to Moses was the same who spoke and the world was made and who was the God of Abraham (Ex 3:14, 15; 6:4). So then if he who was the God of Abraham was only an angel that impersonated God, then he who created the world was a created angel; which, as I have showed, is absurd.

6. It is impossible to explain otherwise what the Jews so unanimously affirm, that God revealed himself face to face to Moses; which is more than he granted any prophet, unless the Word that appeared to Moses was the true God and not a mere angel (see Onk. on Dt 34:10, 11 and the other Targums).

---

[120] *"Yours, O Lord, is the greatness, for with great power you created the world, and the might, for you brought our fathers out of Egypt with many mighty acts and brought them across the sea, and you were revealed in splendor upon the mountain of Sinai, with bands of angels, to give the law to your people. You gave victories over Amalek, Sihon, Og and the kings of the Canaanites; in the majesty of your glory you caused the sun to stand still in Gibeon and the moon in the plain of Ajalon, until your people, the house of Israel, were avenged on those who hated them. For all these things are the works of your hand, in heaven and on earth, and you have authority over them and sustain everything which is in heaven and everything which is on earth. Yours, O Lord, is the dominion in the firmament, and you are exalted above all the angels that are in heaven and above all those who are appointed as leaders on earth."*

[121] The text reads in part, *"...for He revealed Himself in His Word, and with Him the companies of ministering angels..."*

But what, say they, may not an angel bear the name of God, when he represents the Person of God? Was not the ark called *Jehovah*, because it was a symbol of his Person?

Does not Jonathan on Num 11:35, 36 say to the ark, *Revelare Sermo Domini et redi?*[122] This is indeed a notion which the Socinians have borrowed of Abenezra[123] on Exodus 3 and Joseph (*Albo de Fund*, c. 8). And so they pretend that the pillar of cloud is called the Lord (Ex 13:21, 14:19), that the ark is called the Lord (Num 10:35), that the angel is called the Lord (Jdg 6:15), the name being given to the symbol, viz. the ark; and to the second cause, namely, the angel; because of their representing God.

But to the great displeasure of our modern Jews and Socinians who have borrowed from them their weapons, we have still enough of the ancient Jewish

---

[122] *"And it was when the ark should go forward, the Cloud gathered itself together and stood still, not going on, until Mosheh [Moses], standing in prayer, prayed and supplicated mercy from before the Lord, and thus spoke: Let the Word of the Lord be now revealed in the power of Your anger, that the adversaries of Your people may be scattered; and let not the banner of those who hate them be uplifted before You. But when the ark should rest, the Cloud gathered itself to ether and stood, but did not overspread, until Mosheh, standing in prayer, prayed and besought mercy from before the Lord, thus speaking: Return now, Oh Word of the Lord, in the good- ness of Your mercy, and lead Your people Israel, and let the glory of Your Shekinah dwell among them, and (Your) mercy with the myriads of the house of Jakob, and with the multitudes of the thousands of Israel"* (Num 10:35-36 PJE).
[123] Abraham ben Meir Ibn Ezra (1089-1167). One of the most dis- tinguished Jewish biblical commentators and philosophers of the Middle Ages.

texts left, to show how their sentiments in these matters are quite to contrary.

For, 1. they (as has been already observed) believed that the Angel spoken of in Judges 6:15 was the Word and that this Word created the world, as has been largely proved.

2. The ancients held just the reverse of what our moderns say, as we gather from Philo. For instead of an angel's taking the place of God, he says the *Logos* took the place of an angel (*On Dreams* 1.238-39).

As to the ark, it is folly to imagine that because God promised to dwell and to hear prayers there, and enjoined worship toward it, therefore the ark was called Jehovah. The ancient Jews spoke not to the ark, but to God, who resided between the cherubim. This is plainly expressed in those words of Jonathan (Num 10:35-36, *"Let the Word of the Lord be now revealed"* etc.), where the words are not addressed to the ark itself but to him who promised to give them some tokens of his presence, namely, to the Word, who created the world, who redeemed Israel from Egypt, who heard their prayers from over the ark, and who had shut up therein the tables of the Law, which he had given them on mount Sinai.

And thus the Targum on 1Ch 13:6. *"David and all Israel went up to remove the ark of the Lord, who dwells between the cherubim, whose name is called on it;"* or as 2Sam 6:2, *"Whose name is called by the name of the Lord of hosts, who dwells between the cherubim."* In short, the Scripture never gives to any place or creature the name *Jehovah* in the nominative case, either singly or joined with any other noun in apposition. But either in an oblique case, such as *aron YHWH* or with a verb substantive understood, as *Jehovah Nissi, Jehovah Shamma.* Other things that the Socinians have to say against this the reader may see fully answered by Buxtorf in his *Exercitationes ad Historiam*, ch. 1 on the History of the Ark, where the reader shall have a full satisfaction by reading those chapters.

It remains therefore certain that the Word mentioned in Philo and the paraphrases is not an angel but a Divine Person; *Theos* (God) as Philo calls him many times; and if the expression is allowable, *deutros theos* (Second God), as he speaks in Eusebius, *Preparation for the Gospel* 7.13.

But we must now go on to that which will remove all difficulties from this subject and convince the reader, if anything can do it, that the Jews looked upon the *Logos* as a Divine Person. I speak of the appearances of an angel who is called God and worshipped as God under the Old Testament; and I thought it fitting for this very reason to write more upon this subject in order to prevent the objections of the modern Jews and of the Unitarians all at once.

CHAP. XIII.

That all the appearances of God, or of the Angel of the Lord, which are spoken of in the books of Moses, have been referred to the Word by the Jews before Christ's incarnation.

SOME OF THE LATE Jewish commentators that have had disputes with the Christians, particularly those whose comments are collected in the Hebrew Bible printed by Bomberg[124] at Venice, oppose this proposition with all their might. They have laid it down for a rule that wherever God is *said to be present, there all the celestial family is with him*; i.e. the angels, by whose ministry (as they say) God has ordinarily acted in his appearances to men. So Rabbi Solomon Jarchi says on Gen 19:24. Opposed to this were those ancient Jews who followed the tradition of their forefathers. They were not biased by the spirit of dispute with Christians. Rather, they understood the *Chokhmah* (Wisdom) and *Bina* (Understanding) to be Wisdom and the Holy Ghost; as we were admonished

---

[124] Daniel Bomberg (d. 1549). A Christian who printed many important Hebrew books.

by R. Joseph de Karnitol[125] (*Saare Tsedec*, fol. 25. col. 4. and fol 26. col. 2.).

This collection of late commentators are of great use for interpreting the Scriptures. Nevertheless, several divines that have applied themselves to the study of the comments of these Rabbis have been led by them rashly into their same opinion. The renowned Grotius fell into this snare and has had but too many followers. We have no cause to wonder that the Papists do the same, being concerned as they are to find examples in the Old Testament of religious worship paid to angels, the better to cover their idolatry.

But in truth, the modern Jews absolutely depart from the ancient sentiments of their own fathers; and they who follow the modern Jews in this weaken (for lack of due consideration only, I hope) the proofs of the Divinity of Jesus Christ. They do this by yielding to the modern Jews, as an agreed point between them and the Christians, that which is quite contrary to what the Apostles and primitive Christians supposed in their disputes with the Jews of their times, and which our later Jews themselves would never have submitted to if they had known any other way to avoid the arguments that were brought against them out of their own Scriptures.

---

[125] Karnitol is a corruption of Gikatilla. This is R. Joseph b. Abraham Gikatilla.

It behooves us therefore to give just force to those arguments that were used by the Apostles and the Fathers and to restore to the truth all her advantages, by showing how bad of guides our modern Jews are in the matters now before us; and how they have deviated from the constant doctrine of their ancestors in order to find out ways to defend themselves against the Christians.

I affirm then for certain that the appearances of God, or of any Angel who is called Jehovah, or the God of Israel, who is worshipped and spoken of in the Old Testament, were never said by the ancient Jews to refer to created angels who impersonated God. Further, I vouch, that generally the ancient Jews referred these appearances as the Word, whom they distinguished from angels, as they do God from the creature. This thereby justified the patriarchs in paying divine worship and adoration to him that appeared to them, according to these ancient Jews.

To prove this, I must return to Philo's opinion which I have had occasion to speak about in several places. I would willingly spare myself the trouble, and my reader the nauseousness of repeating the same things; but this is a matter of such importance as necessarily obliges me, by a particular enumeration of passages, to produce Philo's judgment on this point, as I have done already. He is indeed so ample, and so much ours in his testimony concerning the dignity of the Angel that appeared to the Fathers, that he could not say more if we had hired him to give evidence on our side:

1. In general, he asserts, that it was the Word who appeared to Adam, Jacob, and Moses; though in the books of Moses it is only an angel that is spoken of [*On Dreams* 189, 192, 194].

2. It was the Word who appeared to Abraham (Gen 18:1) according to Philo; for he says, it was the Word that promised Sarah a son in her old age, and that enabled her to conceive and bring forth [*Allegorical Interpretation III*.217].

3. It was the Word that appeared to Abraham as an angel, and that called to him not to hurt his son when he was about to sacrifice him [*On Dreams* 1.193-94].

4. It was the Word that appeared to Hagar [*On the Cherubim* 3; *On Dreams* 1.239-40].

5. It was the Word that appeared so many times to Jacob, though he is called the Angel that delivered him out of all his trouble [*Allegorical Interpretation* III 177]. It was the Word that appeared to Jacob in Bethel [*On the Migration of Abraham* 4-6; *On Dreams* 1.189-90], afterwards directed him how to manage Laban's flock [*On Dreams* 189-90] and advised him to return to the land of his kindred [*On Dreams* 189-90]. It was the Word that appeared to

Jacob in the form of an angel, and wrestled with him [*On Dreams* 128-29], and changed his name into that of Israel [*On the Changes of Names* 13.87; *On Dreams* 128-29].

6. It was the image of God, which in other places is the same with the Word, that appeared to Moses in the bush [*On the Life of Moses* 12.66]. It was God that called to him at the same time [*On Dreams* 1.194], even the Word [*On Dreams* 1.190-91] whom Moses desired to see [*Allegorical Interpretation* III.100-103].

7. It was the Word who led Israel through the wilderness (Ex 23) [*On Agriculture* 12.51]. He was the Angel in whom God placed his name [*On the Migration of Abraham* 31.174]. That Word who is called the Prince of angels, who was within the cloud [*The Heir of All Things* 42.205], and is called "Divine appearance of fire" [*On the Life of Moses* 46.254]. And he was this Angel that appeared to Moses and the elders of Israel on mount Sinai (Ex 24) [*On the Confusion of Tongues* 20.96; *On Dreams* I.11.62]. It was the Word whom those Jews rejected when they said, Let us make a captain, and return into Egypt (Num 14) [*Allegorical Interpretation* III.61.175].

8. It was the Word that governs the world, that appeared to Balaam like an angel [*On Cherubim* 10.31-33; *On the Unchangeableness of God* 37.181].

9. It was the Word by whom Moses when he was to die was translated [*Sacrifices of Abel and Cain 3.8*].

II. Let us come next to the Chaldee paraphrases, and see how they render those texts that speak of the Divine appearances in Scripture; and let the reader take these remarks to heart,

1. That whatever he finds in those paraphrases, he may be assured that it was the general sense of the Jewish Church in ancient times.
2. That any judicious writer may justly suspect those who first published those Targums of having cut away their many parts in order to favor the new method of their last writers, which I have explained in the beginning of this chapter.

The first appearance of God to man was when he created our first parents (Gen 1:27). He blessed them and said to them, "*Be fruitful, and multiply, and replenish the earth*" (Gen 1:28). The one who gave them this blessing was the one who created them, as we read in the Jerusalem Targum on Gen 1:27, "*The Word of the Lord created man in his own image.*" For his giving them the blessing, we have this in that Targum on Gen 35:9, "*O eternal God ... you have taught us the marriage-blessing of Adam and his wife; for thus the Scripture says expressly, 'And the Word of the Lord blessed them, and the*

Word of the Lord said to them, Be ye fruitful, and multiply, and replenish the earth.'"

God appeared again to our first parents after their sin where it is said, *"They heard the voice of the Lord God walking in the midst of the garden"* (Gen 3:8). Now as Philo said to us, it was the Word of the Lord who appeared to Adam; and both Onkelos and Jonathan agree that Adam and his wife *"heard the voice of the Word of the Lord God walking in the garden."* Likewise in the Jerusalem Targum (vs. 9) it is said, *"The Word of the Lord called to Adam...,"* and again (vs. 10) where Adam makes this answer to God, *"I heard your voice in the garden;"* both Onkelos and Jonathan have it, *"I heard the voice of your Word in the garden."*

In the history of the Deluge, we see that there was a revelation to Noah the preacher of righteousness to build the ark and to warn others while it was being built (1Pe 3:20). But who gave Noah that warning? Jonathan says, *"The Lord said this by his Word."* And the Jerusalem Targum, *"It was the Word of the Lord that said this."* And in the same way, Jonathan has it in Genesis 6:6 that, *"The Lord judged them by his Word;"* and said, *"I will destroy them by my Word."* Likewise, for the saving of Noah all the paraphrasts attributed this to the Word: the Jerusalem Targum says, *"The Word of the Lord spared Noah"* (Gen 7:16). And in Gen 7:1 Jonathan has it, *"The Word of the Lord remembered Noah."* Lastly, according to Onkelos and Jonathan,

"The Lord said by his Word, 'I will not again curse the ground any more for man's sake'" (Gen 8:21).

After the Flood God appeared often to Abraham. According to Jonathan on Genesis 15:6, a promise was made to Abraham that his seed should be as the stars of heaven for number, *"He believed in the Lord, and had faith in the (Memra) Word of the Lord,"* and it was counted to him for righteousness.[126] Therefore it was the Word of the Lord that came to him in a vision (15:1), and that made him that promise (5). It follows (7) that he said to Abraham, *"I am the Lord who brought you out of Ur of the Chaldees."* Who said this to Abraham? The Word of the Lord, according to Jonathan's Targum; for there is no other nominative case of the verb in his paraphrase. You see the same where Abraham divides the beasts in order to make a covenant with God. It was done at God's command, the one who afterward appeared between the pieces to Abraham and then solemnly entered into a covenant with him (Gen 15:9ff.). Here, says the Jerusalem paraphrase on Exodus 12:43, it was *"the Word of the Lord that appeared to Abraham between the pieces."* According to Onkelos and Jonathan, it was *"by his Word"* that God made this covenant with Abraham (Ex 6:8).

---

[126] This point is often missed by many. When Paul and James quote this verse about being justified by faith (Rom 4:9, 22; Gal 3:6; Jam 2:23), there is already a Christocentric, Word-oriented interpretation already present among the Jews. Who justified Abraham by faith? The Word. Who justifies us by faith? Christ Jesus. It's the same thing.

We must take notice that he who appeared then to Abraham says, "*I am El Shaddai,*" which is translated, "*The Almighty God,*" for according to Onkelos on Genesis 49:25, in the blessing of Jacob to his son Joseph, these names—*the Word of God* and *El Shaddai*, are parallel. Thus, it runs according to Onkelos, "*The Word of the God of your Father shall help you; and El Shaddai shall bless you,*" where plainly *El Shaddai* is the same who is called, "*The Word of the God of your Father.*"

As Philo taught us that the appearance of God to Abraham (Gen 18:1) was an appearance of the Word (*Allegorical Interpretation III.*217) where he calls one of the three angels that appeared to Abraham the *Logos*, the Word of God; and Josephus (1. 1. *Ant.* or *Antiquities of the Jews* 1.213) calls him God, so the Jerusalem paraphrase has it in the end of the next verse, "*The Word of the Lord appeared to Abraham in the valley of vision, as he sat warming himself in the sun, because of his circumcision.*" Elsewhere the same paraphrase quotes these words as being the words of Scripture saying, "*The Scripture has declared, 'And the Word of the Lord appeared to him in the valley of vision'*" (Gen 35:9). Jonathan also in his paraphrase on Deuteronomy 34:6 has these words, "*The Lord has taught us to visit the sick, in that he revealed himself by the vision of his Word to Abraham, when he was sick of the cutting of circumcision.*"

When God gave him a command for the sacrificing of his son (Gen 22:2) then, as Abraham was doing it, the Angel of the Lord called to him out of heaven, and told him, "*Now I know that you fear God, seeing you have not withheld your son, your only son, from ME.*" This last word plainly shows that this Angel was God himself, even the same that spoke to Abraham, and gave him that command (vs. 1, 2). And that command was given by the *Logos*, the Word, according to Philo, as it has been already shown. The Jerusalem paraphrase has the same in vs. 8 where, upon Isaac's inquiring for the lamb that was to be sacrificed, Abraham answered him, "*My son, the Word of the Lord will prepare me a sheep.*" And so, when Abraham found that the Word provided him a sheep and accepted that for a sacrifice instead of his son, "*Abraham worshipped, and prayed to the Word of the Lord, saying* (among many other things), '*You, O Lord, spoke to me, that I should offer up Isaac my son.*'"

In the other Targums (vv. 16-17), the Angel of the Lord calls to Abraham out of heaven the second time (the last word shows that this Angel was God himself; for it was God who called to him out of heaven the first time, as it has been already shown), and says to Abraham, "*By myself I have sworn, says the Lord. Because you have done this thing, and have not withheld your only son from me,*[127] *therefore in blessing I will bless you...*" There, both Onkelos and Jonathan say, "'*By my Word I have sworn,' says the Lord.*" What should be their meaning in this? When they say, "*Thus says the*

[127] *From Me* is in the Samaritan and LXX.

Lord," it was properly used by the Word appearing here as an angel, and not according to his own natural being. But for the form of the oath, where, according to the Hebrew text (Gen 20), "*God swore by himself,*" the paraphrasts render it that, "*God swore by his Word.*" and well they might, for they understood that the Word was God. And indeed, these Targums show in other places that where this form of swearing was used, it was the Word of the Lord who swore and held himself obliged to perform what was sworn (compare Ex 6:8 with Dt 26:5 and Num 14:30 with Dt 31:7).

We read of an Angel appearing to Hagar in the wilderness (Gen 16:7). He told her to return and submit to Sarah her mistress (9), telling her all about the child she now bore and what sort of man he would become. But as this Angel spoke in the style of God saying, "*I will greatly multiply your seed*" (10). So she confessed it was the Lord who spoke to her and she said to him, "*You, God, see me*" (13). It is clear that it was God himself who appeared, though he is called an Angel in the text. Therefore, not only does Philo call him the *Logos* in those places above mentioned, but the Targums likewise show that he was the Word of the Lord, according to the sense of the Jewish Church. Thus, Jonathan renders vs. 13, "*She confessed before the Lord Jehovah, whose Word had spoken to her;*" and the Jerusalem Targum, "*She confessed and prayed to the Word of the Lord, who had appeared to her.*"

Again, an Angel called to Hagar out of heaven (Gen 21:16). But he also said to her that which no created angel could say; speaking of her son Ishmael, "*I will make him a great nation*" (18). Philo says that it was the *Logos*. And who performed this promise? It was God the Word, according to the Targums. For whereas the text says, "*God was with the lad;*" it is rendered both by Onkelos and Jonathan as, "*The Word of the Lord was his support or assistance*" (20).

We read also of two Divine appearances to Isaac, one in Gerar (Gen 26:2), and the other at Beersheba (24). In the former place, Isaac was ready to go down into Egypt, but God commanded him to continue in Canaan and gave him a promise in these words, "*I will be with you, and will bless you; for to you and your seed I will give all these countries, and I will perform the oath which I swore to Abraham your father*" (Gen 26:3). So then, he who appeared now to Isaac is the same who swore this to Abraham. So we learn much from this text. But according to the Targums, it was God the Word who swore all this to Abraham. Elsewhere they also tell us that it was the Word who swore to Isaac and to Abraham that he would give them the Promised Land (Ex 6:8; 32:13).

In the second appearance where God promised something to Isaac, he told him, "*I am the God of Abraham your father*" (Gen 26:24). But the Jerusalem Targum says that, "*Abraham worshipped and prayed to the*

Word of the Lord" (Gen 22:14). According to Jonathan's Targum, Isaac prayed for his son Jacob in these
words, *"The Word of the Lord give you of the dew of
heaven"* (Gen 27:28). In the same Targum on Genesis
31:5, where Scripture has Jacob saying, *"The God of
my father has been with me,"* the Targum has, *"The Word
of the God of my father,"*[128] or, *"The Word being the God
of my father."*

Among the Divine appearances to Jacob, those
two at Bethel were more remarkable than the rest:
one at his going to Padan-Aram (Gen 28:13), the other
at his return from there (Gen 35:9), where it is said
expressly, *"then God appeared to him the second time."*

The history of the first of these is given us at large
(Gen 28:13-16). Jacob himself gives this account of
the last to his son Joseph (Gen 48:3-4). *"God Almighty
appeared to me at Luz in the land of Canaan, and blessed me,
and said to me, 'Behold, I will make you fruitful, and multiply you..."* That it was the Word who appeared to him,
we have showed already from Philo in several places;
and that this was the sense of the Jewish Church in his
time, we have much reason to believe. As to this first
appearance in the introduction (vs. 10), where the text
speaks of Jacob's setting out from Beersheba to go to
Haran, there both Jonathan and the Jerusalem Targum tell us of the sun set early that day because the

---

[128] *Of your father*; so the Samaritan and LXX.

Word[129] had a desire to speak with Jacob. Again, in the conclusion of this history (Gen 28:20-21), where Jacob vowed a vow saying, *"If God will be with me ... then shall the Lord be my God,"* here we read in Jonathan's Targum *"that Jacob vowed a vow to the Word, saying, 'If the Word of the Lord will be my help ... then the Lord will be my God."*

Why should the paraphrast say that Jacob made this vow to the Word instead of God, as it is in the Hebrew text? Because they believed that it was the Word who appeared to him. Thus, who is the angel that spoke to Jacob (Gen 31:11)?[130] Where Scripture declares, *"I am the God of Bethel, where you vowed a vow to me"* (13), we see in the Targum on Genesis 28:20 that it was the Word to whom Jacob vowed a vow at Bethel. Therefore, according to this Targum, it must be the Word that is called an angel in this place.

The second time that God appeared to Jacob was in his return from Padan-Aram (Gen 35:9). It is expressly said in the Jerusalem Targum, *"The Word of the Lord appeared to Jacob the second time, when he was coming from Padan-Aram and blessed him,"* which is as clear a testimony as can be desired for our purpose.

---

[129] Jonathan has *Debbira* (Word) here. Scholars often note that *Memra* (Aramaic "Word") is used like John's *Logos*. But here, we have a synonym that is being used the same way.

[130] The sentence here, as well as the 1699 version, is unintelligible. It reads, "This being so, we cannot be to seek who that Angel was who spoke to Jacob…"

Whoever will consider with some attention those appearances of God to Jacob, and compare them with what we read in Genesis 18:15-16, and with what Hosea the Prophet says (Hos 12:3-4) concerning the Angel who was God, cannot but take notice of two things. The first is that the *Logos*, who is called an Angel, was indeed God. The second is, that the wrestling of that Angel with Jacob was a preparation for the belief of the mystery of the incarnation, by which the Apostles were made able to say, "*That which we have looked upon, and our hands have handled, of the Word of life—this is our message*" (1Jn 1:1, 5). But we must say more upon such an important subject.

CHAP. XIV.

That all the appearances of God, or of the Angel of the Lord, which are spoken of in Moses's time, have been referred to the Word of God by the ancient Jewish Church.

WE READ OF NO OTHER appearance of God, or of an Angel of the Lord, until Moses saw him on mount Horeb (Ex 3:2). There we read that "*the Angel of the Lord appeared to him in a flame of fire out of the midst of a bush.*" This is the only place in this story where Moses calls him an Angel that appeared. Elsewhere he always calls him God, particularly in vs. 4, where he says that upon his turning aside to see why the bush did not burn, "*When the Lord saw this, God called to him out of the midst of the bush, and said to him, 'I am the God of your father, the God of Abraham, the God of Isaac, and the God of Jacob'*" (6). Upon seeing this sight, Moses says that he hid his face, for he was afraid to look upon God. After this, he goes on still calling him God, as we read in almost every verse. So, in vs. 16 he says, God commanded him to go to the elders of Israel, and say to them, "*The Lord God of your fathers, the God of Abraham, of Isaac, and of Jacob, appeared to me.*" God would never have commanded him to tell them a lie, and therefore we may be sure that it was not a created angel, but God who appeared to him.

Why then should Moses once call him an Angel as we see he did in the second verse? A created angel he could not be, for the reasons now mentioned. He must therefore be God, and yet he must appear as an angel that came on a message from God. This is what Philo says in one word—he was the *Logos*, or Word, who is both God and the Messenger of God, as we have shown of him in several places.

As for the Targums, the matter is clear. For when Moses was sent to the children of Israel to tell them that their God had appeared to him and sent him to bring them forth out of Egypt, there Moses asked him his name. God said to Moses, "*Tell them, I AM THAT I AM*," or in fewer words, "*I AM has sent me to you.*" That which God calls himself here is the sense of the name Jehovah [Yahweh/LORD]; this signifies the Eternal Being. Now see how this is rendered in the Jerusalem Targum. There we read that "*the Word of the Lord said to Moses, 'He who said to the world, Let it be, and it was, and shall say to it again, Let it be, and it shall be.*" Here Moses asked God, and the Word answered his question. But it is certain that he who answered the question was the same Person who he had been speaking with all this time, even the same who appeared to him in the bush.

Moses being thus commissioned by the Word of God as his messenger to the children of Israel for the discharge of his ministry had both his instructions and credentials from the Word, according to the Targums.

For the first of these, God appeared to him more often than to anyone before him. R. Akiba (50-135 AD) said that Moses acted as mediator between the Gevura,[131] that is the Word of God, and the people of Israel, and observes that God spoke to him a hundred and seventy-five times. The times that God spoke to him from off the mercy-seat, upon the ark of testimony, and between the two cherubim were too many to count (Num 7:89). But those which R. Akiba reckons were appearances upon extraordinary occasions. In these two particular appearances, ordinary and extraordinary, it was the Word of God who spoke to Moses, according to the Targums.

Thus, they speak of God's talking to him from the mercy-seat and from there the Word was appointed to speak with him, according to Onkelos and Jonathan on Exodus 25:22 and 30:36. In Numbers 7:89, Jonathan says it was the Word who spoke to him. And likewise, in those occasional appearances both Jonathan and the Jerusalem Targums tell us once for all (Dt 34:10). "*The Word of the Lord knew Moses*" (*mmrl kl mmll qbvl*), to speak with him word for word.

---

[131] In Kabballah, the Gevura is one of ten Sefirot (emanations) through which the Ein Sof (Infinite) reveals itself and creates all things.

His credentials were all the signs and wonders which the Lord sent him to do (Dt 34:11); or, according to the Targums, which "*the Word of the Lord sent him to do, in Egypt, to Pharaoh, and his servants, and all his land; and in all that mighty land, and that great terror, which Moses showed in the sight of all Israel.*"

For the acts of his ministry, they were chiefly these three: 1. His bringing the people out of Egypt. 2. His giving them laws, and statutes, and judgments from God. 3. His leading them through the wilderness to the confines of Canaan. In each of these it was the Word that appeared to Moses, according to the Targums.

His bringing the people out of Egypt is wholly ascribed to the Word by Onkelos and Jonathan (Dt 20:1), and in Jonathan (Dt 24:18). The people were commanded to teach to their children that it was the Word of the Lord who did all those signs and wonders in Egypt, says Jonathan on Exodus 13:8. It was the Word who sent all those plagues on Pharaoh, and his servants, and all the land of Egypt, says Jonathan on Deuteronomy 29:1-2.[132] Especially, it was the Word that gave that stroke which finished the work, according to the Jerusalem Targum (Ex 12:29), namely, "*It was the Word of the Lord who appeared against the*

---

[132] Allix adds Dt 28:6, but I can find no close match to what this verse is supposed to say. However, this entire chapter is all about "the Word of the LORD" doing various things (see Dt 28:1, 7, 9, 11, 13, 15, 20, 21, 22, 25, 27, 28, 35, 45, 48, 49, 59, 61, 62, 63, 68).

Egyptians at midnight, and his right hand killed the firstborn of the Egyptians, and delivered his own firstborn the children of Israel."

After this, "*the Word of the Lord led the people through the desert to the Red sea,*" says the same Targum (Ex 13:18). "*The Word of the Lord, being their leader, in a pillar of fire by night, and of a cloud by day,*" says Onkelos (Dt 1:32-33). And when the people arrived at the Red sea, and they saw Pharaoh with his army behind them, they were in a rage against Moses and he cried to God (Ex 14:15). According to the Jerusalem Targum, "*The Word of the Lord said to Moses, 'How long will you stand and pray before me? — Tell the children of Israel to come forward, then reach out your rod and divide the Red sea.*" He did so, and according to the Jerusalem Targum on Dt 1:1, "*The Word divided the sea before them; so that the children of Israel went into the midst of the sea on dry ground*" (Ex 14:22), "*the Egyptians following them.*" And at morning, according to the Jerusalem Targum, "The Word of the Lord looked upon the army of the Egyptians, and threw upon them bitumen, and fire, and hail out of heaven" (24). And "*the Egyptians said, 'Let us fly from before the people of Israel, for this is the Word of the Lord that gets them victory*'" (25), but their flight was in vain, for "*by the Word of the Lord the waters were made heaps*" (Onkelos on Ex 15:8). And according to him also, when "*God spoke by his Word, the sea covered them*" (10). Thus, the whole work of the people of Israel's deliverance out of Egypt, every part of it, has been ascribed to the Word of the Lord by the Targums.

For the giving of the laws by which they were be formed into a Church and Kingdom; first, immediately after their coming out of the Red sea (Ex 15:25), according to the Jerusalem Targum, "*The Word of the Lord gave them precepts and orders of judgments,*" particularly, as Jonathan has it, "*The Word of the Lord gave them there the law of the sabbath, and that of honoring father and mother, and judgments concerning bruises and wounds, and for the punishment of transgressors.*" Afterwards, when they had come into the wilderness of Sinai, the text says, "*Moses went up to God, and the Lord called to him out of the mount, saying, 'Thus shall you say to the house of Israel…*" (Ex 19:3). There Onkelos says, according to one of Clark's[133] various readings, "*Moses went up to meet the Word of the Lord*" (Ex 19:8). Moses returns with the People's answer to the Lord, then, according to the Jerusalem Targum, "*The Word of the Lord said to Moses, 'Go to the people, and sanctify them today and tomorrow, and let them wash their clothes, and be ready for the third day, for the third day the Lord will come down in the sight of all the people upon mount Sinai*" (9). Accordingly, the people, having prepared themselves on the third day, according to Onkelos, "*Moses brought the people out of the camp to meet the Word of God*" (17), yet the people

---

[133] Samuel Clark (1626-1701). English Nonconformist, rector at Grendon Underwood, Buckinghamshire, and annotator of the Bible. He was a friend of John Owen, Richard Baxter, and George Whitefield.

only saw thunder and lightning and the mountain smoking and felt the earth quake under them. They also heard the noise of the trumpet, which so frightened them that they removed and stood at a distance and said to Moses, "*You speak to us, and we will hear; but do not let the Word from before the Lord speak with us, lest we die*" (Ex 20:19), according to Onkelos, in one of Clark's various readings. Moses therefore, according to Jonathan on Deuteronomy 5:5 "*stood between them and the Word of the Lord, to show them the Pithgama* [Pithgama is another Aramaic word for "word"], *the matter and words that were spoken to him from the Lord.*" What they were, we read in Exodus 20:1ff. where, according to the Jerusalem Targum, the Word of the Lord spoke the tenor of all these words, saying, "*I am the Lord your God, who brought you out of the land of Egypt, out of the house of bondage.*" After this follow the Ten Commandments, commonly called the Decalogue. That it was God the Word that spoke this to the people, the ancient Church could not doubt, as we see in the Book of Deuteronomy where Jonathan tells us that Moses reminded his people of what they had heard and saw at the giving of the Law (Dt 4:33). "*Is it possible that a people should have heard the voice of the Word of the Lord, the living God, speak out of the middle of the fire, as you have heard, and yet live?*" Again, vs. 36, "*Out of heaven he has made you hear the voice of his Word, — and you have heard his words out of the midst of the fire.*"

Again, he puts them in mind of the fright they were in (Dt 5:23). "*After you had heard the voice of the Word out of the midst of the darkness on the mount burning with fire, all your chiefs came to me, and said, 'Behold, the Word of the Lord our God has shown us the Divine Majesty of his glory, and the excellence of his magnificence, and we have heard the voice of his Word out of the midst of the fire, why should we die, as we must, if we hear any more of the voice of the Word of the Lord our God; for who is there living in flesh, that hears the voice of the Word of the living God speaking out of the middle of the fire, as we do, and yet live?*" Again, in Deuteronomy 18:16 he reminds them of the same thing in some of the same words. Many more such quotations might be added, but these are sufficient to prove that it was the undoubted tradition of the ancient Jewish Church that their Law was given by the Word of God and that it was he who appeared to Moses for this purpose.

As the Word gave the Law, it was also he who made promises in those many appearances to Moses throughout his whole leading of the people of Israel through the wilderness.

I will begin with that Divine appearance, which was continually in sight of all the people of Israel for forty years together throughout their whole travel in the wilderness; namely, the pillar which they saw in the air day and night. In the place this pillar is first spoken of, namely, at the coming of the people of

Israel up out of Egypt, there it is expressly said that *"the Lord went before them in the pillar of cloud by day, and fire by night"* (Ex 13:21). Afterward, he is called the Angel of God (Ex 14:19), where we read that the people, having come to the Red Sea and being in imminent danger of being overtaken by the Egyptians by whom they were closely pursued, the Angel who had gone before the camp of Israel all day, turned at night and went behind them. That this Angel was God is certain, not only because he is called God[134] (Ex 13:21; 14:24; Num 12:5), but also because he was worshipped (Ex 33:10), which was a sure proof of his Divinity. Since he was God himself, and yet the Messenger [Angel] of God, it must be that this was the *Logos* or Word; and that this was the tradition of the ancient Church, we are taught not only by Philo in the place mentioned above,[135] but also by the Jerusalem Targum on Ex 14:24, and Jonathan on Ex 33:9, and by Onkelos on Dt 1:32-33, as has been mentioned.

When the children of Israel, after the first three days' march, found no other waters but those that were too bitter for them to drink, at which time they murmured, Moses cried to the Lord, who immediately showed him a tree, which they threw into the waters to make them sweet (Ex 15:25). Here was a

---

[134] Technically, he is called Yahweh.
[135] *On Husbandry* 51; *The Heir of All Things* 42.201-205.

Divine appearance and it was of the Word of the Lord, according to the Jerusalem Targum.

A month after their coming out of Egypt, they murmured for lack of bread against Moses and Aaron; at which time God showed himself so much concerned that *he made his glory appear to them in the cloud* (Ex 16:7, 10). That according to the sense of the ancient Church, this was the *Shekinah* of the Word, has been just now shown, both from Philo and from all the Targums; and we find the same here in this place where Moses tells them, "*Your murmurings are not against us, but against the Word of the Lord*" (vs. 8), according to Onkelos and Jonathan.

When the Amalekites came against this poor people that had never seen war (Ex 17:8ff.), and smote those at the rear, God not only gave his people a victory over them, but also said to Moses, "*Write this for a memorial in a book … that I will utterly blot out the memory of Amalek from under heaven*" (Ex 17:14). What did Moses then do? In the place where they had fought, he set up an altar with *Jehovah-Nissi*, "*The Lord is My Banner*" (15), meaning that it was the will of God they should be in perpetual war against Amalek. He recorded this reason for it in his book according to Jonathan, "*For the Word of the Lord has sworn by his glory, that he will have war against Amalek for all generations*" (16).

The next Divine appearance we read of was at the giving of the Law on mount Sinai; where we have already said enough, and we must avoid being too long. For this reason, we omit much more that might be said of the following appearances in the wilderness, which are all ascribed to the Word in one or another of the Targums. But I ought not to fail to take notice of some special things.

For their places of worship, God promised according to the Jerusalem Targum, "*In every place that you remember my Name in prayer, I will be revealed to you in my Word and I will bless you,*" and the temple is called "*the place which the Word of the Lord your God will choose to place his Shekinah there,*" according to Jonathan's and the Jerusalem Targums on Deuteronomy 12:5 and Exodus 20:24. Especially at the altar for sacrifice, which was before the door of the tabernacle, God promised Moses, both for himself and the people, according to Onkelos and Jonathan on Exodus 29:42, "*I will appoint my Word to speak with you there, and I will appoint my Word there for the children of Israel.*" Above all, at the mercy seat where the ark stood, God promised to Moses, according to those Targums on Exodus 25:22 and 30:6,[136] "*I will appoint my Word to speak with you there.*" In sum of all the precepts in Leviticus, it is said at the end of that book, according to those Targums, "*These are the statutes and judgments and laws which*

---

[136] Original reads 30:36. This is a typo. Numbers 27:4 is inexplicable, so I have removed it.

the Lord made between his Word and the children of Israel"
(Lev 26:46).

When they entered into covenant with God,
obliging themselves to live according to his laws, they
made the Word to be their King and themselves his
subjects. So Moses tells them, according to the Jerusalem Targum, "*This day you have made the Word of the
Lord King over you so that he may be your glory*" (Dt
26:17). And, "*The Word of the Lord rules over you as king
this day, as over his beloved and peculiar people*" (18). As a
consequence of being their King, he ordered them by
his chief minister Moses to make him a royal pavilion
or tabernacle, and to set it up in the midst of their
camp. Both that and all of its furniture he ordered
Moses to make according to the pattern showed him
in the mount (Ex 25:40). Especially for the presence
of the great King, there was to be an apartment in the
inner part of the tabernacle separated from the rest
with a veil embroidered with cherubim (Ex 27:31).
This part was called the Most Holy Place, or the Holy
of Holies (Ex 27:33).

Here the ark was to be placed, overlaid with pure
gold and having a crown of gold round about it. In
the ark was contained the tablets of the Law. Upon it
was placed the mercy-seat, overshadowed with the
wings of two cherubim that stood on the two ends of
the mercy-seat (Ex 37:9), each one looking at the
other and both of them toward the mercy-seat.

This provision was being made for the place of his *Shekinah*, the Word, who showed himself before in a cloudy pillar by day, and in a fiery pillar by night that stood over the camp. Now from here, he came to take possession of his royal seat in the tabernacle over the ark; from where, out of the void space between these cherubim it was that the Word used to speak to Moses and to give him orders from time to time for the government of his people, according to the para-phrasts on Ex 25:22 and 30:6,[137] and especially Num 7:89, as mentioned above.

From here on out, throughout their whole jour-ney through the wilderness, the pillar was constantly over the tabernacle, and the people attended him. But whenever he gave the commandment, the pillar moved and showed which way the camp was to go. Upon notice of that, Moses first gave the word in a set form of prayer, which we have in the first six verses of the 68th Psalm. The first verse of it is in Numbers 10:35 in these words, according to the Jerusalem Tar-gum, "*Arise now, O Word of the Lord, in the might of your strength.*"[138] According to Jonathan's paraphrase, "*Ap-pear now, O Word of the Lord, in the strength of your wrath.*" In both the Targums it follows, as in the He-brew text, "*And the enemies of your people he shall scatter, and they that hate you shall flee before you.*" When they

---

[137] See note above.
[138] Psalm 68. "*To the choirmaster. A Psalm of David. A Song. God shall arise, his enemies shall be scattered.*"

had performed their journey according to the will of their King, which they knew by seeing the pillar stand still, then Moses used the form for the resting of the ark. According to the forementioned Targums, "*Return now, O Word of the Lord, to your people Israel; make the glory of your Shekinah dwell among them and have mercy on the thousands of Israel*" (Num 10:36). After this was said, the priests (who carried the several pins of the tabernacle) laid down their burdens and set up all things as before; then the pillar returned to its place over the midst of the tabernacle.

In this state of Theocracy, their keeping of God's laws is called by their Targums "*the believing and obeying of the Word.*" Their breaches of his laws are called "*their despising and rebelling against the Word.*" Of the use of both these manners of speaking there might be given more instances than can be easily numbered.

The Targums likewise ascribe to the Word both the rewarding of their obedience and the punishing of their transgressions. On their obedience, according to the Targums, it was the usual promise that the Word should be their help or support (Num 23:8, 21); that he should bless them and multiply them (Dt 24:19); that he should rejoice over them to do them good (Dt 28:63, 30:9). They were told that he would be "*a consuming fire to their enemies*" (Dt 4:24); particularly, that he was so to the Anakims (Dt 9:3); that "*it was he that delivered Og into their hands"* (Dt 3:2); that *"it was he that would cast out all the nations before them"* (Dt 9:23).

On the other hand, according to the sense of the ancient Church, it was the Word who punished them for their disobedience, and also it was he who forgave them upon their repentance. Of both these kinds there are many remarkable instances, as particularly, of the punishing of their disobedience. According to Jonathan on Exodus 32:35, it was the Word who destroyed the people for worshipping the calf that Aaron made. For their lusting at Kibroth-hattaava, Moses told them who it was whom they provoked by it (Num 11:20). (According to Onkelos and Jonathan,) *"You have despised the Word of the Lord, whose Shekinah dwells among you."*

Because of their refusal to go forward into the Promised Land, because of the evil report of the spies, Moses tells them, according to those Targums, *"It was rebelling against the Word of the Lord"* (Dt 1:26). Afterward, when they went up contrary to God's decree, Moses asks them, *"Why do you transgress the decree of the Word of the Lord?"* (Num 14:41). In their murmuring at Zalmona, according to Onkelos in one Polyglot of Clark's various readings, *"They spoke against the Word of the Lord, and against Moses."*[139] Thus, Num 21:6 according to the Jerusalem Targum, *"The Word of the Lord sent fiery serpents among the people."* Upon their

---

[139] Polyglot vol. 4.

whoring with Baal-Peor, according to the Jerusalem Targum, "*The Word of the Lord said to Moses, 'Take all the heads of the people, and hang them up before the Lord'*" (Num 25:4).[140] In short, according to the Targums on Deuteronomy 28:20ff., it was "*the Word of the Lord*" who would send all his judgments and curses that are there denounced against impenitent sinners.

But on the other hand, according to those Targums, it belonged to "*the Word*" to grant pardon to those who were qualified for it. So when Moses begged pardon for his people that had sinned beyond mercy, if it had not been infinite, according to the Jerusalem Targum, "*The Word of the Lord answered him, and said, 'Behold, I have forgiven, and pardoned according to your word'*" (Num 14:20). In case that, upon the inflicting of God's judgments mentioned above, God's people should be brought to repentance, it was promised, according to Jonathan's Targum, that "*then the Word should accept their repentance according to his good pleasure, and should have mercy on them, and gather them out of all nations…*" (Dt 30:3). So likewise 32:36, according to the same Targum, it is promised that "*the Word of the Lord judges mercifully the case of his people, and there will be pity before him for the evil that he will decree upon his servants.*" It would be very easy to add many more such instances out of the Targums; but these are abundantly enough to show the sense of the ancient

---

[140] Or "*You shall crucify them on wood before the Word of the Lord.*"

Church, what they thought of him who so often appeared to their fathers in the wilderness, and spoke to them by his servant Moses.

When Moses understood that God would not let him live to bring his people into the Promised Land; he implored God to send him a successor, in these words, according to Jonathan's Targum, "*Let the Word of the Lord, who has dominion over the souls of men … appoint a faithful man over the congregation of his people*" (Num 27:16). Moses gave him this charge to Joshua, God having appointed Joshua in his stead, in the hearing of the people, according to Onkelos and Jonathan, "*Your eyes have seen what the Lord did to Og and Sihon, so he will do to all the kingdoms that you pass through; therefore do not fear them, for the Word of the Lord your God shall fight for you*" (Dt 3:21-22).

He repeated the same thing later to all the people; telling them first, according to Jonathan, "*The Word of the Lord said to me, 'You shall not pass over this Jordan, but the Lord your God and his Shekinah will go before you'*" (Dt 31:2-3). He adds, "*And Joshua will go over before you, as the Lord has spoken*" (4). And regarding all your enemies, "*the Word of the Lord shall deliver them up before you*" (5). Therefore, it says in Onkelos, "*Do not fear them, for the Word of the Lord your God goes before you; he will not fail nor forsake you*" (6).

After this, Moses calls to Joshua and says to him in front of them all, according to Jonathan, "*Be strong and of a good courage, you must go with this people into the land which the Word of the Lord has sworn to their fathers that he would give them … and the Shekinah of the Word of the Lord shall go before you, and his Word shall he you help; he will not leave you nor forsake you. Do not fear, neither be dismayed"* (7-8). He repeats it again from God to Joshua, according to Onkelos and Jonathan, *"You shall bring the children of Israel into the land which I have sworn to them; and my Word will be your help"* (23).

It was on that same day that he gave this charge to Joshua that Moses also gave them his prophetic song (22-23). God then told Moses that same day, *"Go up to … mount Nebo, and die"* (32:48-49). Moses obeyed and lingered no longer than to give the tribes of Israel his blessing before his death (33:1). When this was finished, he went up to mount Nebo (34:1). There, according to Jonathan, it was *"the Word of the Lord"* who gave satisfaction to his bodily eyes to see all the land of Canaan before they were closed. So, vs. 5, *"Moses the servant of the Lord died there … according to the Word of the Lord."* He was translated by the *Logos*, according to Philo.[141] It was certainly the current tradition of the Church in his age that his soul was taken out of his body *"by a kiss of the Word of the Lord,"* as Jonathan renders it; or, according to the Jerusalem Targum *"at the mouth of the decree of the Word of the Lord."*

---

[141] *The Sacrifices of Abel and Cain* 3.8.

After his death, Joshua took up the reigns of leadership, and according to the Jerusalem Targum, "*The children of Israel obeyed Joshua, and they did as the Word of the Lord had commanded Moses*" (9).

Besides all these Divine appearances to Moses and the children of Israel, there are also a few that were made to Balaam on their account and are therefore recorded in the same sacred history. Where these are first mentioned, both Onkelos and Jonathan have, "*The Word came from before the Lord to Balaam, 'Who are these men who are with you?'*" (Num 22:9). So again, the second time, according to the same Targums, "*The Word came from before the Lord to Balaam by night, and said to him, 'If these men have come to call you...'*" (20). It is plain that the ancient Jewish Church took these appearances to have been made by the Word.

But what opinion did they have of the Angel's appearing to Balaam (vs. 22)? Others may ask what they thought of the dialogue between Balaam and the donkey that he rode upon, which occurred because the beast was frightened at the Angel's appearing to him. All this, as Maimonides says, happened only in vision of prophecy.[142] But it was a thing that really happened, we are assured by St. Peter who tells us, "*God opened the mouth of the dumb beast to rebuke the madness of the Prophet*" (2Pe 2:16). As it cannot be doubted that Balaam used to have communication with devils

---

[142] Maim. *More Nebochim* 11. P. 42.

that spoke to him in various ways, so there is reason to believe they spoke to him sometimes by the mouth of dumb beasts. If so, then to hear the donkey speak could not be strange to him. And why God should order it so? There is a reason given in Jonathan and the Jerusalem Targum. The reader may see other reasons elsewhere, but they are not proper for this place.[143]

We need to consider whether this angel that appeared to Balaam was a created angel or not. It appears by the words to have been the Lord himself who appeared as an angel to Balaam; for thus he says to him, *"Go with the men, but speak only the word that I tell you"* (Num 22:35). Now it does not appear after this that anyone else spoke to him from God, but God himself. Therefore, Philo says plainly that this appearance was of the *Logos*, as has been already shown. And that this was the sense of the Church in his age, we may see in the two following appearances to Balaam, as well as in the two that were before this. The Targums say it was *"the Word that met Balaam, and spoke to him"* (Thus, both Onkelos and Jonathan on Num 23:4, 16).

---

[143] *Muis Varis*, p. 95.

CHAP. XV.

That all the appearances of God, or of the Angel of the Lord, which are spoken of in the books of the Old Testament after Moses's time, have been referred to the Word of God by the Jews before Christ's incarnation.

THUS FAR IT HAS BEEN our business to show that it was the Word who made all those appearances, either of God or of an Angel of God that was worshipped, in any part of the five books of Moses. We have been much larger in this than was necessary for our present occasion. But whatever may seem to have been over-kill in the previous chapter, it is hoped the reader will not wish we had said less, when he comes to reflect upon the use of it, to prove that the Word was a Person and that he was God.

Now, we will try to make amends for the wordiness used previously through the shortness of what we have to say in the rest of this chapter. We will look at those Divine appearances that are recorded in the other books of Scripture after the Pentateuch, and we will find those appearances fewer and fewer, until they basically come to cease in the Jewish Church. For once the *Logos* was settled as the King of Israel between the cherubim, he was not to be looked for in other places. Of those books of Scripture in which the following appearances are mentioned, we do not have as many paraphrases as we had for the five books of Moses.[144] One paraphrase is all that we have of most of the books we now speak of. Yet, we have reason to thank God, that that evidence of the Divine appearances of the Word of God have been so abundantly sufficient, that we have no need for anymore. In what will see in the following appearances of God, or the Angel who was worshipped, it will be enough to show that the ancient Jewish Church had the same notion that they had of those already mentioned out of the five books of Moses.

We read of but one Divine appearance to Joshua, and that is when a man with a drawn sword in his hand came to him, calling himself the captain of the Lord's host (Josh 5:13-14). Some would say that this was a created angel, but certainly Joshua did not take him for one. Otherwise he would not have fallen down on his face and worshipped him as he did (14). Nor would a created angel have received it from him without reproving him, as the angel did to St. John in a similar situation (Rev 19:10; 22:9). But this Divine Person was so far from admonishing him for having done too much that he commanded him to keep going and do

---

[144] Genesis-Deuteronomy have three Targums: Onkelos, Jerusalem/Neofiti, and Pseudo-Jonathan. Most of the other books only have one.

even more, requiring of him the highest acknowledgment of a Divine Presence that was in use among the eastern nations. We see this in these words, *"Take off your sandals from your feet, for the place where you are standing is holy"* (Josh 5:15).

Now, considering that these are the exact same words that God said to Moses in Exodus 3:2-3, we see a plain reason why God should command this to Joshua. It was for the strengthening of his faith, to let him know that as he was now in Moses's role, so God would be the same to him that he had been to Moses. This is particularly so with respect to that trial which required a more than ordinary measure of faith, that is the difficult task of taking the stronghold of Jericho with such an army as he had without any provision for a siege. Thus, the Lord said to him, *"See, I have given Jericho into your hand"* (Josh 6:2). No one but God could say and do this; and the text plainly says, *"It was the Lord."* That the Lord who thus appeared as a warrior and called himself *"the captain of the Lord's host,"* was none other than the Word, as was plainly the sense of the ancient Jewish Church. This appears in what remains of it in their paraphrase on Joshua 10:14, *"For the Lord the God of Israel by his Word waged battle for Israel."* It is also found in later, *"For the Lord your God—his Word—was fighting for you"* (23:3, 10), and also vs. 13 which says, *"It was the Word who cast out the nations before them."*

Indeed, this very judgment of the old synagogue is to be seen not only in their Targums until this day, but in their most ancient books (*Rabboth*, fol. 108. col. 3.; *Zohar*, par. 3. fol. 139. col. 3.; Tanch. *ad Exod.* iii.; Ramb. *ad Exod.* iii., Bach. fol. 69. 2). The learned Masius in Joshua 5:13-14 has translated the words of Ramban,[145] and he has preferred his interpretation, which is the most ancient amongst the Jews, to the sense of the commentators of the Church of Rome.[146]

As for divine appearances in the Book of Judges, we read of one to Gideon that seems to have been of an angel of God, for so he is called (Jdg 6:11-12, 20-22). In this last place it is also said that "*Gideon perceived he was an Angel of the Lord.*" That is, he saw that this was a heavenly person that came to him with a message from God. And yet that he was no created angel it seems, because he is so often simply called the Lord (14, 16, 23, 24, 25, 27). Gideon in that whole story never addressed himself to anyone other than God. The message delivered from God by this Angel to Gideon is thus rendered in the Targum, "*Surely my Word shall be you help, and you shall smite the Midianites as one man*" (16). The Word who helped Gideon against the Midianites was none other than he who appeared to Joshua with a sword in his hand (Josh 5:13).

---

[145] Moses ben Nahman.
[146] Given that Masius was a Roman priest, this is remarkable.

This was now the sword of the Lord and of Gideon (Jdg 7:18, 20).

What the ancient Jewish Church meant by the Word of the Lord in this place one may guess by their Targum on Judges 6:12-13, where the angel says to Gideon, "*The Word of the Lord is at your aid, O mighty warrior.*" And Gideon said to him: "*Please, master, if the Shekinah of the Lord has come to our aid, why has all this happened to us?*" It is plain by this paraphrase that they reckoned the Word of the Lord to be identical with the *Shekinah* of the Lord, even he by whom God had so gloriously appeared for their deliverance. And indeed they could hardly be mistaken in the person of that Angel who says that his name is *Pele*, the Wonderful, which is used among the names of the Messiah (Isaiah 9:6), which name the Jews make a shift to appropriate to God, exclusively to the Messiah.

The angel who appeared to Manoah (Judges 13) could seem to have been none other than a created angel. But the name which he takes of *Pele*, The Wonderful, shows that he was the Word of the Lord, or the Angel of the Lord (Isa 63:8).

In the first Book of Samuel we read of no other such appearance, except that which God made to Samuel (1Sa 3:21). This was only by "*a voice from the temple of the Lord, where the ark was at that time*" (3-4). The word *hekal* signifies a temple or a palace, thus the tabernacle was called where the ark was in those days at Shiloh. It was there that *"God revealed himself to Sam-uel by the Word of the Lord"* (21). But that the Word of the Lord was their King, and the tabernacle was his palace, where his throne was upon the ark between the cherubim, and that from this place the Word gave his oracle in the opinion of the ancient Jewish Church, all this has been so fully proved in the previous chapters, such that to prove it here again would be superfluous. Therefore, I take it for granted that, in their opinion, it was the Word of the Lord from whom this voice came to Samuel.

In the second Book of Samuel we read how, upon David's sin in numbering the people, God sent the Prophet Gad to give him his choice of three punishments: either three years of famine, or three months of destruction by enemies, or three days of pestilence throughout all the coast of Israel. This last one was a judgment from heaven that would fall equally upon a prince or a peasant. And so David made this his choice, rather than of either of the other two. He said, *"Do not let me fall into the hands of man, but rather into the hands of the Lord. For great are his mercies"* (1Ch 21:13). Thus, God sent a pestilence upon all the coasts of Israel and seventy thousand men fell (2Sa 24:15).

To prove to David's bodily eyes this extraordinary instance, as well as God's justice in punishing sinners, and his mercy to them if they repented and prayed, God made him see an angel standing between the earth and the heaven, having a drawn sword in his hand stretched out over Jerusalem to destroy it (2Sa 24:16-17; 1Ch 21:16). When David saw this sight, he fell on his face and prayed. Then God said to the destroying angel, "*It is enough, stay now your hand. Then the angel came down and stood by the floor of Oman the Jebusite*" (2Sa 24:16). (This was on the very place God designed that Solomon should build his temple and he declared it to David at this occasion). There, according to the angel's order by the Prophet Gad, David now built an altar, and sacrificed upon it. Then, "*The Lord commanded the angel, and he put his sword into his sheath*" (17). This was none other than a created angel, whom God employed into his service and appointed to appear in that manner for all those purposes mentioned.[147]

What the ancient Church thought of all this passage of history, we may easily guess by what has already been shown of their ascribing all rewards and punishments to the Word who had the management and government over God's people. And though it seems that care has been taken to conceal this notion of theirs as much as was possible in the Targums of the

---

[147] What Allix says in this sentence is difficult to understand. Is he saying that he believes the angel in this text was created? If so, it why bring this story up? Is he saying that the OT church believed this angel was created? This seems to put the cart before the horse, for he will immediately say that later Jews appear to have tried to conceal the early understanding but have failed to fully eradicate all vestiges of the Word in this story. This means he is proving from this passage that this Angel was in fact the Word, which is consistent with his entire argument.

books now before us; yet there is a passage that seems to have escaped the correctors, by which we may perceive that the sense of the Church here was agreeable to what we find of it in all other places. For in 2 Samuel 24:14, where we find in the text that David said, *"Let us fall now into the hand of the Lord, for his mercies are great,"* the Targum renders these words, *"Let me be delivered into the hand of the Word of the Lord, for great are his mercies."* It was therefore the Word of the Lord into whose hands David fell. It was his Angel by whom the judgment was executed; and it was also his mercy by which the judgment was suspended and revoked. The Targum on this text sufficiently shows that all this was the sense of the Jewish Church.

In short, the ancient Church considered the Word as being their Sovereign Lord, and King of the people of Israel. All those kings whose acts are described in the two Books of Kings, they looked upon them as his lieutenants or deputies, who held their title from and under him by virtue of his covenant with David their father. Solomon declares this in these words, *"Blessed be the Lord God of Israel, who by his Word made a covenant with David my father"* (1Kg 8:15). Whatever God did for his people under their government, in protecting and delivering them from their enemies, they owned that it was *"for his Word's sake, and for his servant David's sake"* (2Kg 19:34; 20:6). When they had broken his covenant, God removed them from before his Word, and gave them up to be a scorn to all nations, as he threatened he would do (1Kg 9:7, according to their Targum).

In these books we read of only two more divine appearances in Solomon's time, and both these to Solomon himself (1Kg 9:2).

The first was at Gibeon (1Kg 3:5), where the Lord appeared to Solomon "*in a dream by night,*" and said to him, "*Ask what I shall give you.*" He asked nothing but wisdom, which so pleased the Lord that he gave him not only that but also riches and honor above all the kings then in the world. The Targum, as it has come to our hands, does not say it was the Word of the Lord that appeared to him, and that gave him all this. But that it was so according to the sense of their Church may be gathered from the text, which tells us that as soon as Solomon was awake, he went immediately to Jerusalem (which was about seven miles distant) and there "*he stood before the ark of the covenant of the Lord*" (which was there in the tabernacle set up by David his father), "*and he offered up both burnt offerings and peace offerings, and made a feast to all his servants*" (15). The haste in which all this was done brings us to the reason he did this. For of all peace offerings for thanksgiving to God, the same day that they were offered, the flesh had to be eaten (Lev 7:15). The breast and the right shoulder by the priests, all the rest by the offeror and those that he had to eat with him.

It is plain, therefore, that this was a sacrifice of thanks-giving to God. But why did Solomon not stay in Gibeon and pay his duty at the place where he had received the vision, especially since the tabernacle which Moses made by God's command, and the brazen altar which Bezaleel made (2Ch 1:2-4), and more were all there at Gibeon? It is because Solomon had come on purpose to Gibeon to sacrifice upon that altar at that time in the first place. The very day before this appearance of God, he had offered a thousand burnt offerings upon it (6), and on that very night God appeared to him (7). Now given that Solomon had found such good success when he sacrificed at Gibeon that God came and appeared to him and gave him so great a blessing, we would think he would certainly have stayed there to have paid his thanksgiving in that place. But instead, he understood that the one who appeared to him was the Word, and his special presence was with the ark at Jerusalem, as we have abundantly proved. Therefore, he quickly hurried to that place to pay his burnt offerings and peace offerings of thanksgiving to the Word of the Lord. This we cannot doubt was the sense of the ancient Jewish Church, though it doth not appear now in their Targums.

If it was the Word who made that first appearance to Solomon, then it must be he who made the second also. For both of these appearances were by the same person. So, it is said expressly in the text, "*The*

Lord appeared to Solomon the second time, as he had appeared to him at Gibeon" (1Kg 9:2). But of this second appearance, that it was the Word of the Lord, there is a clearer proof than of first; as the reader will certainly judge, if he considers the circumstances of this second appearance and the words which God spoke to Solomon on this occasion.

First, the time of this divine appearance to Solomon was when he had finished the building of the house of the Lord (1). He had brought the ark into the most holy place, even under the wings of the cherubim (1Kg 8:6). The glory of the Lord had taken possession of this house (10-11), and Solomon had made his prayer and supplication before it (12-61). Subsequently, God appears and tells him, "*I have heard the prayer and supplication that you have made before me. I have hallowed this house which you have built*" (9:3). That is, I have taken it for my own, "*to put my name there forever*" (1Ch 7:12). "*I have chosen this place to myself for a house of sacrifice.*" This was a plain declaration from God, that it was of this house that he had spoken by Moses in these words, "*There shall be a place which the Lord your God shall choose to place his name there, here shall you bring all that I command you, your burnt offerings and your sacrifices*" etc. (Dt 12:5, 11). Now see how those words of Moses are rendered in Jonathan's Targum on Deuteronomy, "*There will be a place which the Word of the Lord will choose to place his Shekinah, there shall you bring your offerings*" etc. Here we cannot but see that he that appeared to Solomon and said to him, "*I have chosen this place*" etc. Speaking all along in the first person is the same one of whom Moses said all the same things but spoke of him in the third person. As it appears in Jonathan's Targum (both vs. 5. and 11) of that chapter, this was none other than the Word, according to the doctrine of the ancient Jewish Church; though in their Targum on 1 Kings 9 (which also is called Jonathan's, but how truly the reader may see by this instance) there is not the least mention of the Word upon this occasion.

The Word of the Lord now resting at his place in Solomon's temple (2Ch 6:41), and having put an end to his own theocracy by setting up kings of Solomon's lineage that came in by hereditary succession and governed after the manner of the kings of other nations; after this, in the Scripture history of those times, while the first temple was standing, we read of no more divine appearances as we formerly had.

There is only one exception, namely, that when Elijah heard that "*still small voice*" (1Kg 19), of which something ought to be said more particularly. It may be observed that this was in that part of Israel which had no communion with the temple. It was in Ahab's time, when the children of Israel had not only cast off the seed of David but seemed to have quite forsaken the covenant which God had made with their fathers by his servant Moses. To bring them back to their duty, God had now sent Elijah, who was a kind of second Moses. God showed this by putting him into so many of Moses's circumstances. For example, after a fast of forty days, which no one except Moses had ever kept before him, he comes to Horeb, the mount of God (1Kg 19:8).

We first read of this mountain in Exodus 3:1, when God first appeared to Moses at this same place. There (Ex 3:6), Moses hid his face because he was afraid to look upon God. Elijah did the same thing in this same place (1Kg 19:13). He wrapped his face in his cloak and then God spoke to him, just as he had done first to Moses. He who spoke now was the same who spoke then. This is made clear by comparing the circumstances. He who spoke then was God the Word, as we have proved before in the former chapter. This was the sense of the ancient Jewish Church. And to us Christians, it cannot but look very agreeable that just as when Moses and Elijah were upon the earth, the Word appeared to them and spoke with them on mount Horeb; so also when he was made flesh and dwelt among us, Moses and Elijah came to him on mount Tabor[148] and spoke with him at his transfiguration.

---

[148] There is good reason to believe this was actually on Mt. Hermon. The text does not say, but it is clear that they were just at Caesarea Philippi, which is at the base of Mt. Hermon.

Of those appearances of angels to Elijah (1Kg 19:5, 7; 2Kg 1) and the angel who slaughtered so many of Sennacherib's army (2Kg 19:35), we have no more to say in this place; because they seem to have been created angels, and neither of them is called the Word of the Lord in their Targum.

But we can say something about that vision of God which was seen by the prophet Micaiah (1Kg 22:19ff.). Although he does not say that God appeared to him, nor that he saw anything more of God than a mere resemblance of a king sitting in state, which was at that moment visibly represented before him, we must take notice of one thing. It is of some importance that when he says, *"I saw the Lord sitting on his throne, and all the host of heaven standing by him on his right hand and on his left"* etc., the most learned Jews conceive that he saw the *Shekinah* with the angels of his attendance, and that this vision of Micaiah is the same which was showed to Isaiah (Isa 6:1ff.), and to some of the other prophets.

In the prophetical books of Isaiah and Ezekiel, there are two appearances of God, or of the *Shekinah* in his temple, which we are obliged to give some account. Of these, as I will show, we have no reason to doubt but that it was the Word who appeared to those prophets according to the sense of the ancient Jewish Church.

First, in Isaiah 6:1ff. the prophet says, "*I saw the Lord sitting upon a throne, high and lifted up, and his train filled the temple. Above him stood the seraphim*[149] *... And one called to another and said, 'Holy, holy, holy Lord of hosts, the whole earth is full of his glory' ... And the house was filled with smoke.*" That this house was the temple is expressly said at the end of the first verse. And the smoke was the sign of the *Shekinah* of God, with which the temple was now filled, as it was when he first entered into it (1Kg 8:10-11). In this way here, the Lord sitting upon his throne, was none other than God sitting upon his mercy-seat over the ark. That is, he was the Word of the Lord according to the opinion of the ancient Jewish Church, as has been abundantly proved before in this chapter. But this can also be seen here in their paraphrase; for whereas the prophet still speaking of the Lord whom he saw sitting on his throne (Isa 6:1), says, "*Then I heard the voice of the Lord, saying, 'Whom shall I send?*" (8), the Targum renders it, "*I heard the voice of the Word of the Lord, saying, 'Whom shall I send?'*" We Christians need not thank them for this, being fully assured, as we are by what the Apostle says in John 12:41 that this was none other than our Lord Jesus Christ. For there the Apostle, having quoted the words that Isaiah heard from the Lord that spoke to him (Isa 6:9-10) tells us, "*These things Isaiah said when he saw his glory, and spoke of him.*" That the

---

[149] Allix reads "cherubims."

Apostle here speaks of the Word made flesh, it is clear enough from the text. But besides, it has been proved by our writers beyond all contradiction.[150]

In the same way, that which the prophet Ezekiel saw was an appearance of God represented to him as a man sitting on a throne of glory (Ezek 1:26, 28; 10:1). The throne was upon wheels, after the manner of a *sella curulis*.[151] These were living wheels, animated and supported by cherubim (1:21), each of which had four faces (1:6) such as were carved on the walls of the temple (41:19). In short, even though he was in Chaldea (Babylon), that which Ezekiel saw was nothing other than the appearance of God still dwelling in his temple at Jerusalem. This, even though God was weary of it and was soon about to abandon it, to leave his dwelling place and allow it to be destroyed by the Chaldeans. To show that this was the meaning of it, he saw this glorious appearance of God, first, *"in his place"* (3:12), i.e. on the mercy-seat, in the temple (9:3).

Next, he saw him having left his place, gone to the *"threshold of the house."* Judges use to give judgment in the gate; so there, over the threshold of his house,

---

[150] See Plac. *Lib. ii. Disput.* 1. It should be noted that the Hebrew text does not talk about the "glory" or the shekinah in Isaiah 6. However, the Targum does. Thus, some scholars have argued that John is actually either targuming himself or was familiar with the old Targum on Isaiah 6:1 and is alluding to it. Either way, he is tapping into this ancient tradition, and this supports Allix's argument all the more.

[151] This refers to the Roman Emperor's "Chariot Seat," which basically represented political and military authority.

God pronounced sentence against his rebellious people (5-7). Afterwards, from the threshold of the house (10:4), the prophet saw the glory departing even farther. It *"mounted up from the earth over the midst of the city"* (10:18-19). Lastly, he saw it go from there and *"stand upon the mountain on the east side of the city"* (11:23), that is on the Mt. of Olives, which is before Jerusalem on the east (Zech 14:4), and so the Targum has it on this place.

After this departure of the Divine Presence, Ezekiel saw his forsaken temple and city destroyed and his people carried away into captivity (33:21ff.). After this he saw no more appearances of God until his people's return from his captivity; and then, the temple being rebuilt according to the measures given from God (chs. 40-42). The prophet could not but expect that God would return to it as of old. So, he saw it come to pass in his vision, *"Behold the glory of the God of Israel came from the way of the east* (where the prophet saw it last, at the Mt. of Olives, 43:2). So again, *"The glory of the Lord came into the house by the way of the gate whose prospect is toward the east"* (4). And, *"Behold the glory of the Lord filled the house"* (5). So again, *"It filled the house"* (44:4) now, as it had done in Solomon's time (1Kg 8:11).

All along in this prophecy of Ezekiel, there was but one Person who appeared, from the beginning to the end. In the beginning of this prophecy, it was God who appeared in his temple over the cherubim; and there we find him again at the end of this prophecy. But that it was none other but the Word who appeared in the temple, according to the sense of the ancient Jewish Church, has been proved so fully out of their Targums elsewhere, that we need not trouble ourselves about that any farther, though we cannot find it in the Targum on this book.[152]

In the books of Chronicles there is nothing remarkable of this kind, but except what has been considered already, in the account that we have given of the Divine appearances in the books of Kings. And there is no mention made of any such appearance in any of the other books that were written after the Babylonian captivity, except in the books of Daniel and Zechariah.[153] Of Daniel the Jews have not given us any Targum, therefore we have nothing to say of that book. They have given us a Targum, such as it is, of the book of Zechariah, which is the last we have to consider.

---

[152] The Memra does appear frequently in the Ezekiel Targum. A possible example that might have satisfied Allix could be, "… *by placing their threshold beside the threshold of My Holy Temple, and their buildings beside My Temple Court, with only a wall of My Holy Temple between My Memra and them. They defiled My holy name with their abominations which they committed, so I destroyed them. in My anger. Now let them put their idols and the corpses of their kings far away, so as not to sin before Me, and I will cause My Shekinah to dwell among them forever*" (Ezek 43:8-9).

[153] This again does not mean that the Memra is not to be found in these books. He appears quite often, but mostly in prophecy or in some kind of theological way. Allix is concerned with actual appearances.

In this book of Zechariah, we read of three angels who appeared to the prophet. The first appeared to him as a man (Zech 1:8, 10), but he is called an angel (9). In Zechariah's words, "*The angel who talked with me,*" is the title he is often given to distinguish him from all others in the same book (1:13, 14, 19; 2:3; 5:5, 6; 6:4). A second angel appeared to him also as "*a man*" with a measuring line in his hand (2:1). But whoever compares this text with Ezekiel 40:3-5 etc. will find that this, who appeared as "*a man,*" was truly an angel of God.

Next, the first angel going forth from the place where he appeared (Zech 2:3), "*another angel*" comes to meet him, and tells him, "*Run, speak to this young man*" (whether to the angel surveyor, or whether to Zechariah himself) and tell him, "*Jerusalem shall he inhabited*" etc. (2:4). He who commands another should be his superior. And yet this superior says that he himself was sent from God. But he said it in such terms that it showed he was God himself. This the reader will see more than once in his speech, which is continued from vs. 4 to the end of the chapter.

It appears especially in vv. 8, 9, and 11 of this chapter. First, in vs. 9. having declared what God would do for Jerusalem in these words, according to the Targum, "*The Lord has said, 'My Word shall be a wall of fire about her, and my Shekinah will I place in the midst of her.'*" He goes on to vs. 12, and there he delivers a message from God to his people in these words: "*Thus says the Lord of hosts (after the glory[154] which it was promised to bring upon you...).*" Here the sense is ambiguous; for it seems strange that the Lord of hosts should say another has sent me. But so it is again, and much more clearly expressed in vs. 13 where he says, "*Behold, I will shake my hand upon them, and they shall be spoil for those who served me.*" No one but God could say this, but he adds in the next words, "*And you shall know that the Lord of hosts has sent me,*" which plainly shows that though he styled himself God, yet he came as a Messenger from God.

This is plainer still when he says, "*Many nations shall be joined to the Lord in that day, and I [my Shekinah] will dwell in your midst*" (15). This again no one but God could say, and yet it follows, "*You (O Zion)[155] shall know that the Lord of hosts has sent me to you.*" Here we plainly see two persons called by the name of Jehovah; namely, one that sends, and another that is sent; so that this second Person is God, and yet he is also the Messenger of God.

So likewise, in the next chapter the angel that used to talk with the prophet showed him Joshua the high priest standing before the Angel of the Lord, and

---

[154] The note reads, "After the glory of his Shekinah being returned into the temple, when that was rebuilt, they should soon after see Babylon itself taken, and spoiled by their ancient servants the Persians."

[155] The original has a note that all of the pronouns are feminine and therefore refer to Zion.

Satan standing over against Joshua as his adversary (Zech 3:1). In vs. 2 the prophet hears the Lord say to Satan not once but twice, "*The Lord rebuke you*," for he was maliciously bent against Joshua who has just come out of the captivity "*like a brand plucked out of the fire.*" He that was called the Angel (1) is now called the Lord (2), and this Lord intercedes with the Lord for his protecting Joshua against Satan. That which gave the Devil advantage against Joshua was his sins; which, as the Targum says, were the marriages of his sons to strange wives. Whatever his sins may have been, they are here called "*filthy garments*;" and Joshua is clothed in them before the angel (3-4). The angel commands all who stood about him, saying, "*Take away the filthy garments from him.*" Here again, by commanding the angels, he shows himself their superior. Afterwards, when the filthy garments are taken off, this Angel says to Joshua, "*Behold, I have caused your iniquity to pass from you*;" words, which, if a man had said them to another, the Jews would have accounted it blasphemy (Matt 9:2-3). "*For who* (say they) *can forgive sins but God alone?*"

But here was one who exercised that authority over the high priest himself. This could be none other than he who was called of God, a priest for ever after the order of Melchizedek (Ps 110:4), of whom the Jewish high priest, even Joshua himself, was but a figure. But he goes farther, adding, "*I will clothe you with pure vestments,"* that is, according to the Targum, *"I will clothe you with righteousness"* (5). And he said,[156] (again commanding the angels), *"Let them set a clean turban on his head; and they did so, and clothed him with garments, and the Angel of the Lord stood by."* Here again he is called an Angel, at last, as he was at first (Zech 2:3). It is an angel's office to be the messenger of God; and so he often owned himself to be, in saying, *"The Lord sent me."* And yet this Messenger of God commands the angels (2:4; 3:4-5) and himself stands by to see them do his commands (5).

This Angel calls Israel his people, and says, he will dwell among them (Zech 2:10-11). He takes it upon himself to protect his people (5), and to avenge them on their enemies (10). He intercedes with God (3:2). He forgives sin and confers righteousness (3:4). If all these things cannot be truly said of one and the same person, then here are two chapters together that are each of them half nonsense, and there is no way to reconcile them with sense, but by putting some kind of force upon the text, whether by changing the words, or by putting in other words, as Socinus honestly confesses he has done in his interpretation.[157] He says they must do it to make sense of the words. This is absolutely certain, since they only want to interpret the words as they see fit. But he and his followers bring this

---

[156] The note reads *and he said*, Jon. Targ.
[157] Socin. in *Wick*. 1.ii. p. 565.

necessity upon themselves. Those who feel compelled to set up new opinions must defend them with new Scriptures. For our part, we change nothing in the words; and in our way of understanding them we follow the judgment of the ancient Jewish Church which makes all these things perfectly agree to the *Logos*. This we see in Philo,[158] who often calls the *Logos* God; and yet as often calls him an angel, the messenger of God; and our high priest, and our mediator with God. The same has been shown of the Word elsewhere out of the Targums. And here in this Targum, though no doubt it has been carefully purged, yet by some oversight it is said that, "*The Word shall be a wall of fire about Jerusalem.*" And if the modern Jews had not changed the third person into the first, it would have followed, that his Shekinah should be in the midst of her; as he himself says afterward (10-11), "*He would dwell in the midst of her;*" meaning in the temple, where the Word of God had his dwelling-place always before its destruction, as has been abundantly shown in this chapter, and as we showed from Ezekiel it was promised he should dwell there again after its restoration.

---

[158] *On Dreams 1.238*-41; Eusebius, *Preparation for the Gospel* 7.15. *Deuteros Theos* [Second God]: Philo, *Questions on Genesis* 2.62. As Philo calls the Father, *protos theos* [First God]: *On the Migration of Abraham 194*. The Word as Angel: *The Heir of All Things* 205. Two Powers: *On Dreams* 162-63; *On the Unchangeableness of God* 109. Allix gives several more references, but we are unsure to which attribute these pertain. See *The Heir of All Things* 42.205; *De Somn.* p. 463. F. *De Prof.* p. 364. B; *De Prof.* 466. B; *De Somniss*, p. 594. E; *The Heir of All Things* 205; *Vit. Mos.* iii. P. 521. B.

Gerard De Gols

Excerpts from:
A Vindication of the Worship of the Lord Jesus Christ as the Supreme God

By
Gerard De Gols

CHAP. V.

THAT DIVINE ADORATION IS DUE TO CHRIST, BECAUSE HE IS GOD.

We come now to demonstrate that this holy worship, this divine adoration, which is God's due and his incommunicable attributes, are applied to the Lord Christ in the Scriptures and required of us to be paid to Christ by the Scriptures. This I shall demonstrate, by showing that Christ is that God who is to be worshiped.

We Christians profess that there is one and only one God. This is the fundamental article of all religion. And we believe that this God, whose highest perfection is that he cannot lie, can no more deceive us than he can be deceived by us. We believe that this God is one only, and that in the unity of that divinity there are three Persons: the Father, the Son, and the Holy Ghost who are that one God. This we believe although we cannot understand it, because that great God, who alone knows himself, has to reveal himself to us. Yet, we are assured that this great God is too holy to deceive us, too good to lead us into error, and too jealous of his honor to make anyone else who is not God a sharer of his prerogatives or a partaker of his worship and adoration.

Thus, we find ourselves obliged to believe this Trinity of Persons in the unity of the divinity from most express words of Scripture. For those sacred pages assure us both in the Old and New Testament:

That there is but One True God.

In the Old Testament	**In the New Testament**
Deut 6:4. *Hear Israel, the Lord our God is one Lord.*	Mark 12:29. *And Jesus answered him— "Hear O Israel, the Lord our God is one Lord."*
Isaiah 46:8. *Is there a God besides me? There is no Rock; I know not any.*	1Co 8:4. *There is no God but One.*
	Gal 3:20. *God is one.*

The same holy pages assure us, both in the Old and New Testament:

That there are Three Persons in the Unity of the Divinity, the Father, Son, and Holy Spirit.

In the Old Testament

Gen 1:26. *Let us make man in our image, after our Likeness.*[159]

Ps 33:6. *By the Word of the LORD the heavens were made, and by the Breath [Spirit] of his mouth all their host.*

Ps 45:6. *Your throne, O God, is forever and ever. The scepter of your kingdom is a scepter of uprightness ... God, your God has anointed you.*

In the New Testament

Matt 3:16-17. *And behold, the heavens were opened to him, and he saw the Spirit of God descending like a dove and coming to rest on him; and behold, a voice from heaven said, "This is my beloved Son, in whom I am well pleased."*

Matt 28:19. *Go therefore and make disciples of all nations, baptizing them in the name of the Father and of the Son and of the Holy Spirit.*

---

[159] Original note: "God speaking in the plural number ["us"] here expresses a plurality of Persons in the unity of the divinity; for that God spoke not to the angels is certain, because they had no hand in the creation, neither was man made after their image, but only God's: And that God did not speak in the plural number after the manner of princes, is as certain, because it is evident that the eastern princes spoke in the singular (Dan 4:4, 18, 20; 5:14; 6:26). And God always spoke by the prophets in the singular number (Gen 17:1; Ex 20:2; Num 14:35; and elsewhere)." Editor's note. Many scholars have questioned this assumption that God did not speak to angels (i.e. in the divine council) here. However, even if they are correct and God is here addressing the divine council, we find all three Persons associated with the council elsewhere in Scripture, they are all three clearly in Genesis 1:1-3, and therefore the point of this being a proof-text for the three Persons is still valid.

Ps 110:1. *The LORD said to my Lord.*

Isa 61:1. *The Spirit of the Lord GOD is upon me, because the LORD has anointed.*

Isa 63:9,10, 11, 14. *The Angel of his Presence saved them ... but they rebelled and grieved his Holy Spirit ... The Spirit of the LORD gave them rest.*

[Num 6:24, 25, 26. Isa 6:3, 8; 33:22].

John 10:30. *I am my Father are One.*

John 14:17. *I will ask the Father, and He will give you another Helper ... even the Spirit of Truth.*

2Co 13:14. *The Grace of the Lord Jesus Christ and the love of God and the fellowship of the Holy Spirit be with you all.*

1Jn 5:7. *For there are three that bear record in heaven, the Father, the Word, and the Holy Ghost: and these three are one.*[160]

The same holy Scriptures tell us both in the Old and New Testament:

---

[160] The original note here is an apologetic for the authenticity of these words in the original manuscript. He cites one "Mr. Whiston" who "imposes a most horrid falsehood upon the world, in asserting that this verse never was in the text until about the middle of the reign of Queen Elizabeth, and that no Greek copy in the world that was really written before printing ever had it otherwise than in the margin." De Gols is quite certain that it is found all the way back to the second century. Modern scholarship has shown that these words were in fact a later addition. Metzger explains that no Greek Fathers ever quoted it; it is absent in all ancient versions of the Syriac, Coptic, Armenian, Ethiopic, Arabic, and Slavonic texts. It appears to have been a marginal note that was added because the copiest interpreted the original text to symbolize the Trinity. This then made its way into one line of Latin texts. It doesn't really matter, because there are plenty of other passages that clearly show three Persons sharing one divine Nature. See Bruce Manning Metzger, United Bible Societies, *A Textual Commentary on the Greek New Testament, Second Edition a Companion Volume to the United Bible Societies' Greek New Testament (4th Rev. Ed.)* (London; New York: United Bible Societies, 1994), 647-48.

That this God is holy and just,
that he cannot lie nor deceive us.

In the Old Testament	In the New Testament
Ps 89:35. *Once for all I have sworn by my holiness; I will not lie.*	Tit 1:2. *God, who never lies.* Heb 6:18. *It is impossible for God to lie.*

And lastly, the same Scriptures assure us, both in the Old and New Testament:

That God will not give his Honor to any created Being.

In the Old Testament	In the New Testament
Isa 42:8. *I am the LORD; that is my Name; my Glory I give to no other.*	Php 2:10. *That at the Name of Jesus every knee should bow.* Jude 25. *To the only wise God, our Savior, through Jesus Christ our Lord, be Glory, Majesty, Dominion, and Power, both now and forever. Amen.*

Having therefore this foundation of God's veracity and concern for his own honor, and he having so plainly revealed to us that there are three Persons in the unity of the divine majesty, we humbly receive his revelation with all due regard and most awful [profoundly reverential] submission. And this we believe, although we do not have a full perception of it. We believe it on the authority and fidelity of the most holy God who has revealed it, although we do not understand how that can be. We are not desirous of searching into that secret which God has withheld from us, and reserved for a brighter light, and a more exalted station. We are satisfied it is so, though we do not know how.

Even with respect to the creation, we believe the creatures are made, though we do not understand how they were made. We jangle not with the works of God, because we do not know how he made them; for it is my opinion that if we perfectly understood how any of the creatures were made, we should be able to make them too. Since we are therefore satisfied about the one, why should we not be about the other? For if we do not know the architecture of a fly, nor understand the formation of a gnat, which surpasses our understanding as much as our power to make them, how much more unable are we to comprehend the nature of that Being, who infinitely exceeds all beings, the Lord and giver of life?

In confidence therefore of God's truthfulness, and in reliance on his wisdom, holiness, and truth, we believe that there are three Persons in the undivided unity of the divinity; and that Jesus Christ, whom we, and all the host of heaven, and all the churches on earth adore, is the true God. We adore him as God with the same honor and worship as we honor the Father, and that not rashly, not unadvisedly, not inconsiderately, but according to and in obedience to God's own command, *"That all may honor the Son, just as they honor the Father. Whoever does not honor the Son does not honor the Father who sent him"* (John 5:22, 23). These words most positively instruct that the very same honor must be paid to the Son as is paid to the Father, and that whatever pretense men may make, that honor is due to the Father only, that God here himself testifies that he is dishonored if the same honor that is due to him is not paid to the Son. The reason and foundation is because this Son, this Jesus Christ, is very God—is really and truly God.

That Christ is that very God that is to be worshiped, appears:

From the Divine Names.

All the names and titles which belong to the glorious majesty of God are given to the Lord Christ; and these are not given once, but always; not only without, but with the distinguishing article; not barely, but with the most glorious attributes in the very same manner as they are given to God the Father. He is called God absolutely, the incommunicable Name of *JEHOVAH* [YHWH] is given to him. He is called the true God, the mighty God, the great God and Saviour. All the sublime titles whereby the only true God is dignified and distinguished are given to him.

Jesus Christ is Jehovah God.

The Jews say that *JEHOVAH* is God's proper name, and so peculiarly God's name, that it never was nor can be communicated to any created being.[161] And this is grounded upon the Scriptures: Isa 42:8, "*I am the Lord [Jehovah], that is my Name; my Glory I give to no other, nor my praise to carved idols;*" and Hosea 12:5, "*The LORD God of Hosts, the LORD is his memorial Name,*" where the word "*memorial*" excludes all created beings from participating in that name, and appropriates it to God alone. God himself insists upon his being Jehovah alone, in opposition to all other gods, glorying, in a manner, and triumphing in it as the distinguishing character by which he would be known to be infinitely superior to all the gods of the nations. Ex 12:12, "*On all the Gods of Egypt I will execute judgments, I am the LORD (Jehovah);*" Jer 32:27, "*I am the LORD (Jehovah), the God of all flesh. Is there anything too hard for me?*"

The Jews further say[162] that in the letters of the name Jehovah, the three tenses (past, present, and future) are contained: was, is, and shall be. We add that St. John from this interprets it, "*Who is, who was, and is to come*" (Rev 1:18). Thus, it is called the name of

---

[161] De Gols cites Boxtorf. *Lexicon Hebraicum* (1607), p. 157 here. This refers to Johannes Buxtorf (1564-1629), a Hebraist and professor of Hebrew for thirty-nine years at Basel. He was known as the "Master of the Rabbis."
[162] Buxtorf, Ibid.

God's existence; for when God had said, "*I AM WHAT I AM*" (Ex 3:14), he then immediately calls himself *JEHOVAH* (vs. 15), and he says that this is his peculiar name. "*This is my Name for ever, and this is my Memorial unto all Generations.*" Our adversaries [the Socinians][163] do allow that the name Jehovah has reference to the necessary existence of the Person so named in his own right.[164]

And this name JEHOVAH, this peculiar name, which the Psalmist says is God's name alone (Ps 83:18) is given to the Son of God, even to Jesus Christ. This name is distinguished in our translation by capital letters, though the word *Jah*, which is a contraction of Jehovah, is noted with the same capitals and also rendered LORD.[165]

In the Old Testament	**In the New Testament**
Isa 45:21-25. *There is no other god besides me, a righteous God and a Savior; there is none besides me. Turn to me and be saved, all the ends of the earth! For I am God, and there is no other. By*	Rom 14:10-11. *For we will all stand before the judgment seat of God; for it is written, "As I live, says the Lord, every knee shall bow to*

---

[163] Named for Italian theologian Fausto Sozzini (Lat: Faustus Socinus). Socinianism is nontrinitarian in its view of Christ and precursor to many forms of Unitarianism within Protestantism.

[164] Original note: Clarke's *Reply*, p. 164. Editor's note. This is Samuel Clarke (1675-1729), a Socinian and anti-Trinitarian leader of the Enlightenment. He believed that Christ was merely a man.

[165] Original note: Ex 15:2; 17:16; in the Psalms often; Isa 38:11; Song of Solomon 8:6.

myself I have sworn; from my mouth has gone out in righteousness a word that shall not return: "To me every knee shall bow, every tongue shall swear allegiance." Only in the LORD, it shall be said of me, are righteousness and strength; to him shall come and be ashamed all who were incensed against him. In the LORD all the offspring of Israel shall be justified and shall glory.
Isa 44:6. *Thus says the LORD, the King of Israel and his Redeemer, the LORD of hosts: "I am the first and I am the last; besides me there is no god."*

me, and every tongue shall confess to God."
Php 2:9-11. *Therefore God has highly exalted him and bestowed on him the name that is above every name, so that at the name of Jesus every knee should bow, in heaven and on earth and under the earth, and every tongue confess that Jesus Christ is Lord, to the glory of God the Father.*
Rev 1:8. *"I am the Alpha and the Omega," says the Lord God, "who is and who was and who is to come, the Almighty."*

It would never end if we enumerated all the texts of Scripture, for it is observed that the name Jehovah is more than sixty times given to Christ in the Old Testament, and all such places, as by the authority of Christ and the Apostles, are applied to Christ in the New Testament, as the Son of God and the Savior of the world. I shall only take notice of one more.

In the Old Testament
Jer 23:6. *In his days Judah will be saved, and Israel will dwell securely. And this is the name by*

In the New Testament
1Co 1:30. *And because of him you are in Christ Jesus, who became to us wisdom from*

which he will be called: "The
LORD is our righteousness."

God, righteousness and sanc-
tification and redemption.

Here, I observe that the *"Lord our Righteousness"* is not all the name of Christ, but Jehovah alone; and *"our Righteousness"* is a description both of his divine nature, and of the mercy mankind should receive from him. In the original it is *tzidkenu* ("righteousness") and Buxtorf tells us that the word *tsedeq* ("righteous") was a common addition to the titles of the kings of Jerusalem.[166] And so here Christ is called *"Jehovah the righteous,"* and particularly *"our Righteousness,"* to declare his government and what mankind should receive from him, who is both their King and their God. This text is explained by Jer 33:16 where it is not said to be his name, but his title, and description of his nature.

I shall only add, that the Jews say[167] the name Jehovah is not only God's great and glorious name, but that it is also the name of grace and mercy from Exodus 34:6. *"The LORD, the LORD, a God merciful and gracious, slow to anger, and abounding in steadfast love and faithfulness."* That this name of grace belongs to the Messiah, the same Jews acknowledge when they say, "Why do the Israelites pray, and are not heard? The answer is because they do not understand (*Shemhamphorash*) the name of Jehovah explained, but in the age

---

[166] Buxtorf, *Lex.* 638.
[167] Ibid., 30 & 167.

of the Messiah God shall make it known to them, and then shall they be heard."

And again, "The Scripture says, the name of the Messiah is the LORD OUR RIGHTEOUSNESS, or Jehovah our Righteousness. And why? Because he is to be God the mediator, by whose hand we shall obtain [the] righteousness of God. God therefore calls him by the name of Jehovah."[168]

From what has been said, it appears that Jesus Christ the Messiah is Jehovah. For since that title is in Scripture a principal note of distinction by which the true God was pleased to manifest himself and to set forth his own superior excellency in opposition to all pretended deities; and since this name is given to Christ and applied to Christ so frequently; it follows, and the consequence is undeniable, that Christ is that God, that only true God, who is possessed of all those distinguishing powers and perfections which go along with that sublime title.

Jesus Christ is the First and Last.

In the Old Testament	**In the New Testament**
Isa 44:6. *I am the first and I am the last; besides me there is no god.*	Rev 22:13. *I am the Alpha and the Omega, the first and the last.*[169]

---

[168] Buxtorf, *Lexic.*, 164.
[169] The original reads Rev 1:11 and De Gols was probably thinking of 1:8, but the closest (and actual) text that he quotes is Rev 22:13.

I cited this text of Isaiah before to prove that Christ is Jehovah. Now I reproduce it because it expresses the eternal greatness and infinite majesty of God, and to prove that Christ is that God, because this most glorious title is given to him: a title which expresses the eternity not only of the divine Being, but his supreme power, dignity, and glory, and his government of all things (Isa 44:6-8).

Maimonides[170] tells us, that it is the fourth article of the Jewish Faith to believe, "That God is the First and the Last."[171] But the Gospel has made it the first, the principal, the fundamental article of the Christian Faith, that our Lord Jesus Christ is the first and the last, is the supreme God, with the Father and the Holy Ghost, the only one God.

Jesus Christ is called God absolutely.

In Acts 20:28 we find Christ called God absolutely. *"Care for the church of God, which he obtained with his own blood."* There is also 1Ti 3:16, *"God is manifest in the Flesh."*[172] In both these places the name of God is

---

[170] Moses ben Maimon (1135-1204). Spanish born rabbi who became one of the most influential of all medieval Torah scholars.

[171] Maimon, *Sanh.* C. 10.

[172] The ESV reads, *"He was manifest in the flesh."* There is a textual difficulty here. The pronoun "he" translates a Greek word that has two letters, *o* and *s*. When they are together, this means "who." Many manuscripts have *th* for *o*, making it possible to read *theos* (God). Even though the "who" is almost certainly original, it is still vague. Who is the "who?" It can refer to either God or to Christ (who is also God).

given to Christ in the most strict and proper sense, in the same manner as it is given to the Father.

Jesus Christ is the True God.

1 John 5:20. "*We are in him that is true, even in his Son Jesus Christ.*"[173] This is the true God and eternal life. That this was spoken of Jesus Christ is most certain from the scope of the whole Epistle, wherein the Apostle purposed to speak of Christ's divinity; for there were heretics at that time, namely Cerinthus and the Ebonites, who taught that Christ was merely a man. The Apostle, therefore, in opposition to these heretics, asserts this of Jesus Christ, for nobody can doubt it of the Father.

He asserts therefore that Christians are in God, because Jesus Christ is God, and he calls God "*the true*" (*alēthinon*). He then explains that "*even in his Son*" (*en tō huiō autou*) is said here to be the true God and eternal life. This is evident from the pronoun "*this*" (*houtos*). All grammar obliges us to refer that to both predicates.

For these two predicates are of great weight, the first "*this is the true God*" and the next "*and eternal life.*" Now it has been acknowledged even by an adversary,

---

[173] The ESV reads, "*So that we may know him who is true, in his Son Jesus Christ.*"

that Eternal Life is a name of Jesus Christ,[174] and appropriated to him; and it is as certain that the other predicate pertains to the same Person. For had it been intended of the Father, that he is the true God, and Christ the Eternal Life, the text should have run *houtos*, "this" is the true God, and *ekeinos*, "that" other is Eternal Life; but the words are, "*This is the true God, and Eternal Life.*" There is but one subject to both predicates.

Some copies read the first part of this verse, "*We are in him that is the true God*," *alēthinon theon*, and this strengthens the Apostle's assertion, for then the sense must be this, "*We know that the Son of God is come, and has given us an understanding that we may know the true God; and we are in him that is the true God, even in his Son Jesus Christ. This is the true God and Eternal Life.*"

This construction most powerfully asserts that there is no way of knowing the true God for certain, except by such a Teacher who is God himself. And Christ has both taught us the true God, and united us to the true God, himself being the true God. This is agreeable to the whole design of St. John, which is both in his Gospel and Epistles to vindicate the divinity of Christ, against the heretics of those times. Therefore, as he began his Gospel, so he ends this Epistle, averting the divine nature of Christ; and in both,

---

[174] *Modest Plea*, 264. Vide Becman. Exercit. X. Amst. 1643. This is most likely the book written by Samuel Clarke.

he frequently inculcates the necessity of believing Christ to be the true God.

Jesus Christ is the Great God and Saviour.

Titus 2:13. "*Waiting for our blessed hope, the appearing of the glory of our great God and Savior Jesus Christ.*" In this text the titles of great God and Savior are given to Christ. That they concern Christ alone is certain because there is no mention of the Father, but only Christ in the following part of the discourse. It is evident further from the article *ta* ("*the*") which is used only once, whereby one and the same Person only is spoken of. For had two different persons been designed, the article would have been put before "Savior," and because the *epiphaneian* ("*the appearing*") is always ascribed to the Son alone and never to the Father.[175] Therefore, with submission, the version could and ought to be rendered, "*the glorious appearing of our great God and Saviour Jesus Christ.*" Our old translation, though it does not come up to the force of the Greek, still comes nearer than this one. "*Looking for that blessed hope and appearing of that glory of that mighty God, and of our Saviour Jesus Christ.*" Our adversaries themselves confess that the grammatical construction requires both to be ascribed to Christ.[176]

---

[175] 2Th 2:8; 1Ti 6:14; 2Tim 1:10; 4:1, 8.
[176] Clarke's *Scripture-Doctrine*, 77, 2nd edition.

Jesus Christ is the only Sovereign God and Lord.

Jude 4. "*For certain people have crept in unnoticed ... deny our only Master and Lord, Jesus Christ.*" The one article denotes that Jesus Christ is that only Lord and God. The force of the word *despotēn* ("Master") is not sufficiently explained. The words may thus be rendered, "*that only*" sovereign God and Lord of ours, Jesus Christ. The Complutensian Codex[177] reads it as, "*that only God and our sovereign Lord*" (*ton monon theon kai despotēn ton kurion*), And Mr. Perkins has it, "*the only Ruler who is God, and our Lord Jesus Christ.*"[178]

Jesus Christ is the Mighty God.

Isaiah 9:6. "*His name shall be called Wonderful, Counsellor, the Mighty God.*" Before I explain this text, I must observe that the LXX has everywhere rendered the Hebrew *El* and *Elohim* by "*God*" (*theon*). Aquila has rendered it by *ischuron*, from its proper signification, "*the powerful*" *God*; though some rather derive it from a word expressing God's omnipresence, according to Jer 23:23. "*Am I a God at hand, declares the LORD, and not a God far away?*" But whatever the etymon (derivation of the word) is, this is the proper name of God, and St. Jerome says that it is the proper title of the

---

[177] Original note: Beza in loc. Editor's note. Printed 1502-1517, this is the first full polyglot (multiple language side-by-side) Bible ever printed.
[178] [William] Perkins, *Exposit.* in loc.

only true God, because he alone possesses almighty power.[179] This is given to the Child Christ Jesus, as well as to the eternal Father.

To the Father	To Christ Jesus
Isa 10:21. *The remnant shall return, even the remnant of Jacob to the mighty God, the El Gibbor.*	Isa 9:6. *Unto us a child is born, a Son is given—and his name shall be the El Gibbor, the mighty God.*

The LXX has taken a strange liberty in translating this, for instead of saying "the mighty God," they have made a comment and turned it into, *"the Angel of the great council"* (*megalēs boulēs aggelos*). St. Jerome thinks the reason was because they thought it was strange to apply the name of God and *"mighty"* to a child.[180] Some are of the opinion that the latter Jews had corrupted some copies of the LXX, and that after this several of the most ancient Christian writers, who highly valued the Septuagint version, quoted this text, not as that has it, but as it is in the Hebrew text.[181] And as this name of *El* is given to Christ in the singular, so it is also in the plural number.

---

[179] Jerome, in *Esa.*, 85. Ed. Bened.
[180] Jerome, in Esa., 86.
[181] Dr. Waterland, *Sermon* 6, 219. This is Daniel Waterland (1683-1740), an English theologian who became Master of Magdalene College, Cambridge in 1714, Chancellor of the Diocese of York in 1722, and Archdeacon of Middlesex in 1730.

*Jesus Christ is Jehovah Elohim, the Lord God,
and El Elohim, the God of gods.*

This word [Elohim] is used in the plural, both to denote the Trinity of Persons in the unity of the divine Essence, as also to signify the exceeding greatness of God's power; and though it is given sometimes analogically to angels and princes,[182] it is notwithstanding the proper name of God.

This name is construed with a verb of the singular number, and has the name of Jehovah added to it, to denote the Trinity of Persons in the unity of the Divinity.[183]

This name is given to Christ (Ps 48:8, 9, 10). "*As we have heard, so we have seen in the city of the Lord of hosts, in the city of our God, which God will establish forever. Selah. We have thought on your steadfast love, O God, in the midst of your temple. As your Name, O God, so your praise…*" Here the name of Elohim is given to Christ four times, and twice in the last verse. "*This is God, our God forever and ever. He will guide us forever (KJV: unto death).*" And so again in Hosea 1:7, "*I will have mercy on the house of Judah, and I will save them by the LORD their God,*" by "*Jehovah their Elohim.*" The Jews themselves acknowledge this text is about the Messiah, and accordingly the Chaldee paraphrase [that is, the Targum] reads it, "*by his Word which is their God.*"

---

[182] Psalm 96:5; The original reads 97:5 (a typo). It also has Gen 6:13 and Ex 4:5, both of which are inexplicable.
[183] He cites here Johannes Hoornbeck (1617-1666), *Confut. Socin.* 1.2.c.5., p. 420.

In the New Testament we find the same title of "*Lord God*" given to Christ (Luke 1:16, 17). We find the angel speaking of John the Baptist, "*And he will turn many of the children of Israel to the Lord their God, and he will go before him,*" namely before Christ, who is that Lord God. In the strictest construction, the words "*Lord their God*" are so immediately connected to "*him,*" that they cannot possibly be understood of any person but Christ. If this is compared with Luke 3:4 and Malachi 3:1, it is impossible that any person can be understood but Christ, who is the Lord.

As Christ is called *Jehovah Elohim,* "*the Lord God,*" so he is also called *El Elohim,* "*the God of Gods.*" Ps 50:1, as our old translation has it, is a Psalm that has always been looked upon as relating to Christ and his coming to judgment, and as such it must necessarily pertain to Christ. "*For the Father judges no one but has given all judgment to the Son*" (John 5:22). And so the Psalmist speaks to Christ, "*Arise, O God, and judge the earth*" (Ps 82:8). Upon this text the Jews have this comment, "When the judgment goes forth in mercy and favor, the Judge is called Jehovah; but when he punishes, he is called Elohim."[184]

Jesus Christ is over all God blessed forever.

Rom 9:5. "*To them belong the patriarchs, and from their race, according to the flesh, is the Christ, who is God*

---

[184] Buxtorf, *Lexicon*, 30.

over all, blessed forever. Amen." That St. Paul speaks this of Christ is so plain from the whole context that no expression whatsoever could be plainer; for the Father is not so much as named in the foregoing part of the chapter. And "*who is*" (*ho ōn*) naturally refers to the person spoken of immediately before it, and that is Christ. The antithesis between what he is according to the flesh and according to the Spirit requires it.

It is pretended as an objection to the force of this text that some manuscripts read, "*who is over all blessed forever,*" without the word God; and that Erasmus has observed that some of the Fathers do not have the word "*God*" in this text.[185]

But Dr. Mill[186] says that the manuscripts have it, as also the Syriac version; and Erasmus,[187] his pretense from the Fathers is vain, for he names but two, only Cyprian and Hilary, and are they of weight against the whole Catholic[188] church? And as Beza[189] has observed,

---

[185] Metzger's discussion of this verse is lengthy, but only because the punctuation is difficult. There is no hint that the word "God" does not belong in the passage according to modern scholars.

[186] John Mill, *in loc.*

[187] Erasmus *in loc.*

[188] Original note: "That the Word of God was in the Greek copies in the time of Noetus, is evident from his quoting the text with it at his second appearance." Epiph. *Haer.* 57. P. 114. Edit. Billii Col. Agrip. 1617. Editor's note. "Catholic" refers not to Rome but to "universal" here. Noetus was a presbyter in Asia Minor around 230 A.D. and was a proponent of the heresy called modalistic Monarchianism or Patripassianism. Epiphanius of Salamis (310-403 A.D) was a bishop of Salamis, Cyprus and defended the orthodox faith against heresies. His work *Panarion* (also known as Adversus Haereses or "Against Heresies") is what De Gols is citing here.

[189] Beza, in loc.

though the word God is not in the text, the sense would be the same, and the divinity of Christ sufficiently expressed by "*being over all*," and by "*blessed forever*." I will not turn to the significance of these phrases.

Our author pretends from the Socinians that this is a doxology, and that it is a form used by the Jews, God be blessed forever; and therefore, the evidence of this text vanishes by an ellipsis.[190]

That the Jews used such a form is true, but that this is the case here, all the figures of speech in the world can never make out, and nothing but open violence to grammar can pretend to be done to the text. When all is done, all they do is make the sense broken and confused, for neither the grammar nor the antithesis will allow such an ellipsis. The antithesis absolutely requires that both the divine and human natures should be expressed. This is what we find in Romans 1:3 where he says that, "*Christ was made of the Seed of*" David. In Romans 9:5 he says, "*of the Fathers,*" but in both it reads "*according to the flesh*" (*kata sarka*), creating the parallel. Again, in 1:3 it says that he was "*declared with power to the Son of God according to the Spirit of Holiness*" (*kata pneuma agiōsunēs*), and in 9:5 that he is "*over all God blessed forever.*" So that this is no doxology, but a plain description of the divine nature of Jesus Christ,

---

[190] William Staunton, *The Sincere Thoughts of a Private Christian*, 63. An ellipsis is the omission from speech or writing of a word or words that are superfluous or able to be understood from contextual clues.

such that as certain as he is of the Father, so surely is Jesus Christ *"over all God blessed forever."*

Having defended the text, I will now show you the significance of the expression *"over all God blessed forever,"* which is the most lofty expression that can be made; for Christ is not only here called God, but God with the most exalted epithet, "over all," even as it is given to God the Father.

To the Father	To the Son
Eph 4:6. *One God and Father of all, who is above all.*	Rom 9:5. *Christ, who is over all God blessed forever.*

Besides this, he is called "blessed forever," (*eulogētos eis tous aiōnas*); which is also exactly the same as is given to God the Father.

To the Father	To the Son
Rom 1:25. *The Creator who is blessed forever, Amen.*	Rom 9:5. *Christ, who is God blessed forever, Amen.*

Here we must observe that this phrase *"blessed forever"* was always used by the Jews as a name of God. Through it they expressed the One God of Israel.[191] Therefore, there were no other words to express the divinity of Christ. This alone should be enough to

---

[191] Bishop Pearson, *On The Creed*, Art. 2, p. 133. Bishop Bull, *Defense of the Nicene Creed.* S.2.C.3.§10. This is John Pearson (1613-1686), Bishop of Chester and George Bull (1634-1710), Bishop of St. David's.

prove the point; for according to the Jewish phrase, which the Jews certainly understood, he is God, that is *"blessed forever,"* and he that is *"blessed forever"* is most certainly God.

In the Old Testament	In the New Testament
Ps 24:8. *Who is this King of glory? The LORD, strong and mighty, the LORD mighty in battle! ... Who is this King of glory? The LORD of hosts, he is the King of glory.*	1Co 2:8. *None of the rulers of this age understood this, for if they had, they would not have crucified the Lord of God of glory.*

Jesus Christ is King of Kings, and Lord of Lords.

With these titles St. Paul makes the distinguishing characters of the one true God; and these are given and ascribed to the Son, with the same pomp and magnificence, as they are to the Father.

To the Father	To the Son
1Ti 6:15. *He who is the blessed and only Sovereign, the King of kings and Lord of lords.*	Rev 17:14. *The Lamb will conquer them, for he is Lord of lords and King of kings."*
	Rev 19:16. *On his robe and on his thigh he has a name written, "King of kings and Lord of lords."*

Jesus Christ is Life.

This title, which is not the least of God's glorious titles, is equally ascribed to Jesus Christ as to the Father.

To the Father	To the Son
John 5:26. *The Father has life in himself.*	Rev 5:26. *As the Father has life in himself, so he has granted the Son also to have life in himself.*
Dt 32:40. *I live forever.*[192]	
Jer 10:10. *The LORD is the true God; he is the living God.*	Job 19:25. *I know that my Redeemer lives.*
	John 1:4. In him was life.
	John 11:25. *I am ... the life.*
	Acts 3:15. *The Author of life.*

Jesus Christ is the Fullness of the Godhead.

Col 2:9. "*For in him the whole fullness of deity dwells bodily.*" These words of St. Paul are very extraordinary; for the Apostle, foreseeing that heretics would arise that should speak of a secondary God, a God made of a creature, he purposely expressed himself in in this way concerning Christ's divinity, so that we would understand him to be the real and true God, the very supreme God, and not a nominal or contrived god. The Apostle therefore did not say that Christ was God, because that word might be liable to exception,

---

[192] Editor's note. I would tend to think that this one is about the Son, not the Father, for the verse has the Person lifting up his hand to heaven and swearing that he will carry out vengeance upon his enemies. This is the duty of the Captain of the Host, the Angel of the LORD.

having been given to men, princes, and prophets;[193] but to put that matter above all exception, he says that in Jesus all the fullness of the Godhead dwelt bodily; and although he appeared as a man, he was God also; for he expresses two natures in the same Person, the divine inhabiting and the human inhabited.

St. Paul did not say *plērōma theotētos*, which might have been understood for the "fullness" of gifts and graces, wisdom, power, mercy, and the like, a fullness of gifts greater than any created being enjoyed. He expressly says, *tēs theotētos*, of the very Godhead, of the Divinity itself. This is a distinguishing expression. The other signifies the qualities. This the very essence of Divinity, but more, he speaks of the fullness of the Godhead, to let us know that Christ is in all respects the very God, the eternal and supreme God. He then adds *pan to plērōma*, "all the fullness" of the Godhead, to assure us that as the Father is, so also is the Son; and that the Godhead of the Father and of the Son is all one, the glory equal, the majesty co-eternal.

Secondly, that Christ is the very God that is to be worshiped, appears from:

---

[193] A good case can be made that the term "god" is never used of human beings anywhere in the Bible. It is, however, used of various supernatural beings (with a little "g"). See Cyrus Gordon, "אלהים (Elohim) in Its Reputed Meaning of *Rulers, Judges*," *Journal of Biblical Literature* 54 (1935): 139–144.

The Divine Attributes.

By the word "attributes" I mean such perfections and excellencies of the divine Nature, where God is distinguished from the creatures, and where God makes himself known to his creatures. Now these are all ascribed to Christ.

First, Eternity is ascribed to Jesus Christ.[194]

Rev 1:8. "'*I am the Alpha and the Omega,*' says the Lord God, '*who is and who was and who is to come, the Almighty.*'" This is the very description which the prophet gives to the one God of Israel (Isa 43:10).[195] But having spoken to this before, I pass to other texts.

Micah 5:2. "*But you, O Bethlehem Ephrathah, who are too little to be among the clans of Judah, from you shall come forth for me one who is to be ruler in Israel, whose coming forth is from of old, from ancient days.*" In these words, we plainly find two "comings-forth," the one promised to be in Bethlehem, the other from eternity. This is not only a plain proof that Christ was pre-existing before his birth of the virgin but is as full a proof as words can express of his eternity also.

Prov 8:22-23. "*But you, O Bethlehem Ephrathah, who are too little to be among the clans of Judah, from you*

---

[194] In this and the following sections on the attributes of God, De Gols cites Johannis Marckii's Latin *Compendium theologiæ Christianæ*, 1690 ed.

[195] The original has Isa 43:20. This is a typo. It is probably 43:10.

shall come forth for me one who is to be ruler in Israel, whose coming forth is from of old, from ancient days." I will speak more of this text later.

Jesus Christ is Omnipresent.

This is the divine perfection where God cannot be contained by any kind of created thing; he cannot be created; he is present with all creatures; and he infinitely exceeds the limits of the creatures. And so, the third article of the Jewish Faith, expresses God's ubiquity [omnipresence]. "I perfectly believe, that the Creator is not a body. Neither can he be known or understood by any bodily comprehensions. There is nothing else like him."[196]

This is ascribed to God the Father, and also in the same manner to God the Son.

To the Father	To the Son
Jer 23:23-24. *"Am I a God at hand, declares the LORD, and not a God far away? Can a man hide himself in secret places so that I cannot see him?"* declares the LORD. *"Do I not fill heaven and earth? declares the LORD."*	Matt 18:20. *Where two or three are gathered in my name, there am I among them.* Matt 28:20. *Behold, I am with you always, to the end of the age.* Col 1:17. *In him all things hold together.*

---

[196] Maimonid. *In Sanhedr.* C. 10.

Acts 17:28. *In him we live and move and have our being.*

Heb 1:3. *He upholds the universe.*

Jesus Christ is Immutable.

Immutability is that most perfect constancy of God whereby he is perfectly free from all change actual or possible. This is God's prerogative, and is ascribed to the Son, in the same pomp and magnificence, as it is to the Father.

To the Father	To the Son
Ps 102:25-27. *Of old you laid the foundation of the earth, and the heavens are the work of your hands. They will perish, but you will remain; they will all wear out like a garment. You will change them like a robe, and they will pass away, but you are the same, and your years have no end.* James 1:17. *The Father of lights, with whom there is no variation or shadow due to change.*	Heb 1:10-12. *You, Lord, laid the foundation of the earth in the beginning, and the heavens are the work of your hands; they will perish, but you remain; they will all wear out like a garment, like a robe you will roll them up, like a garment they will be changed. But you are the same, and your years will have no end.* Mal 3:6. *I am the LORD, I do not change.*

Before I proceed, let me make a remark on those admirable words of David (Ps 102) applied by St. Paul to Christ. No words can be devised that more emphatically describe the eternity and immutability of the one only true and eternal God. since they are here ascribed, and that by an Apostle, without any reserve, without the least restriction to Jesus Christ, we are obliged to believe that this Jesus Christ is the eternal and immutable God. When David first expressed these words, he spoke of Jehovah, the God of Israel. When the Apostle applies them, it is to Christ. The great actions mentioned there are the actions of Christ He expands the heavens and lays the foundations of the earth. Those great attributes of the divine Nature there related, namely immutability and eternity, are the perfections of Jesus Christ. Christ therefore is Jehovah, the God of Israel, the one and only God, as well as the Father.

It is very observable that this text is co-penned by the sacred writer and that therefore all reasons for criticism of prepositions or articles are prevented. Whatever doubt there may be by them, or because of them in other texts, there can be none in this—Christ is the eternal God, Christ is God immutable.

Jesus Christ is the Independent God

Independency is that perfection of God where he is sufficient in himself and is the only cause of all things. It is a divine perfection that declares the all-sufficiency and happiness of the divine Nature. This is ascribed to the Son equally as to the Father.

To the Father	To the Son
Gen 17:1. "*I am the Almighty God;*" or, as the old translation has it, according to the Hebrews, "*I am the all-sufficient.*"	John 5:26. *As the Father has life in himself, so he has granted the Son also to have life in himself.*

This text of St. John is very well worthy of our consideration, as it does most admirably assert Christ's divinity, and explain his independency. This text clearly intimates that although he had his divine life and nature from the Father, as the fountain of the Deity, yet he received it not by participation, but by communication. He did not only participate of it, but it was wholly communicated to him. Hence, the Christian Fathers have called Christ "self-perfection," self-power," "self-God," "self-light," "self-understanding," and the like.[197]

All of these expressions, Epiphanius seems to explain most clearly, plainly showing that those expressions signify not that Christ has them of himself, but in himself, and that though he is God of God, yet he is God in himself.[198] This is sufficient to title him "Self-God," one who is God in himself, and so is God himself; not another God, but another Person from the Father, having the same Essence communicated to him.

---

[197] Gregory of Nyssa, *Catech. Major.* Basil, 1.2. *Contra Eunomium*, 740. Tom. I. Ed. Par. 1638.
[198] Epiph. *Haer.* 77. P. 243. Edit. Colon. 1617.

Jesus Christ is the Omniscient God.

Omniscience is that perfection of God where he most perfectly knows all things in himself, by one eternal act. This is most certainly a divine perfection, and the divine privilege; and is in the Scriptures ascribed to the Son equally as to the Father.

To the Father	To the Son
1Kg 8:39. *For you, you only, know the hearts of all the children of mankind.* Acts 15:8. *God, who knows the heart.* Jer 17:10. *I the LORD search the heart and test the mind.*	John 16:30. *Now we know that you know all things.* John 21:17. *Lord, you know everything.* Rev 2:23. *I am he who searches mind and heart.* Acts 1:24. *You, Lord, who know the hearts of all.* Col 2:3. *In whom are hidden all the treasures of wisdom and knowledge.*

Jesus Christ is the Almighty God.

Omnipotence is a divine attribute according to all men. It is the perfection of the Son as well as of the Father. The Scriptures assure us of this, as they ascribe it to the Father and to the Son with the same strength of expression.

Before I show you that it is applied to the Son, I must observe, that the word "Almighty," (*pantokratōr*), translates the Hebrew *Shadday*, the all-sufficient (Gen 17:1). It also translates another phrase used in Scripture to express almighty power, and that is the Lord of Hosts, *Jehovah Sabaoth*. St. Ambrose and Jerome[199] have observed that the LXX has rendered Jehovah Sabaoth indifferently by the Lord of Hosts and Almighty. And St. John in Revelation 4:8 alludes to the thrice holy of Isaiah (6:3). Instead of (*kurios sabaōth*), as the Septuagint has it,[200] which is "*Lord of Hosts*," it has "*Lord God Almighty*" (*kurios o theos o pantokratōr*).

That this attribute is the property of the Father needs no proof; but that it is applied only to the Father is not true, for it is applied to the Son both in the Old and New Testaments.

To the Father	To the Son
Isa 6:5. *Woe is me ... for my eyes have seen the King, the LORD of hosts!*[201]	John 12:41. *Isaiah said these things because he saw (Christ) his glory and spoke of him.*
Zech 12:5, 10. *The inhabitants of Jerusalem have strength through the LORD of hosts, their God*	John 19:34, 37. *One of the soldiers pierced his side with a spear ... Against another Scripture says, "They will look on him whom they have pierced."*

---

[199] Ambrose, *de fide*, l.4. c. 1. P. 314. Edit. Par. Anno 1569; Jerome, tom. 3. P. 519.

[200] De Gols says the LXX reads, *kurios dunameōn*. But there are not variants that have this reading.

[201] This is not a good proof-text for the Father, as Jesus says Isaiah saw him (John 12:41). Curiously, this is the passage that De Gols cites right beside it for the Son.

... *I will pour out on the house of David and the inhabitants of Jerusalem a spirit of grace and pleas for mercy, so that, when they look on me, on him whom they have pierced.*[202]

Rev 1:7-8. *Behold, he is coming with the clouds, and every eye will see him, even those who pierced him, and all tribes of the earth will wail on account of him. Even so. Amen. "I am the Alpha and the Omega," says the Lord God, "who is and who was and who is to come, the Almighty."*

Thirdly, that Christ is the very God and is therefore to be worshiped appears from:

The Divine Operations.

All the works of God are ascribed to Christ in the same manner as they are to the Father. John 5:19, *"Truly, truly, I say to you, the Son can do nothing of his own accord, but only what he sees the Father doing. For whatever the Father does, that the Son does likewise."*

The adversaries of the divinity of Christ make use of this very text against Christ as an argument against his almighty power. But then, I must observe to you that they divide the text and take only the first part. Be well assured, they do not take it as it is. It is most positively against them. The full meaning of the

---

[202] This verse is also cited in the NT as referring to Christ rather than the Father, and therefore would seem not to be referring to the Father (John 19:37). Again, De Gols cites the NT quotation for Christ. De Gols seems to imply that the NT is changing the meaning from the Father to the Son.

text is that God the Son is intimately united with the Father, never separate from him, and therefore never acts except in concert with him. Their operation is undivided, and their work is one. Then it appears that this text is so far from denoting any imperfection in the power of the Son, that, on the contrary, it sets forth the greatness and unmeasurable perfection of his power as being inseparably linked with, and indeed one and the same in extent and degree, with the power of the Father.

Jesus Christ is the Creator of the World.

That the creating of the world is an act of God, of Almighty power is a truth known to all mankind and acknowledged by the very light of nature. This is ascribed to Jesus Christ in the Scriptures exactly as it is to the eternal Father.

To the Father	To the Son
Gen 1:1. *In the beginning God created the heaven and the earth.*	John 1:3, 10. *All things were made through him (Christ the Word) and without him was not anything made that was made ... He was in the world, and the world was made through him.*
Ex 20:11. *In six days the LORD made heaven and earth, the sea, and all that is in them.*	Col 1:15-17. *He is the image of the invisible God, the firstborn of all creation. For by him all things were created, in heaven and on*
2Kg 19:15. *You are the God, you alone, of all the kingdoms of the earth; you*	

have made heaven and earth.

Heb 3:4. *The builder of all things is God.*

earth, visible and invisible, whether thrones or dominions or rulers or authorities—all things were created through him and for him. And he is before all things, and in him all things hold together.

Before I proceed, I must observe that several of the ancients, namely Origen, Basil, and Ambrose, have rendered the word *reshith* in Gen 1:1 as "*The Beginning*," "*by the Son*."[203] And, the Chaldee Paraphrase (i.e. the Targum) for *in principio*, in the Beginning, has in *Sapentia*, on or by his Wisdom. This Wisdom is the Logos, the Son of God, and this agrees excellently well with Solomon in Prov 8:22. "*The LORD possessed me (reshith darko)*, "*the beginning of his way*" (*principium*

---

[203] Jerome says, "Most people think that in the Hebrew is contained in the Son, God made heaven and earth" (Jerome, *Questions in Hebrew*, in Genesis ii. 507. Quoted in Saint Jerome's, *Hebrew Questions on Genesis*, trans. C. T. R. Hayward [Oxford: Oxford University Press, 1995], 30).

The Fathers get it from the meaning of *reshith* as either "beginning" or "first." What if the Hebrew was talking about first as preeminence? The word carries this meaning in places in the OT. "*Amalek was the first (reshith) among the nations*" (Num 24:20). "*[Leviathan] is the first of the works of God*" (Job 40:19). Sometimes the first-born was the *reshith* as in "*Reuben, you are my first-born (bekor); My might and the beginning (reshith) of my strength*" (Gen 49:3). Paul seems to be taking very Jewish ideas like this and applying them to Jesus at creation when he says, "*He is the image of the invisible God, the firstborn of all creation. For by him all things were created, in heaven and on earth, visible and invisible, whether thrones of dominions or rulers or authorities—all things were created through him and for him. And he is before all things, and in him all things hold together*" (Col 1:15-17). So the translation idea of Genesis 1:1 is that In the First, that is in the Firstborn Son, God began creating.

via suae), that is, of his works, as Vatablus[204] expounds it. The text makes it good, for the same verse has, "*I was before his works of old;*" where the Word *qedem* adverbially signifies "before," as we have rendered it, but substantively signifies an orientation, i.e. the "*sunrise of his words of old.*" There is no necessity to make *reshith* an adverb either, as they are both substantives. Therefore *reshith* is the essential Wisdom of God, not a property but a substance; for true Wisdom is substance, according to Plotinus, "The true wisdom is substance and the true substance is wisdom." This substantial Wisdom is the Logos, Jesus Christ, the Son of God, called by St. Paul, "*The firstborn of every creature.*" This is the Wisdom of God, or the idea according to which he framed all things, and therefore must be before all things. Answerable to this are the two attributes Philo gives to the same subject, calling him "the firstborn Word of God" (*prologonon theos logon*) and "*the Beginning*" (*archēn*).[205]

I must observe further that our translation, which has rendered by "*the firstborn of every creature*" (*prōtotokos pasēs ktiseōs*), does not come up to the force of the Greek; for the original signifies "*firstborn before all the creation*" (Col 1:15). And St. Paul himself shows it must be so understood, because in vs. 17 he says,

---

[204] François Vatable (d. 1547) was a French humanist scholar, a Hellenist, and a Hebraist.
[205] De Gols cites Henry More (1614-1687) here and his work on the Cabala.

"*He is before all things,*" which positively exempts him from being one of the creatures, because "*all things were made by him.*" Therefore, our version ought to be corrected, with submission to grammar and consistency in this place, as it is does not agree with the text, and as it may give a foothold to our adversaries to believe Christ to be a created being, though the first of the creation. St. Paul intended to signify the exact opposite, that Christ is no creature. this is so far from the firstborn of every creature that he existed before all things, and that all the creatures in heaven and earth were made and created by him.

- Eph 3:9. "*God, who created all things by Jesus Christ.*"[206]
- Heb 1:2. "*Through whom also he created the world.*"
- 1Co 8:6. "*To us there is one God, the Father, from whom are all things and for whom we exist, and one Lord, Jesus Christ, through whom are all things and through whom we exist.*"

In this last text, St. Paul opposes both Father and Son to the many gods and many lords. There is but one Lord to us, namely Jesus Christ. Does this mean that the Father is excluded among the many Lords,

---

[206] Some manuscripts do not have "by Christ Jesus." The ESV follows that tradition.

since he is also the Lord *"by whom are all things"* (Rom 11:34, 36)? God forbid, but Father and Son are one Lord. So again, to us there is but one God, namely the Father.

Is the Son then excluded among the many gods, since it is the Son who *"is over all, God blessed forever"* (Rom 9:5)? God forbid, but Father and Son are one God. For St. Paul in this place not only tells us that the Father and Son are one God and one Lord, but also intimates the reason why. For this reason they are one—because all things flow from both. There is nothing of the Father but by the Son; nor any thing by the Son but what is also of the Father, so that the original of all creatures is referred to both, as to one individual fountain and cause of their existence.

I must further observe, that the expressions "in him" (*en autō*), "by him" (*di autou*), and "for him" (*eis auton*) are used both in respect to the Father as to the Son. So also *eis auton ta panta* and *di autou ta panta* are equally applied to the Father and to the Son, *"all things are for him, and all things are by him."* These expressions are equally applied to Father and Son and did not drop by chance from the pen of inspired writers, but they have a certain and full meaning to signify that these two Persons are the same God and Creator. As a consequence, this effectually takes off any pretense the Arians [those who taught that Christ is only a human] can have merely from the force of the prepositions, as if they were intended for a note of inferiority, when they are nothing more than a note of distinction. The operation of one is of equal extent with the operation of the other. Indeed, all is but one work of both.

Before I leave this matter, I shall only mention[207] that the work of creation is everywhere represented as the certain mark or characteristic of the true God. It is the favorite topic which God is pleased to insist most upon, whenever he would either distinguish his own peculiar majesty and power above and beyond all the gods of the nations; or when he would excite in his people the highest idea possible, suitable to his transcendent excellency, and peerless perfections.

For instance, Isaiah 40:26. "*Lift up your eyes on high and see: who created these? He who brings out their host by number.*" And Job 12:7-9. "*But ask the beasts, and they will teach you; the birds of the heavens, and they will tell you; or the bushes of the earth, and they will teach you; and the fish of the sea will declare to you. Who among all these does not know that the hand of the LORD has done this?*"

Creation is the distinguishing character of the one true God. Whenever the Scripture intended to raise in men's minds such esteem and veneration as they ought to have for the supreme God, nothing higher nor greater could be said than this, that he is the Creator, that he created the universe, that he had laid the foundations of the earth, and that the heavens are the works

---

[207] Dr. Waterland, *On the Divinity of Christ*, Sermon 3, p. 93.

of his hands. Therefore Socinus, to evade the force of that argument and of the consequence St. Paul draws from it for divine worship (Rom 1:25), fell into this mad notion that God is not to be known from the creation.[208] After him, others followed.

But if some are so blind that they cannot see, and others so prejudiced that they will not see, they are but few; and these perhaps express their wishes rather than their thoughts, and are no argument against universal consent; unless we must conclude that nature is not regular in its course, because it produces some monsters and prodigies. No! These few are rather to be deemed delirious than that all the world should be fools.

Jesus Christ is the Preserver of the World.

Although preservation is always included in creation, as it is in a sense a continual creation, the Scriptures have often singled it out by name and laid a very great stress upon it. Therefore, I thought it best to mention it by itself.

This is a divine act which none but infinite power can perform; for there is no less power and wisdom and goodness in the preservation of the creatures than in their first creation, and God is as greatly to be praised for our well-being as for our initial being. The Scholastics have happily called this *manutenentia*, that is a

---

[208] Socinus, *prolect.* Cs2. "*Negamus Deum aliquo modo ex operibus agnosci posse.*"

continual holding his hand to his work; for should God withdraw his aid, how soon would all things perish?

This act of divine power and mercy is ascribed to God the Father. So it is also, with great force and emphasis, ascribed to God the Son in the holy Scriptures.

To the Father	To the Son
Neh 9:6. *You are the LORD, you alone. You have made heaven, the heaven of heavens, with all their host, the earth and all that is on it, the seas and all that is in them; and you preserve all of them.*	John 5:17. *My Father is working until now, and I am working.*
Ps 36:6. *Man and beast you preserve, O LORD.*	Col 1:17. *In him all things hold together.*
Ps 145:15. *The eyes of all look to you, and you give them their food in due season.*	

Jesus Christ is the Worker of Miracles.

The working of miracles has been esteemed by all men to be the peculiar prerogative of God, because no one but he has the springs of nature in his hands; and only he can bend them to such ends, as his will and wisdom shall direct them. Miracles are such acts which are above and contrary to the course of nature. The holy Scriptures ascribe them to God and God alone. Yet, they also ascribe them to Jesus Christ, the Son of God, as a demonstration of his almighty power, and his divine nature, that he with the Father is that One only God.

To the Father	To the Son
Ps 72:18. *Blessed be the LORD, the God of Israel, who alone does wondrous things.*	Luke 6:19. *For power came out of him and healed them all.*
Ps 86:10. For you are great and do wondrous things; you alone are God.	Matt 11:5. *The blind receive their sight and the lame walk, lepers are cleansed and the deaf hear, and the dead are raised up, and the poor have good news preached to them.*
Ps 136:4. *O give thanks ... to him who alone does great wonders.*	
1Co 12:6. *And there are varieties of activities, but it is the same God who empowers them all in everyone.*	

And Christ not only brought about miracles himself, but as a further demonstration of his divinity, he empowered his Apostles to do the same.

- Luke 10:19. *"Behold, I give unto you authority to tread on serpents and scorpions, and over all the power of the enemy."*
- Acts 4:10. *"Let it be known to all of you and to all the people of Israel that by the name of Jesus Christ of Nazareth, whom you crucified, whom God raised from the dead-- by him this man is standing before you well."*

Jesus Christ is the God of all Mercy & Grace, the Redeemer.

The word grace not only signifies pity and compassion, but aid and assistance which we receive from God. Through it, we are enabled to do those things that please God. It also signifies the whole work of redemption and all the blessings and favors which flow from it, which God was pleased to effect by Jesus Christ.

Redemption is the highest act of God's wisdom, power, and mercy. It is an act far exceeding the work of creation. In the creation there was nothing to withstand almighty power; God spoke, and it was done: *"He commanded, and they were created"* (Ps 32:9; cf. Ps 148:5). But in the redemption, God's justice was to be satisfied. His law, which was violated by man's transgression, was to be fulfilled. Atonement was to be made for transgressors, before mankind could be received into favor and God become gracious to them. For God is a law to himself, his attributes are a rule and measure to his works. God set forth Christ Jesus therefore, *"For a demonstration of his righteousness against sin"* and *"God made him to be sin for us who knew no sin, that we might be made the righteousness of God in him"* (Rom 3:25; 2Co 5:21).

As this is the highest demonstration of God's love, that he *"gave his Son for our redemption"* (John 3:16), so the whole act of redemption by Christ is the demonstration of the sublimest wisdom and the greatest power. Thus, Christ is called both the Wisdom and Power of God (1Co 1:24).

And as it was only God's power that could redeem mankind, so the Scriptures, God's revelation of that redemption, ascribe it to God only, yet both to the Father and to the Son, including the Holy Ghost, who are that one God who has redeemed us.

To the Father	To the Son
Isa 63:16. *For you are our Father, our Redeemer.*	Isa 25:9. *It will be said on that day, "Behold, this is our God; we have waited for him, that he might save us. This is the LORD; we have waited for him; let us be glad and rejoice in his salvation."*
Eph 2:4-5. *But God, being rich in mercy, because of the great love with which he loved us, even when we were dead in our trespasses, made us alive together with Christ.*	
Hos 1:7. *But I will have mercy on the house of Judah, and I will save them by the LORD their God.*	Acts 20:28. *Care for the church of God, which he obtained with his own blood.*
Luke 1:68. *Blessed be the Lord God of Israel, for he has visited and redeemed his people.*	1Co 1:30. *Because of him you are in Christ Jesus, who became to us wisdom from God, righteousness and sanctification and redemption.*
	John 1:16. *For from his fullness we have all received, grace upon grace.*

Jesus Christ is the God that Forgives Sins.

"*Sin is lawlessness*" (1Jn 3:4). The law is God's image, his will. Therefore, all sin is against God, and it is God's right and privilege alone to forgive sins. So, the holy Scriptures ascribe it only to God, as an act of God and of God alone. Yet, this they ascribe both to Father and Son and also to the Holy Ghost, who are that one and only God.

To the Father	To the Son
Ex 34:6-7. *The LORD, the LORD, a God merciful and gracious, slow to anger, and abounding in steadfast love and faithfulness, keeping steadfast love for thousands, forgiving iniquity and transgression and sin.*	Matt 9:2, 6. *Take heart, my son; your sins are forgiven. ... But that you may know that the Son of Man has authority on earth to forgive sins—he then said to the paralytic—"Rise, pick up your bed and go home."*
Isa 43:25. *I, I am he who blots out your transgressions for my own sake, and I will not remember your sins.*	Matt 26:28. *This is my blood of the covenant, which is poured out for many for the forgiveness of sins.*
Jer 31:34. *I will forgive their iniquity, and I will remember their sin no more.*	Col 1:14. *In whom we have redemption, the forgiveness of sins.*
Luke 5:21. *Who can forgive sins but God alone?*	

Jesus Christ is God who Regenerates and Sanctifies.

Regeneration and sanctification are as much out of man's power as his creation. Men, spiritually dead in sin, can no more raise themselves to a new life than a man naturally dead can raise himself to natural life. Regeneration is the gift of God and of God alone; and the holy Scripture ascribes it to God alone, as his own act and deed and his alone. Yet, it is ascribed to God the Father and in the same manner to God the Son, who, with the Holy Ghost, is that one God who is the Lord and Giver of Life.

To the Father	To the Son
1Th 5:23. *Now may the God of peace himself sanctify you completely.*	John 17:19. *For their sake I consecrate myself, that they also may be sanctified in truth.*
	1Co 6:2. *You were sanctified, you were justified in the Name of the Lord Jesus Christ and by the Spirit of our God.*
	Heb 2:11. *He who sanctifies and those who are sanctified all have one source. That is why he is not ashamed to call them brothers.*

Jesus Christ is God the Sanctifier.

Therefore St. Paul calls Christ the *"Lord from heaven,"* and the *"quickening Spirit,"* when he compares him to the first Adam (1Co 15:22). *"For as in Adam all die, so also in Christ shall all be made alive."* How so? Because Christ is the *"Lord from heaven"* (vs. 47), and in vs. 45 he is *"the quickening Spirit;"* where the expressions "The Lord from heaven" (*ho kurios*[209] *ex ouranou*) and "the quickening Spirit" (*pneuma zōopoioun*) signify his divine Nature and can signify nothing else.

For that *"Lord from heaven"* signifies God is beyond dispute and appears evidently from John 3:31, *"He who comes from above is above all ... He who comes from*

---

[209] *Ho kurios* ("the Lord") is only found in some manuscripts. Thus, if you took out an ESV, you would not read "the Lord from heaven," but the "man from heaven." Though a disputed reading, the theology is certainly not disputed.

heaven is above all." The Jews used to call God, "*The Adam above who is blessed,*" and the Cabalists say that this "*Adam above*" was married to the "*congregation of Israel,*" where the marriage between Adam and Eve was a representation. This is what St. Paul applies "*to Christ and his church*" (Eph 5:32).[210]

The other phrase also signifies the divinity of Christ; for in this verse Adam, who was only a man, is fully distinguished from the last Adam, who was more than a man, who was also God. "*The first man Adam was made a living soul, the last Adam was made a life-giving Spirit*" (1Co 15:45). In both the Scriptures and the ancient Jews, by "Spirit" refers to the divine Nature of the Messiah; for this is how they interpret Gen 1:2: "The Spirit of the Lord moved upon the face of the waters ... This is the Spirit of King Messiah."[211]

Jesus Christ is God, the Judge of the World.

That God is judge of the whole world is a truth we have received from God, not merely by revelation, but God has imprinted it in the law of nature and wrote it in the hearts of all mankind.[212] That God

---

[210] Bishop Bull, *Jud. Eccl.* Cath. C.5.§.5.
[211] John Lightfoot, *A Commentary on the New Testament from the Talmud and Hebraica, Matthew-1 Corinthians, Acts-1 Corinthians*, vol. 4 (Bellingham, WA: Logos Bible Software, 2010), 274.
[212] Ridderus, *The Faith and Morality of the Gentiles* (Amsterdam: 1670), 54. This refers to Franciscus Ridderus (1618-1683), a Dutch Reformed minister who served at Schermorhorn, Brielle, and Rotterdam. He wrote religious poems and devotional books.

alone is judge is as certain, and the Scriptures have ascribed the judgment to God, both to the Father and to the Son as God, as that one God.

Because the judgment is to be executed in a visible manner, the Scripture tells us that God has appointed Jesus Christ the Son of God, and the Son of Man, God and man, to hold that judgment visibly. *"For the Father judges no man but has committed all judgment to the Son"* (John 5:22).

To the Father	To the Son
Ecc 12:16. *For God will bring every act to judgment, everything which is hidden, whether it is good or evil.*	John 5:27. *He gave Him authority to execute judgment, because He is the Son of Man.*
Ecc 11:9. *God will bring you into judgment.*	Acts 17:31. *Because he has fixed a day on which he will judge the world in righteousness by a man whom he has appointed; and of this he has given assurance to all by raising him from the dead.*
Gen 18:25. *Shall not the Judge of all the earth do what is just?*[213]	1Co 5:10. *For we must all appear before the judgment seat of Christ, so that each one may receive what is due for what he has done in the body, whether good or evil.*

Now if we examine the texts of the Old Testament and compare them with those of the New, we will find the descriptions of this Judge described the same way.

---

[213] Technically, this verse refers to the Son, as Abraham is having a conversation with the Angel of the LORD.

Ps 50:1. The Judge is called *El Elohim*, Jehovah, the God of Gods, the Lord, or as our version reads, *"the mighty God, even the Lord;"* or as the other translation, *"the Lord, even the most mighty God."* In Ps 96:13 and Ps 98:9 we find that it is Jehovah, the Lord, who *"comes to judge the earth. He will judge the world in righteousness, and the peoples in faithfulness."*

Now from the New Testament we learn that the Father judges no man but has committed all judgment to the Son (John 5:22), and that Christ is the Judge. So, it necessarily follows that Christ the Judge is both God and Man; that Christ the Judge is Jehovah, the God of Gods, the mighty God who comes to judge the earth.

Jesus Christ the Supreme God.

Having thus far seen that all the high titles, all the divine attributes, and all the divine works which are ascribed to God the Father are ascribed to Christ the Son of God also, we must conclude that this Christ is the very God, the one supreme God with the Father, whose glory is equal, whose majesty is co-eternal.

Every title, every attribute, every work proclaims Christ to be God. All these together make it so clear, so full, so irrefutable a demonstration of his divinity, that one may justly wonder how any who retain the least regard to the Scriptures ever doubt it.

For if these names, attributes, and operations are God's prerogative, and God is by them made known to us, and God is by them distinguished from us; and we have no other criteria to know the divine Nature than by these; we must conclude that wherever these are found, there we find God; and where these are not found, God is not there.

Therefore, if these attributes declare God, we must declare Jesus Christ to be God. For they are all found in him and ascribed to him. If these criteria are not conclusive in regard to Christ, notwithstanding they are found in him, then they cannot be conclusive in any other person, not even for the Father, for we have no other criteria given to us with which we can know the only true God than these. If these are not sufficient for the one, they cannot be for the other; and if they are conclusive for one, they must also be for the other.

To pretend that they are given to the Father in a more eminent manner[214] than to the Son is false and frivolous. Where do they think they have come up with that distinction, and where is it found? They are given exactly alike, and in the most solemn and majestic manner to the Son as they are to the Father. Our adversaries will be eternally at a loss to discover a difference. For instance, in John 1:1, the Word is called God in the same verse as the Father is called God. Should not every man believe that it is to be understood in the same strict and proper sense for two?

---

[214] Clarke, *Modest Plea*, 148.

How shall any judicious reader ever be able to understand language if, in the same verse and same sentence, the same word should stand for two ideas or bear two senses so vastly different from each other? What could move any one in reading this verse to understand one as the true God and the other an inferior God, which is a contradiction in terms? When all the circumstances of the context give us no suspicion of any such different meaning, but the whole thing tends to confirm us that the Word is to be understood in the strict sense to the true God, that is to both, then on what basis does anyone disagree?

The Socinians were at least sensible to the force of the names and attributes of God that to evade it rather than acknowledge Christ to be God, they pretend that the attributes of God are no criteria of the divine Nature. They deny that these attributes are such perfections of the Divinity, as we declare them to be. But, they say they are rather something different from God, something between God and a creature (see Adam Goslavius[215] and others). For them, the divine attributes are something, some third thing between God and the creature, the faculties of God, and the powers of God. They say it is impossible that God can

---

[215] Adam Goslavius was a 17th century Socinian pupil of Nicholas Taurelli. He was a Polish Knight from Bebeln, Germany and had a brother named Andrew who was also a Socinian. De Gols cites here his work *Against Kecherman*, p. 71. In a moment he will cite another Socinian, Jonas Schlichtingius (b. 1592), *Against Meisner*, 12.

be the attribute "eternity;" eternity cannot be God himself. But is this not a total distraction? Oh, when men are wise beyond revelation, how does God give them up to a reprobate mind! When men willfully depart from the right way, what amazing folly and madness do they run into![216]

But no more of this. I shall only observe that it is a peculiar providence of God that he has bestowed to us so many numbers of evidences for the proof of our Lord's Divinity that less of them would have sufficed. But divine Wisdom, foreseeing what opposition the Gospel of "*God manifest in the flesh*" would meet with, purposely guarded it by giving us so many, these great and powerful arguments, so that were it possible for some single evidence by the craft of the Devil to be eluded, the power of the whole would never be overcome.

God's providence is most distinguished in this, because the consequence is so very great. For God would never have brought so many concurring testimonies of a creature's dignity to rob himself of his honor and to deceive the world. For if we are deceived in this article of Faith, it is not man but God who has

---

[216] There is some deep philosophy going on here. Traditionally, the Church has stated that God "simple." This means that he is indivisible and is not made up of different attributes. Thus, he is not the sum of his attributes, but each attribute simply is what God is. De Gols is affirming this ancient distinction but is not pressing it other than to say that the Socinians were playing with philosophical doctrines surrounding the attributes of God in order to deny that Jesus Christ is God!

deceived us. But this is not reconcilable to eternal justice, truthfulness, and goodness. So God, for the honor of his own eternal Son, took all this care and pains to convince us of his Divinity, and furnished us with so many excellent arguments that plead in his behalf, that we might *"honor the Son, even as we honor the Father"* (John 5:23).

Accordingly, all the churches of God in all the dispensations, in all ages of the world, whether Patriarchal, Jewish, or Christian were trained up in the knowledge of the Son of God to know him as the God of their salvation, though in different degrees by those very criteria that are here given of the Divinity of Christ. Truly, upon full consideration we may believe that all mankind would deem it the highest blasphemy to ascribe these lofty titles, these sublime attributes, these almighty works to any created being, which are the only characteristics whereby the Nature of the one only and true God can be made known to us.

And yet we find that from the very age that Christ himself lived, all Christians have ascribed them to Christ, and have stoutly defended them against the heretics in every age. They have accordingly adored and worshiped Christ as the eternal God, the only one and God, to whom all honor and veneration is due.

These evidences, which the holy Scriptures have given us in words as plain and intelligible as could ever possibly be expressed, have had such powerful influence upon men's minds—and not the unthinking part of mankind, but on the most learned,[217] judicious, prudent, and scrupulous, the wisest, and most considerate—that they were forced to embrace the evidence of truth and stooped down with joy and gladness to give glory to the Son of God and to adore God in the Trinity of Persons, in the Unity of the divine Majesty, and worshiped the Father, Son, and Holy Ghost, as the one and only God.

---

[217] De Gols cites Grotius, *de Veritat. Rel. Char.* 1.2. §.3.4.

CHAP. VI.

PRECEPTS OF THE SCRIPTURE THAT ENJOIN US TO WORSHIP CHRIST AS GOD.

Perhaps it will be said, that all that I have said to this point is nothing to the point; that this is neither commanded nor shown by example. I come therefore now to show you both command and example; and shall give you enough of both to convince any man.

But what I have thus far proved concerning the Divinity of Christ was very much to the point, that point being the very foundation, ground, and reason of adoration. For we do not have a god who is a creature, a god made in time, a god of yesterday, a nominal god such as Socinus and most of his followers worship. We worship the true God, and glory in the truth that we do not have a created being, but the eternal God for the object of our worship and adoration.

But before I come to particulars, I must observe that we in our adoration worship the Triune God, the three Persons in the unity of the divine majesty, not excluding but always including the Son and Holy Spirit. And though we sometimes, no and often, pray to God the Father only, without praying directly to the Son or Spirit, we do not therefore exclude them. Rather, we pray this way because the Father is the frontal Divinity, and because we are directed to pray even this way by his Son.

Divines observe that the word "God" is sometimes used "essentially" (*ousiōdōs*, that is, of the essence), and then the three Persons—Father, Son, and Holy Ghost are included and invoked. Whenever the word "God" is used with particular reference to the Father, or Son, or Spirit, this is expressed "personally" (*hupasatikos*, of the persons). For example, Matt 4:7, "*You shall not tempt the Lord your God,*" and vs. 10, "*You shall worship the Lord your God,*" and John 4:24, "*God is a Spirit.*" In these and other places the word is taken essentially, for the Father, Son, and Holy Ghost, three Persons in the unity of the divine Nature. It is used personally, in places like John 14:1. "*You believe in God,*" for the Father; 1Ti 3:16, "*God is manifest in the flesh,*" for the Son; Acts 5:4, "*You have lied to God,*" for the Holy Ghost, as it is explained in vs. 3.

The same is observed of the word Father also, that it is essentially used for God, who is called the Father of spirits (Heb 12:9), and the Father of all (1Co 8:6); and the Gentiles used to call God by the name of Father. But by the revelation God has given us of his own Nature, that word Father so essentially used, includes all the three Persons, the Father, Son, and Holy Ghost. And so, God is "*our Father*" (Matt 6:4) and "*our heavenly Father*" (Matt 5:16). And so, it is also used personally for the first Person of the sacred Trinity, "The

Father," in a hundred places of Scripture. Yet, is it used of the Son also in Isaiah 9:6, "*The everlasting Father*," where, under correction, the Hebrew signifies the Father of Eternity, and so Junius and Tremellius[218] render it, and the marginal notes of our old version have it, "the Author of Eternity;" and the last Belgic version, and the French.[219]

But that we may pray to the Son of God Christ Jesus, and to the Holy Spirit directly, we have not only warrants from examples in Scripture, but we are commanded so to do. These injunctions will appear as bright as the sun in full glory. For there is no act of adoration so exalted, nor supplication so low, nor veneration so high, nor honor, glory, praise, thanksgiving, or obedience, required of us to be paid to the Father, but what is also required of us, in words of equal weight, and by equal strength of expression, to be paid to Christ the Son of God.

I come now to particulars. The first command is of:

Faith and Reliance.

I begin with this first, because St. Paul has laid it as the foundation of all worship and the principal article of adoration (Heb 11:6). "*For without Faith it is*

---

[218] The Junius-Tremellius Bible (1575). Immanuel Tremellius (1510-80) was an Italian Jewish convert to Christianity, a leading Hebraist and Bible translator. Franciscus Junius was his son-in-law and together they worked on a Latin translation of the Bible from the Hebrew and Syriac.
[219] Of 1618. *Vader der eeuwighent*; *Pere d'Eternite*.

impossible to please him; for he that comes to God must believe that he is, and that he is a rewarder of those that diligently seek him." This faith and reliance, which we are bound to have in the Father, we are by the same Scriptures required to have in the Son.

In the Father	In the Son
John 17:3. *And this is eternal life, that they know you, the only true God.*	John 17:3. *And this is eternal life, that they know you, the only true God, and Jesus Christ whom you have sent.*
John 14:1. *Let not your hearts be troubled. Believe in God.*	John 14:1. *Let not your hearts be troubled. Believe in God; believe also in me.*

Here I must observe, if there is any extraordinary strength or singular significance in the expression of *believing in*, as St. Augustine, the schoolmen after him, and several eminent protestants assert, then it is the highest and most excellent act or degree of faith. The *"full assurance"* (*plērophoria*) of the understanding, which St. Paul speaks of Col 2:2, is the highest thing a Christian grasps in this present life. I say, if there is any strength in that expression, which, however, I dare not say,[220] but if there is, then it is here equally used of the Son as of the Father. But whether there is or is not anything extraordinary in the form of words, I am very

---

[220] De Gols cites Peter Haylin (1599-1662) on the Apostle's Creed here.

sure there is in the duty required. That is, namely, that whatever faith, reliance, hope, trust, or confidence we are to exercise in God by virtue of God's excellencies and his dominion over us, we are to put the same faith, reliance, hope, trust, and confidence in the Lord Jesus, because of his divine excellencies and his dominion over us as God, and our Redeemer.

We should consider Jer 17:7, "*Blessed is the Man that trusts in the Lord, whose trust is the LORD;*" and on the contrary, "*Cursed is the man who trusts in man and makes flesh his strength, whose heart turns away from the LORD*" (vs. 5). When we duly weigh this and compare it with the text of St. John, who requires our faith and reliance in Jesus Christ equally as in the Father, must we not conclude that Jesus is the same God with the Father, or that his gospel draws us away from God and exposes us to the direst curses?

But as we know that the end of the gospel is to bring us to God, and speaks peace to believers, so we are assured that this Jesus in whom we must believe equally as in the Father, is God, is the Son of God, of the same divine nature with the Father, whose glory is equal, whose majesty is co-eternal. And we are further assured by the same Scriptures that God the Father, for the highest demonstration of his love towards us, has given us this very Jesus, that we might believe in him and be happy through by faith. I am sure our Saviour says so. John 3:16, "*For God so loved the world that he gave his only begotten Son, that whosoever believes in him should not perish but have everlasting life. For God did not send his Son into the world to condemn the world, but in order that the world might be saved through him.*" It is very remarkable that St. John, who wrote his Gospel purposely to vindicate and prove the divinity of Christ more than the other Evangelists, insists on this duty of believing in him in a very extraordinary manner. As John 3:36 says, "*Whoever believes in the Son has eternal life; whoever does not obey the Son shall not see life, but the wrath of God remains on him.*" Or John 6:29, "*This is the work of God, that you believe in him whom he has sent*" (cf. John 6:35, 43, 47; 9:35, 36, 38; 20:31, etc.). For of this Christ it says, "*to him all the prophets bear witness that everyone who believes in him receives forgiveness of sins through his name*" (Acts 10:43). From these and many more places in the New Testament, we have a sufficient warrant and command for believing in Christ, which is the principle part of worship and adoration.

Yes, the Scriptures prove that believing in Christ is actually believing in God; for when Paul and Silas had exhorted the keeper of the prison "*to believe on the Lord Jesus Christ*" (Acts 16:31), it is said, "*That when he was baptized he rejoiced, believing in God with all his house*" (34).

The second precept is, to love God.

This duty God requires of us as our God, Creator and Benefactor; and also for our own sakes, that our love of God may return with a blessing back to us. The Scripture requires this duty of us as part of that worship we owe God, and it requires it equally to the Son of God as to God the Father.

To the Father	To the Son
Deut 6:5. *You shall love the LORD your God with all your heart and with all your soul and with all your might.*	Mat 10:37. *Whoever loves father or mother more than me is not worthy of me.*
Jdg 5:31. *Let all your enemies perish, O Lord, but let them that love him be as when the sun goes forth in his might* (NKJV).	John 8:42. *If God were your Father, you would love me, for I came from God and I am here. I came not of my own accord, but he sent me.*
Ps 5:11. *That those who love your Name may exult in you.*	1Pe 1:8. *Though you have not seen him, you love him. Though you do not now see him, you believe in him and rejoice with joy that is inexpressible and filled with glory.*
Matt 22:37. *You shall love the Lord your God with all your heart and with all your soul and with all your mind.*	Eph 6:24. *Grace be with all who love our Lord Jesus Christ with love incorruptible.*
	1Co 16:22. *If anyone has no love for the Lord, let him be accursed. Our Lord, come!*

Now if any man will consider and compare these texts, he will see that the duty of loving Christ is not only enjoined, but is enforced with a benediction to the obedient and with the penalty of a dreadful curse to the disobedient.

Anathema Maranatha (*Cursed. Our Lord, come*). Our English version of [Geneva Bible] 1599, reads this verse, "*Let him be had in execration, maranatha.*" The margin note explains it,

> By these words is betokened the severest kind of curse and excommunication that was amongst the Jews; and the words are as much as to say, as "our Lord cometh": So that his meaning may be this, Let him be accursed even to the coming of the Lord, that is to say, to his death's day, even forever.

The first word, "anathema," signifies an eternal curse, condemnation, or being doomed to destruction. It is used this way in Rom 1:9; Gal 1:8, 9. The other word, "maranatha," whether Syrian[221] or Chaldean, which signifies the Lord's Coming, is added to show that the doom is certain, that the Lord will come to confirm the condemnation. This imprecation therefore is the highest that words are able to express; in the same manner as the duty is enforced by the highest blessing that can be conceived, "*If any Man love me, he will keep my words, and my Father will love him, and we will come to him, and make our dwelling with him*" (John 14:23).

---

[221] De Gols cites Ravanel, *Bibliotheca*, vol. 2, p. 35 here.

Thirdly, Another Precept is, to Honor God.

That honor is due to God is a principle of natural as well as revealed religion. Hence God expostulates with the Jews, through the Prophet Malachi, "*A son honors his father, and a servant his master. If then I am a father, where is my honor? And if I am a master, where is my fear? says the LORD of hosts*" (Mal 1:6).

The duty therefore of honoring God is required of us in the holy Scriptures in the most express terms; and the same honor which is to be paid to the Father, is also required to be paid to the Son, in terms equally strong, and by motives equally cogent.

To the Father	To the Son
Ps 86:9-10, 12. *All the nations you have made shall come and worship before you, O Lord, and shall glorify your name. For you are great and do wondrous things; you alone are God … I give thanks to you, O Lord my God, with my whole heart, and I will glorify your name forever.*	John 5:23. *That all may honor the Son, just as they honor the Father. Whoever does not honor the Son does not honor the Father who sent him.*
Ps 96:7-8. *Ascribe to the LORD, O families of the peoples, ascribe to the LORD glory and strength! Ascribe to the LORD the glory due his name.*	Rev 5:12. *Worthy is the Lamb who was slain, to receive power and wealth and wisdom and might and honor and glory and blessing!*
	Php 2:10-11. *That at the name of Jesus every knee should bow, in heaven and on earth and under the earth, and every tongue confess that Jesus Christ is Lord, to the glory of God the Father.*

Here I must take leave to consider a little more particularly that last admirable citation of St. Paul to the Philippians, where the Apostle sets forth the great condescension of Christ, and the glory that ensued, and the duty required of us to honor the Lord Christ.

The condescension is all the greater because of the state of honor which the Lord Christ had before, which was nothing less than divine glory; for he was in the form of God (*en morphē Theou*), such a one as God is, that is, the true God, or truly God.[222] This expression is only found in this place and is illustrated by what follows, to be equal with God; and that without robbery or prejudice to the divine Majesty. St. Paul explains this in Col 1:15 by being the image of the invisible God, and by being born before the very creation; that is, that he was the eternal Son with the eternal Father, eternal God.

And yet he humbled himself, a humiliation which has several gradations. *He made himself of no reputation; he took upon him the form of a servant; he was made in the likeness of men, and being in fashion as a man, he humbled himself and became obedient unto death, even the death of the cross.* And here it is to be observed, that the Apostle expresses the *form of a servant, and the likeness of men,* in opposition to the other expression of *the form of God*; that he was as truly God, as he was truly man.

---

[222] Beza, in loc.

When Christ is said to have made himself of *no rep-utation*, or when *he emptied himself* or *divested himself*, we must not suppose that he lost anything which he had before, or that he was no more in the *form of God* because he had taken upon him the *form of man*. No, he still retained the same essential glory, the same divine dignity, which he always had. But he concealed it for a time. He did appear among men in the brightness of his divine nature, but laid aside his glory, and divested himself of his splendor, and appeared in our nature as a miserable man, as a *man of sorrows*, to become the sacrifice for our sins.

Then follows the exaltation, *wherefore God also has highly exalted him*. This was an exaltation as high as his humiliation was low; and therefore the Apostle expressly says, *highly exalted him*. The Word in the original is *huperupsen*, raised to the highest degree of glory; which the Psalmist expresses in these words, *For you, O LORD, are most high over all the earth; you are exalted far above all gods* (Ps 97:9).

But how was Christ capable of such an exaltation if he was already God? Can the divine nature be exalted, or can infinity receive a further degree of glory? Some therefore explain this exaltation as pertaining to the human nature of Christ, and very rightly: for the divine nature cannot be exalted. He that was God before the worlds were made could not receive an addition of greatness; *from everlasting to everlasting you are God*: He that was adored by angels and men before his incarnation could not receive a new privilege of worship. And therefore, this exaltation is a new investiture upon his late condescension, a recognition of his rights and privileges which he had from eternity as God, but has now as *Theanthropos*—God and man.

Because Christ, who is the eternal God, condescended so low as to die on a cross for man's redemption, it was fitting that God the Father should declare that it was he who made atonement and paid the price of redemption. It was fitting moreover that the Father should declare that this Redeemer was none less than the very Son of God, that he was now set before the world as their God and their Lord, and that all men might honor him as such, as their God and as their Lord; that they might honor him as their God always, but now as their Lord, their Redeemer by a new claim and a new title.

For this title as Savior was certainly new; for although Christ was ever blessed in his divine nature and perfections, yet had he remained so, and not become our Savior by taking our nature upon him and dying for our sins, he could never have received that title of Savior. For that was subsequent to his sufferings, according to what St. Paul says in Heb 2:9: *But we see Jesus, who was made a little lower than the angels, for the suffering of death, crowned with glory and honor.* And St. Peter in Acts 2:36: *Therefore, let all the house of Israel know assuredly, that God has made that same Jesus whom you have crucified, both Lord and Christ.*

This exaltation is declaring and proclaiming the excellency of this great Person—who he is, and what he is, namely, God eternal. It tells us that he has become the author of salvation and that all must obey him. St. Paul tells us that this exaltation consisted in giving him a *Name above every name*; that is, declaring his divine nature, that he is the eternal God. That the Word "exalting" will bear this meaning is plain from Psalm 128:28, *You are my God, and I will give thanks to you; you are my God; I will extol you*; and from Psalm 18:46, *The LORD lives, and blessed be my rock, and exalted be the God of my salvation*.

For what end was this declaration of the transcendent excellency of the Lord Jesus? This the Apostle tells us, *that at the name of Jesus every knee should bow, in heaven and on earth and under the earth, and every tongue confess that Jesus Christ is Lord, to the glory of God the Father* (Php 2:10-11).

Is this not a precept? Is this not a command? Is this not an injunction for worshiping Christ as God, he who is in the *form of God*, who is *equal with God*, and that *without robbing* God of divine glory? If this is not a precept, no words can express any. No words can more fully express a command than to tell us that the whole design of this exaltation and declaration of his divine nature was that all rational creatures should adore him, that all men should worship him as God and Savior, whether moved by fear or by love.

This worship we are to pay to Christ, to the glory of God the Father. The Apostle has added this on purpose, so that we, while admiring the greatness of the Son, should not forget the Father whose Son he is. Rather, he did it so that we should glorify the Father who has created us, and the Son who has redeemed us with his blood, and to whom, with the Holy Spirit the One God might be all honor and glory for ever and ever. Amen.

Another Duty is, To serve and obey God

God is the Sovereign Lord of the world. He has a right to our service and may command our obedience. The Scriptures require our service and obedience under the highest penalty, even of eternal damnation.

This service and obedience is in and by the same Scriptures required to be paid to the Lord Christ, God the Son, as it is to God the Father.

To the Father	To the Son
Dt 13:4. *You shall walk after the LORD your God and fear him and keep his commandments and obey his voice, and you shall serve him and hold fast to him.*	Ex 23:20-22. *Behold, I send an angel before you to guard you on the way ... Pay careful attention to him and obey his voice; do not rebel against him, for he will not pardon your transgression, for my name is in him. But if you carefully obey his voice and do all that I say, then I will be an enemy to your enemies and an adversary to your adversaries.*

Dt 27:10. *You shall therefore obey the voice of the LORD your God, keeping his commandments.*

Matt 17:5. *This is my beloved Son, with whom I am well pleased; listen to him.*
John 12:26. *If anyone serves me, he must follow me; and where I am, there will my servant be also. If anyone serves me, the Father will honor him.*

It would never end if we were to quote all the texts of the New Testament which require our obedience to Christ. We may only observe the gracious manner of these injunctions. They are not in the harsh terms of a lawgiver, not in the severe dictates of a judge, but in the terms of love and with the motives of our own happiness. But though the terms are gentler, the duty is the same; and indeed the obligation from the grace and goodness of God ties us down all the more to the duty.

The inanimate part of the world obeys Christ; the *very wind and the sea obey him* (Matt 8:27). Nay, the very devils are forced to obey him (Mark 1:27). How much more are we obliged to serve him, whose service is perfect freedom, him who is our God and Savior, him who proposes his laws to us in the strains of mercy and of love!

Christ *the Object of Love, not of Fear*

I know it is objected that there is no precept to fear him. But that is easily accounted for, because Christ is proposed to us as the object of our love and not our fear; as our Saviour, our Redeemer; not primarily as our Judge, and therefore not the object of fear, but of love, hope, joy, and consolation. Though I am very sure that they who do not love him have the greatest reason in the world to fear him; but those that love and obey him, fear him with a reverential fear, though they dread him not. *For you have not received the Spirit of bondage again to fear; but you have received the Spirit of Adoption, whereby we cry, Abba, Father* (Rom 8:15).

Those who neglect the soft voice of love and mercy and peace, will find the day of his Second Coming terrible enough and will have reason to fear him, *when the Lord Jesus is revealed from heaven with his mighty angels in flaming fire, inflicting vengeance on those who do not know God and on those who do not obey the gospel of our Lord Jesus. They will suffer the punishment of eternal destruction, away from the presence of the Lord and from the glory of his might, when he comes on that day to be glorified in his saints, and to be marveled at among all who have believed, because our testimony to you was believed* (2Th 1:7-10; cf. Rev 1:7; 6:15-17).

Another duty required by positive precept is, To pray to God.

Prayer and supplication are certainly the principal acts of divine worship, and God requires them from us. When we do them, we acknowledge him to be the Fountain of all good, and own our continual dependency upon his favor.

That this duty of prayer was not known nor required in the Old Testament is Socinus's opinion, who says it is an additional precept of Christ to the First Commandment. Smalcius[223] is of the same opinion, that prayer was not required by Almighty God in the Old Testament. As to the worshiping of Christ, this they allow also to be an additional precept of Christ to the First Commandment. But how? Christ has enjoined us that we are to acknowledge him as God (that is, for such a one that has divine power over us) and to pay him religious worship, as the Racovian Catechism expresses it.[224]

This is strange, that Christ should enjoin this, that this should be the peculiar precept of Christ, and yet there should be no precept of worshiping Christ anywhere found in the Scriptures, as Socinus claims, and Staunton from him.

How inconsistent are these men with themselves, at one time to assert, at another time to deny what they asserted before! But in answer to their proportions:

First, it is entirely false that the duty of prayer was never commanded in the Old Testament. For in Dt 6:5 we find, *You shall love the Lord your God with all your heart, and with all your soul, and with all your might,*

---

[223] Valentinus Smalcius (1572-1622) was a German Socinian. DeGols gives locations and Latin quotes for both men.
[224] This is Socinius' catechism.

which cannot be done without prayer and adoration; and Vs. 13. *You shall fear the Lord your God and serve him, and shall swear by his Name* which cannot be done without invocation. What is the meaning of this precept in Ps 50:15? *Call upon me in the day of trouble*; or in Isa 55:6, *Seek the Lord while he may be found, call upon him while he is near*; or in Isa 56:7, *My house shall be called a house of prayer for all people?*

The examples of people praying, and the prayers recorded, are so frequent that I need not name them.

As to a form of prayer, there never was any age of the church without a form: Before the Flood, as soon as the sons of God had separated themselves from the sons of men,[225] they had a form of worship, certain rites, certain sacrifices, and certain prayers; and no doubt but the prayers were equally revealed as the sacrifices were. It appears from the Epistle of Jude that there was even in his time some remains of the antediluvian [pre-Flood] liturgy called the Book of Enoch.[226] This book contained the prayers of the first world, as Tertullian (*habit. Mulier.*) and Augustine (*City of God*) thought. The Jews are of opinion that several of the Psalms were composed before the Flood and reserved for the use of the Jewish Church.

---

[225] De Gols takes "sons of God" here in the traditional Reformed-Augustinian interpretation to mean godly men as opposed to the "sons of men" who were ungodly men.

[226] Since DeGol's time, the book of Enoch has been rediscovered.

After the Flood, we find a Prayer of Abraham (Gen 18:27), the Liturgy of Isaac (Gen 32:9), and the form of Moses (Ex 34:9), all which are recorded, not only to assure us that God is the God of order in all the churches, but to confront those men who, with falsehood and lies, go about to deceive.

As soon as God had given the Jews his laws as the form of obedience, he gave them also a form of prayer (Ex 34:9; Num 6:24); and we find that Moses used it, and it was used by the kings of Israel many years after (1Kg 8; Ezra 9). The prophets composed forms of prayer suitable to particular occasions; as the prayer for the Sabbath (Ps 92), the prayer for the Feast of Tabernacles (Ps 98), and that it was used on the festival we find in Ezra 3:11, the prayer for the sick (Ps 102), and the Psalms of Degrees were the daily form of common prayer throughout the year. And the Jews tell us, and it appears also from Jeremiah 32, Habakkuk 3, Joel 2 and other of the prophets, that they had peculiar forms of prayer when in captivity, in war, or in times of pestilence, or famine; and Agur's prayer seems to have been composed for daily devotion (Prov 30:7).

After the Prophets, John the Baptist taught the Jews another form of prayer, which although it is not in existence today, we believe was in the name of the Messiah, not to come, as the prophets (Dan 9:17), but as already come.

And when Christ the eternal Son of God came, and gave us his most excellent form, he had no misgivings about collecting the petitions out of the several forms of prayer, then in use among the Jews.

So much in answer to the first proposition, which the Socinians borrowed from the ancient Manichees who held that Christ made Prayer an addition to the First Commandment; and that Prayer was not known to the Fathers, nor required under the Mosaic dispensation. But that this is most notoriously false, appears from what has been said.

As to the second proposition, that the worship of Christ is an additional precept to the First Commandment, a precept added by Jesus Christ himself; how this can be reconciled to the assertion and positive expression of Socinus and of Mr. Staunton from him, that there is neither command nor example to worship Christ as God. I cannot tell, nor do I believe any man living can resolve this. Both cannot be true, that's certain; and that there is neither command nor example, I have in part and shall further prove the contrary.

If it were true, that Christ added to the law for his own worship, that would be no addition to the law, but a total destruction of the law. There could be nothing more contrary to the law. For the First Commandment is, *You shall have no other gods before me.* This forbids every kind of divine worship that could be paid to any being whatsoever, except God. Therefore, to make a created being to be God, exalting him to the highest degree of honor, and giving divine adoration to him, if that is not contrary to and a violation of the First Commandment, then that commandment cannot be violated.

As a matter of fact, that Christ was worshiped in the Old Testament and that there are commands relating to his worship, nothing is plainer: Psalm 2:12 *Kiss the Son*; Psalm 45:11 *Since he is your Lord, bow to him*. Daniel prayed for the Lord's sake (Dan 9:17) and all the Jews prayed for the mediation of the Messiah, for which reason they prayed towards the temple and towards the Ark of the Covenant—the type and figure of Christ, This is beyond all doubt, and that Christ was worshiped in the Old Testament, and before, as well as in the New, I shall now show.

For a plain and positive precept for worshiping Christ as God, nothing can be more plain and positive than Rom 10:13. *Everyone who calls on the name of the Lord will be saved.*

And that this was spoken of Christ appears from the context, for no other person but Christ is mentioned. For at the 4th verse, Christ is called the end of the law, and at the 12th verse he is Lord over all. The necessity of believing in and confessing him is urged at the 9th verse, *If you confess with your mouth that Jesus is Lord and believe in your heart that God raised him from the dead, you will be saved.* Importantly, the Apostle, in citing several texts out of the Old Testament, does not signify that person to be anyone other than Christ. Instead, he fully demonstrates that this Christ was known and called upon by the Fathers of the Old Testament. The duty of calling upon Christ in this text, is commanded not simply, but under a penalty nothing less than damnation.

What must we think therefore of such men as dare openly declare the contrary? What front must we suppose them to have, to impose upon the world such notorious falsehoods? Is there no precept to worship Christ as God? Are faith, love, honor, service, and invocation not worship? Why then what is worship? Of what does divine worship consist, if not in these duties? What peculiar worship does the Scripture ascribe to the only one God, which it does not ascribe and require us to pay to the Lord Jesus Christ? No, I dare be so bold as to challenge any Socinian or Anti-trinitarian, any enemy to Christ, to show me any act of worship, or homage, or adoration, or obedience which is to be paid to the supreme God, which is not by the Scriptures also given to Jesus Christ and required of us by positive precept to be paid to the Lord Christ.

That Christ was worshiped as God, their great master Socinus has more than once acknowledged; and either that, or the fear of the civil power, moved him to do the same, whatever he taught others, or denied before. What must we think of these men? Are they judicially blinded that they cannot see, or are they willfully blind that they will not understand? Either is dreadful. I would have them remember that those who first refuse to know and worship Christ, may afterwards be given over to a reprobate mind and judicially hardened. It is justice for God to withdraw his light and grace which men have abused, and which they have applied to affront and dishonor their God and Saviour.

CHAP. VII

CHRIST ADORED AS GOD, BY INSTANCES IN THE SCRIPTURE

I come now to the matter where I shall demonstrate that the Lord Jesus Christ has been adored and worshiped as God, as the true and eternal God, by numerous instances recorded in the Scriptures.

Christ adored as God by the Angels.

St. Paul assures us that all the angels of God worshiped him at his incarnation. *When he brings the firstborn into the world, he says, "Let all God's angels worship him"* (Heb 1:6; Dt 32:43 LXX).

David tells us that the Angels of God worshiped him before his incarnation, *Worship him all you gods* (Ps 97:7), which the Septuagint has rendered *worship him all his angels*; for the Hebrew *elohim,* "gods," is a name sometimes given to angels because of their exalted strength and power.[227] They are called upon in that Psalm, which is a prophecy of the kingdom of Christ the Messiah, to worship and adore him. If this worship had not been paid by the angels to Christ, the Apostle could not have produced that psalm for the proof of

---

[227] DeGols cites Buxtorf. *Lex.,* p. 29.

it; but from that allegation it is evident that the gods, or angels, worshiped Christ as well before as at his incarnation.

Jesus Christ worshiped as God by Men.

As Christ was worshiped by the angels, so he was likewise worshiped by the sons of men as their God, as the only true and eternal God. The Scriptures are as clear in this as words can express or demonstrate.

Christ was worshiped as God in every Dispensation, by Adam, by the Antediluvian Fathers, by Noah in the Ark, by the Patriarchs, by Moses and Joshua, by the Israelites in the wilderness, by David and the prophets, by the Apostles and Christians to this very time. The matter of fact of this adoration is recorded with so much care, caution, and concern, that after all, if God the Son was not worshiped equally with the Father as God, we must conclude that then neither has God the Father been worshiped from the creation of the world to this day.

But before I proceed, I must lay down this axiom, that God the Father in all the appearances God was pleased to make to mankind, never appeared visible himself, but always by the *Memra* (*mmr'*), that is, the *Word*, as St. John expressly calls him (John 1:1). This is according to what is said in Exodus 33:20, *You cannot see my face, for man shall not see me and live*; and to what our Saviour says, that *no man hath seen the Father*

(John 6:46) and *His voice you have never heard, his form you have never seen* (5:37). Every revelation of God is through Christ his Son, who is the revealer and interpreter of the otherwise unknown Father, and his will to men. This order and economy in the Persons of the sacred Trinity is what we ought humbly to adore and reverence, rather than pry too curiously into. We must not pretend to be wise above what is written, lest we fall into errors and lose ourselves in inextricable mazes. For to say (Eusebius, *Demonstration of the Gospel*) that the *to theion*, the frontal Divinity, became visible, is extreme erroneous, *for no man has seen God at any time, the only begotten Son, which is in the bosom of the Father, he has made him known* (John 1:18).

The Logos, or Word, explained.

Because our adversaries have with a world of art endeavored to perplex and entangle men's minds, about the true meaning of the *Logos*, or Word, I shall give a clear explication of the phrase and show,

> That it was a term and expression to signify a Divine Person, both by Jews and Gentiles; and that it was used long before and after the age that St. John wrote his Gospel; and that it was that very expression whereby the Jews understood the Messiah.

The Word, or Logos, taken by the Jews for a Divine Person.

As for the Jews, how and in what sense they used it is evident from the Septuagint, and Philo, and the Chaldee paraphrase (i.e. the Targums) namely, for a Divine Person. For example, in Ezek 1:24, the LXX has changed *Shaddai*, the undoubted Name of the omnipotent God, into *logos*, the Word. This they would never have done had they not thought this Word a divine Person.

Philo the Jew, who lived in the age St. John wrote his Gospel, expressly calls this Word *deutron theon*, the Second God, next to the "Father of all things." Elsewhere he wrote that the Word is superior to the whole World and more ancient and general than anything that is made. Again, speaking of the world's being the temple of God, he says, in this temple the High Priest is the Firstborn Divine Word of God. In another book he says this Divine Word is superior to all things; it has no visible species by which it may be likened to any sensible thing, but is itself the Image of God, the most ancient of all intelligibles, and next to the most High, between whom and him there is no medium.

Grotius says, that Philo taught that the Word of God is the Maker of the world, not unbegotten as is God the Father of all, nor yet begotten in like manner as men are. And again, that the Word of God is the Angel or Ambassador of God, who takes care of the universe. And he further quotes some ancient Cabalists who distinguish God into three Lights, which some of them call by the same names we Christians do: Father, Son or Word, and Holy Ghost.

The Chaldee Paraphrase, which is one of the most ancient monuments of Jewish learning, constantly by the Word signifies a divine Person. For instead of Jehovah or God as we have in the Hebrew text, it commonly has *the Word of Jehovah.* "Word" is attributed with personal actions. Thus, it is evident that they looked upon it as a divine Person. For instance,

The Hebrew Text	The Targum
Gen 1:27. *And God made man in his own image.*	Gen 1:27. *And the Word of God made man in his own image.*
Gen 3:8. *And they heard the voice of the Lord.*	Gen 3:8. *And they heard the voice of the Word of the Lord.*
Gen 3:22. *And the Lord God said, "Behold, the man has become like one of us."*	Gen 3:22. *The Word of Jehovah God said, "Behold, Adam whom I created, is the only begotten in the world, even as I am the only begotten in the highest heavens."*[228]
Gen 28:20-21. *If God will be with me ... then shall the Lord be my God.*	Gen 28:20-21. *If the Word of the Lord will be with me ... the Word of the Lord shall be my God*
Ex 20:1. *And God spoke.*	Ex 20:1. *The Word of the Lord God spoke.*

---

[228] De Gols translation here is different from modern translations, which do not have "begotten." His should be considered!

Num 11:20. *You have despised the Lord who is among you.*	Num 11:20. *You have despised the Word of Jehovah, whose divinity dwells among you.*
Dt 1:30, 32. *The Lord your God who goes before you, he shall fight for you ... You did not believe the Lord your God.*	Dt 1:30, 32. *The Word of Jehovah, he shall fight for you ... You did not believe in the Word Jehovah your God.*
Isa 45:17. *Israel is saved by the LORD with everlasting salvation.*	Isa 45:17. *Israel shall be saved by the Word of God with everlasting salvation.*

Those who desire more may consult Rittangel, who had been a Jew, and was well skilled in the Jewish learning.[229] There they may find that Memra is a divine Person, and divine Subsistence, and never used by the Chaldee Paraphrasts otherwise.

Since therefore it is evident that by this Word they meant a person; and since to this person they ascribe not only the name, but the worship of God, it is plain they believed him to be a divine Person. Accordingly, *Chalcidius ad Timæum*, in that book where he professes to explain the doctrines of the Jews, whom he calls the holy sect, delivers this as their sense of this divine Word.

---

[229] Johann Stephan Rittangel (1602-1652), a German Jew who converted to Roman Catholicism, then became a Calvinist, and later a Lutheran. He was professor of Oriental languages at Königsberg. De Gols cites a work *Jesirah*, p. 96. This is probably *Sefer Yezira* (1642). But he also wrote works called *Bilibra Veritatis* and *Veritas Religionis Christianæ* (1699) to substantiate the claim that the Targums prove the Trinity.

This *Word of God* is God, taking care of human affairs, and is the Cause or Principle by which men may live well and happily, if they do not neglect this gift which the supreme God has granted to them.

And to the same purpose Celsus,[230] speaking the sense of the Jews, expressly tells us, "*We agree with you, that the Word is the Son of God.*"

I come now to see how the Gentiles used it and that they also understood by it a divine Person. What the Gentiles knew of the Trinity is not my present business to examine. What they had, they received from the Hebrews, but so grievously depraved and adulterated that nothing can be made of it but confusion. However, those who desire to know may consult Agrippa, Gale, and others.[231] It is enough for my purpose to know what they understood by Word.

---

[230] Celsus (2nd Cent. AD), Greek philosopher and opponent of Christianity. The work was called *A True Discourse*, but it now lost, known to us through passages preserved by Origen. Someone else quotes Celsus as saying, "We agree with you Jews, that the Word is the Son of God." David Simpson, *A Plea for the Deity of Jesus and the Doctrine of the Trinity* (London, 1812), 448.

[231] Henry Cornelius Agrippa (1486-1535), *Three Books of Occult Philosophy or Magic*, 1.3.c.8; Theophilus Gale (1628-1678), *The Court of the Gentiles*, Part IV. 1.2. This is a point made by Peter Allix. For example, "It is certain, that Plato himself, by conversing with the Jews in Egypt, borrowed of them the best notions he had of God." Peter Allix, *The Judgment of the Ancient Jewish Church Against the Unitarians*, second edition (Oxford: Clarendon Press, 1821), 2. This idea goes back at least as far as Justin Martyr. "Plato clearly and openly alludes to the law of Moses, but, fearing the hemlock, he did not dare mention him by name whose teaching, he well knew, was hateful to the Greeks."(Justin Martyr, *Exhortation to the Greeks* 25).

The Logos or Word, how used by the Gentiles.

Tertullian (*Apologet.* 36) will tell us, Zeno has declared that the Logos, the Word, is a maker of the world, who formed all things in due temper, and is called Fate and God, and the Soul of Jupiter.

Orpheus (see Clement, *Strom.* 1.5) says, that the Word is the divine and immortal King.

Numenius the Pythagorean, as he is quoted by St. Cyril (*Against Julian* 1.8), calls the Father the First, and the Word the Second God. And Plotinus (Enn. 5.1.5.c.3) also, speaking of this divine Mind or Word, says this Nature is God, a Second God.

The Logos, or Word, is the very Expression used by the Jews to signify the Messiah.

That the Jews meant not only a divine Person by the Word, but even the very Messiah whom they looked for is evident, not only because they give him the very same characters which the New Testament gives to our Savior, but also because they attribute to him the very same offices that the New Testament attributes to Christ.

First, the Jews give the Word the same characters the Gospel gives Christ.

Philo says the Word is the "character of God" (*On Agriculture* 1.2) and the "image of God" (possibly *Allegorical Interpretation* or *On Agriculture*); answerable to St.

Paul (Heb 1:3): *The express image of his Person*. The bread and food which God has given to the soul; answerable to John 6:33, 35. *I am the Bread of Life*. He says the Word is the house of the Father in which he dwells (*On the Migration of Abraham*), agreeable to John 14:10. "*Do you not believe that I am in the Father and the Father is in me? ... but the Father who dwells in me does his works.*"

Secondly, The Jews attribute to the Word the same offices that the New Testament ascribes to Christ.

So they say, the Word or divine Logos is the Governor of all things, and the Viceroy of the great King (Philo, *On Dreams* & *On Agriculture* 1.2). They say that God, who is King and Pastor of the world, has appointed the Word, his first-begotten Son, to undertake the care of his sacred flock as his own Viceroy and Substitute (*ibid*). The same Philo has a passage relating to the Word, as the intercessor between God and Man, which is highly worthy of our observation (*ibid*).

> This excellent gift (of Intercessor), the Father of all things has bestowed upon the Prince of Angels, the most ancient Word, that standing in the middle, he might judge between the creature and the Creator. He always supplicates the immortal God for mortals, and is the ambassador from the supreme King to his subjects. In this gift he rejoices as highly valuing himself upon it, saying, I stood in the middle between you and the Lord, as being neither unbegotten as God, nor yet

begotten as you, but am a middle between the extremes, and a pledge for both; for the creature with the Creator, that he shall not wholly apostatize from him, so as to prefer disorder before order and beauty; for the Creator with the creatures, to give him an assured hope that the most merciful God will never abandon his own workmanship. For I declare peace to the creature from him who makes wars to cease, even God, who is the King of Peace.

The same Philo (*The Worse Attacks the Better*) himself understood the Messiah by the Word; for he applied those Words of Ezekiel, which the ancient Jews unanimously understood of the Messiah, to the Word. The Words of Ezekiel are these, *And you shall know that I am the LORD, when their slain lie among their idols around their altars* (Ezek 6:13).

But to put all out of doubt, the Targums use the *Word of the Lord*, and the Messiah promiscuously. For so on those words, *I wait for your salvation, O Lord* (Gen 49:18), the Targum says,

> Our Father Jacob said, "I expect not the salvation of Gideon, son of Joash, which is a temporal salvation; nor the salvation of Samson, son of Manoah, which is a transitory salvation; but I expect the redemption of

Messiah, the son of God, who shall come and gather to-
gether the sons of Israel; his redemption my soul ex-
pects."[232]

The Jerusalem Targum has almost the same
Words, with only this difference, that instead of *"I ex-*
pect the Redemption of Messiah the Son of David," it has,
"But I expect the Redemption which you have promised to give us by your Word.[233] So also on these
Words, *"See now that I, even I, am he, and there is no god*
beside me; I kill and I make alive; I wound and I heal" (Dt
32:39); the Targum of Jonathan runs thus, "When the
Word of the Lord shall be manifested to redeem his
people, he, the Word of the Lord, shall say to all the
people, 'See now because I am he, who was, and is,
and is to come, and there is no other God beside me; I
kill in my revenge, and reviving do revive the people
of the house of Israel. I will heal them in the last days."
And nothing is more common with the Jews than to
call the days of the Messiah the last days.

---

[232] Most translations do not render anything about David. De Gols is
getting this from the Neofiti Targum CTg X (a Tosefta) or Cairo Ge-
nizah (Pal.) manuscript. See Kevin Cathcart, Michael Maher, and Martin McNamara, eds., *The Aramaic BibleA: Targum Neofiti 1: Genesis,*
trans. Martin McNamara, vol. 1 (Collegeville, MN: The Liturgical
Press, 1992), Gen 49:18, p. 222, note j.

[233] The Tosefta fragmentary text says: "Their father said to them: Not
for the redemption of Gideon bar Joash do I wait, for it is a transient
redemption and not for the redemption of Samson bar Manoah, which
is a transient redemption, but for the redemption of the King Messiah,
which is the eternal redemption which you have promised (lit.: "said")
in your Memra to br(ing)."

Having seen that this Word was used both by Jews and Gentiles for a divine Person, and that it was a term whereby the Jews understood the Messiah the Savior; I shall now demonstrate that St. John used the same expression as it had been understood and received both by Jews and Gentiles before, and that he put no new meaning nor different signification upon it, but only such as was already known and received by all men.

But this will better appear by comparing the expressions of St. John and the Jews and Gentiles together.

St. John	Jews and Gentiles
John 1:1. *In the beginning was the Word.*	Porphryr, quoted by St. Cyril (*Against Jul. 1.1*) says that the Logos or Word, is *"always without time, and alone eternal."* *And the Word of God made man in his own image. Philo* says, he is the most ancient Word of God (*On Dreams*), and the most ancient of all things that are (*Ibid.*, 16; *Allegorical Interpretation* 1.2).
John 1:2. *He was in the beginning with God.*	So the Jews and Gentiles affirm (Plotin. *En.* 5.1.i.c.6), that their Word is not separated from the First Good, or Father, but of necessity is together with him.
John 1:3. *All things were made by him, and without*	All the Platonic schools call the Word the "Artificer of the world" and Plato himself speaking of the world said, "Which world the word, which of all things is the

him was not anything made that was made. | most divine, framed and set in order. And Philo calls him, the Instrument by whom God made the world (*On the Cherubim*).

John 1:4. In him was Life. | Jew and Gentile affirm that their Word is the *to on*, the Being, the Existence, and that this Being is not a dead Being, that is (Plotin, *Enn.* 1.5.c.2) neither Life nor Mind, but is Life, and Mind, and Being itself.

John 1:4. And the Life was the Light of men. | So they affirm that the Life of their Word was Knowledge and Understanding (Plotin, *Enn.* 1.3.c.5), neither is this Mind or Word *in potentia*, neither is itself one thing, and its Knowledge another, but its Knowledge is itself, or its own Being.

John 1:9. The true light, which gives light to everyone, was coming into the world. | So they, Jews and Gentiles say, that intelligible Light proceeded from the Word (Philo, *On the Creation of the World*), and that all Light is from this Word or Wisdom (Aristob. in Euseb. *Preparation for the Gospel*).

John 1:14. The Word … the only begotten of the Father. | The Jews and Gentiles style their Word the Son of God (Plotin, *Enn.* 5.1.8.c.5); and again the Son or child of God, the full beautiful Mind, even the Mind that is full of God (Philo, *l. de perfectiore*); as also the most ancient Son of the Father of the universe (Philo, ibid.), and the first-born Son of God (Philo, *de agricult.* 1.1).

John 1:18. The only begotten Son. |

Thus, you see St. John speaks of Christ in such a manner, as both Jews and Gentiles might understand of whom he spoke, namely of a divine Person, a divine Subsistence. The Apostles, when they preached Christ to the Jews and Gentiles, used such words as were known to them and understood by them. They coined no new ones, nor did they put new constructions upon them unknown to the world before. They spoke in the plainest and most intelligible manner and made use of such words as Jews and Gentiles had used before, that both Jews and Gentiles might understand them.

When, therefore, St. John speaks of his Word, and in the same phrase and language gives the same account of him as the Jewish and Gentile divines did of theirs, he must be taken to mean the same thing, namely that the Word is a divine eternal Person. How else would anyone take him? For he who speaks or writes in common phrases must use those words according to the common meaning of those words and phrases. If he does not, he must be a most notorious juggler and hypocrite.

Thus, if St. John wrote sincerely what he thought of Christ, every man who reads him and understands his words must believe that that Christ is a divine Person, and that he is the Savior. That John was so understood by Amelius (3rd cent), a pagan philosopher (who understood the language and doctrine of the Gentile schools very well concerning the divine

Word so often mentioned in their writings) appears; for he calls his eyes upon the text of St. John, and then does with all confidence affirm that this was that Word, who, according to Heraclitus (500 BC), existed from eternity, and made all things, and whom, by Jupiter, the Barbarian (meaning the Evangelist) places in the order and dignity of a Principal, declaring him to have been with God, and to be God, and that all things were made by him, and that in him all things that were had life and being (Euseb. *Prep. Gospel*).

And now having proved at large that this Memra, this Logos, this Word is a divine Person, is the Messiah, is the Son of God, the eternal God which is the great hinge upon which this whole Discourse turns; I proceed to assert that it is certain from Moses that God appeared to several of the Patriarchs, which must necessarily therefore be this Memra, the Word of God. And this is what the Christian Fathers assert, that Christ the Son of God made several appearances to the ancient Patriarchs, in the assumption of human bodies, which were momentary assumptions only, and figurative of the perfect and lasting union of the divine Nature of the Son of God with Humanity.[234]

---

[234] De Gols seems to cite Leo the Great here (Ep. 27. Ad Pulcher c.2). I think there is much reason to disagree that the body was either human (it was angelic) or temporary (it went back up to heaven, a real and permanent place where the Angel was worshiped as God in the heavenly throne-room; see Isaiah 6:1).

Our Saviour, telling the Jews that *they had not heard the Father's voice at any time, nor seen his shape or appearance* (John 5:37), is full proof that that divine Person who appeared and spoke to the patriarchs in a human voice or shape was not God the Father. Yet, it is as positively said that Moses, and Aaron, and the elders of the Jews, and several others saw God. It necessarily follows that the God who appeared to them was the Second Person, distinct from the Father, and yet the self-same God. And this is Jesus, whose name is called the Word of God (Rev 19:13).

CHAP. VIII.

CHRIST WORSHIPED BY THE PATRI-
ARCHS FROM ADAM TO MOSES

I come now to the facts, and these I shall take leave to divide into three great epochs.

First, the age of the Patriarchs, from Adam to Moses. Second, the epoch of the Mosaic dispensation from Moses to Christ. Third, the great epoch of the Gospel from Christ to this day.

In all these periods of time Jesus Christ has been adored as God, and worshiped with the Father, and the Holy Spirit, as the one only true and supreme God.

First, The Age of the Patriarchs.

Eusebius asserts that all the Patriarchs were the Christians of the old world, who had the same faith, religion, worship, and the same Name of Christians too. This he endeavors to prove from Psalm 105:15, *Touch not my anointed (tōn Christōn mou) my Christians,* or *my Christs* (Eus. *Prep. Gospel* 1.4.9). But more particularly,

Adam worshiped Christ as God.

It is generally agreed among Divines, that Adam in the state of perfection knew God in Trinity and

Unity.[235] Epiphanius (*Panario*) is most positive in this point. He says Adam was not an idolater, for he knew the Father God, and the Son, and the Holy Ghost; for he was a prophet, and knew that the Father had said to the Son, *Let US make Man*. The same Epiphanius carries that matter a great deal higher and says that Adam, even in the state of perfection, was a Christian, having the form of Christianity, for he was not circumcised; neither was he an idolater, but had the form of Christianity. And Jerome Zanchi (*de creat* 1.1.c.1§12) thinks it very injurious to Adam to believe that he had not as great favor shown him before the Fall as Abraham, Moses, and others had since the Fall. He thus asserts that Adam was sure of the beloved of God, because Jehovah the Son exhibited himself visibly to him, and talked with him, and made himself known to him as his God and Governor before he gave him the precepts of obedience, as he did to the Jews before he gave the Law to Moses. He tells us that several of the ancients (Justin, Irenaeus, Tertullian, and many more) were of that mind that it was Jehovah the Son who created Adam, placed him in Paradise, appeared visibly to him, discoursed with him, and whose voice he heard, and at which he trembled when he had transgressed.

---

[235] Johanni Markii, *Compendium Theol. Christianæ* (C. 1. § 16); Herman Witsius, *The Economy of the Covenants between God and Man: Comprehending a Complete Body of Divinity*, I.2.5.

If, therefore, Adam was so well acquainted with the Son of God before his fall and knew and feared him after he had fallen, there is no doubt but he very well understood the gracious promise of Genesis 3:15, namely that by the promised Seed the same God, Jehovah the Son, would restore him and his offspring from that misery they had brought upon themselves. Because Eve had been first in the transgression, he would restore them by the *Seed of the Woman.*

This promise was the first Gospel, the only Article of Faith that the Serpent's head by whom they fell should be bruised by the Seed of the Woman. It was a promise. It was the first promise. As a promise, it was made *in Christ, in whom all the promises are Yes and Amen* (2Co 1:20).

The Jews in their Targums acknowledge that the Seed of the woman is the Messiah. So we find it in the Jerusalem Targum: "And it shall be when the Children of the Woman shall study the Law, and perform the commandments, that they shall be ready to strike you (O Serpent) upon the Head, and kill you, but when the children of the woman shall forsake the commands of the Lord, and not perform the statutes, you shalt be ready to bite them upon the heels, and hurt them. But there shall be a remedy for the children of the woman. But for you, O Serpent, there shall be no remedy. But the time shall come that they shall from one to another apply remedies to their heels, at the end of the extremity of days, in the days of King Messiah."

In Jonathan's Targum, "And they will have a remedy for their heels in the days of the Messiah."

It is evident that mother Eve herself understood that that Seed of the woman was to be God; for being so forward as to think that the restoration from the fall was to be performed presently by her first-born, she cried out immediately upon the birth of her first child, *I have gotten that Man which is Jehovah the Lord*, or else, *I have gotten that man from the Lord, who was promised to be the Deliverer.*

Why our version reads it, *I have gotten a man from the Lord*, when the words will bear, and ought to bear the other construction,[236] I doubt not. For there is no doubt, as Dr. Lightfoot observes, but Eve had regard to the promise of a Saviour, and therefore said she had obtained that man the Jehovah (*ish et-yhwh*; *ton anthrōpon ton kurion*), that God, that Jehovah, which should become man.[237] The Chaldee paraphrase of Jonathan reads that verse this way, "And Adam knew Eve his wife, who exceedingly longed for that Angel (who was to restore them to happiness) and she conceived and bore Cain, and said, 'I have gotten that

---

[236] He cites a work from the Reformer Paul Fagius (1504-49), *Commentary on Genesis 4*.

[237] John Lightfoot, *A Commentary on the New Testament from the Talmud and Hebraica, Matthew-1 Corinthians, Acts-1 Corinthians*, vol. 4 (Bellingham, WA: Logos Bible Software, 2010), 275.

Man that is the Angel of Jehovah'" (TGen 4:1). And an ancient Belgic, "I have obtained that man of the Lord." And in the annotations has this paraphrase, that is, "Blessed be God, here I have the Lord, the Man, that Seed, who shall bruise the Head of Satan, or the Serpent, he shall perform it."[238]

This is certain however, that mother Eve made a very singular confession of the person of the Messiah, that she looked for him as the *Theanthropos*—God and man. She declares him a man when she calls him *ish*, a man; not Adam, but *virum*, to signify his excellency. For those words differ, Adam-man signifying the weakness of human nature, but *ish*-man signifying the excellency of human nature. She professes his divine nature when she calls him Jehovah. That those natures were to be united in one person, the Redeemer, when she joins these two *ish et-yhwh*, *the man that is the Lord*; which St. Paul expresses by *Theon ephanerōthē en sarki* (1Ti 3:16).[239]

It is very remarkable that Adam did not call his wife *Chava*, or Eve, the mother of all livings until after he had received the promise of the Messiah. Before this, he called her *Ishah*, Woman. But when God had assured him of a Saviour, a Deliverer, then he calls her Eve, or Life, for so the LXX rendered it, *kai ekalesen Adam to onoma tes gunaikos autou Zōē* (Gen 3:20). And

---

[238] He cites the *biblia Belgic*, 1581 at Delft, annot. In c. iv. 1 and older Belgicc versions of 1559 and 1562 read the same way.
[239] See Witsius, *Economy* 2.4.19.

why so? Why must she be called Life, who was in the Introducer of Death? The reason is because Adam knew that in the promised Seed, the "last Adam" (*eschatos Adam*) was included and signified; and that he should be "quickening Spirit" (*pneuma zōopoioun*), as St. Paul calls Christ (1Co 15:45), that he should introduce a better life; thus he is also called Life (John 1:4).[240]

Cain and Abel worshiped Christ as God.

That Cain and Abel believed that same gospel or promise of a Saviour cannot be doubted; for upon faith in the Seed of the woman, the man Jehovah (as their mother had explained it), they both offered their sacrifices to God.

The word sacrifice, though it has often been used for all the duties of divine worship, yet seems here to relate to that external form of worship which is called "expiation" (*hilasmos*), which they offered to God in all probability in order to obtain pardon for their parents transgression, and the release of that misery which their sin had brought upon them and their offspring.

And though we do not find when God was first pleased to institute these sacrificial rites, yet it is piously believed they were of his own appointment,[241] because of his acceptance and confirmation, and

---

[240] Lightfoot, ibid., and Witsius, ibid.
[241] Dr. Heylin *on the Creed*, p. 93.

because he afterwards instituted them by most positive precepts. And no doubt but these very first sacrifices, as they were offered up to God with a view to the promised Seed, the Man-Jehovah, were figures of that one only real and propitiatory sacrifice of Christ, who, through the eternal Spirit, was to offer up himself without spot to God for the redemption of the world (Heb 9:14). For these sacrificial rites had no propitiatory power in them by themselves, of their own nature, but only by virtue of the divine institution, by the ordinance of Almighty God, and by the relation they had to the Messiah the Saviour. Such is should not be doubted were the sacrifices of Cain and Abel, and therefore as such offered to the Son of God as believing in him as the promised Seed—the Man-Jehovah.

Though it may be said that Cain's offering seemed rather to be a "Sacrifice of Thanksgiving" (*eucharistia*), which he offered to God as a quit-rent,[242] in testimony that he held his estate from him as the supreme Landlord, and that Abel's seemed only expiatory; I shall only answer that we know so little of that matter that all we can say is but conjecture. But it is

---

[242] Effectively but not formally a tax or land tax imposed on freehold or leased land by a higher landowning authority, usually a government or its assigns. Under feudal law, the payment of quit rent freed the tenant of a holding from the obligation to perform such other services as were obligatory under feudal tenure or freed the occupier of the land from the burden of having others use their own distinct rights that affected the land.

plain that Cain's offering was not accepted, and this was not from any mistake in the object of his worship, nor in the subject of his oblation, but through the default of his own heart; and St. Paul I think tells us that his faith was not so strong as Abel's (Heb 11:4). "*By faith Abel offered to God a more excellent sacrifice than Cain,*" so that Cain's crime was unbelief. Of what? Of the promised Seed of the Man-Jehovah, the Redeemer, of Christ, as the Apostle there recommends from the happy examples of the elders. And if St. Paul is a good expositor of the Faith of the elders, as he undoubtedly is, then according to him they believed in, and offered to Jesus Christ, and of faith in him: and if we continue in that faith, it will produce the same happy effects in us as it did in the worthies mentioned in the 11th Chapter, who believed in Christ Jesus, and by that faith received the testimony that they pleased God. That they all believed in Christ, is sure from that instance of Moses, of whom it is said expressly that he believed in Christ (vs. 26). "*He considered the reproach of Christ greater wealth than the treasures of Egypt, for he was looking to the reward.*"

That they both believed a Savior to come seems to be plain from Gen 4:7. "*If you do well, will you not be accepted? And if you do not do well, sin is crouching at the door.*" You must observe that the original word "sin" can also signify an expiation for sin, so that the verse will bear this reading: "*If you do not do well, then not only the sin itself, not only the guilt and punishment, but also the expiation for sin, the sacrifice of propitiation, lies ready at the door: for if you do well, you may be sure of being rewarded, but if you do otherwise you ought not to despair of being forgiven, nor be terribly dejected, because the mercy of God is greater than your sin; and for your countenance to fall is not right, seeing that the atonement is ready by faith as the Lamb of God is represented in the sacrifice of Abel, which is a most acceptable sin-offering.*" For the design of this text is evidently the silencing and quieting of the spirit criminally agitated by violent commotions.[243]

The paraphrase of Onkelos proves what we have just said. "*If you will do well, shall you not be pardoned? But if you will not do well, shall not your sin be reserved against the Day of Judgment, when it shall be revenged upon you, if you will not be converted? Whereas if you will be converted, it shall be forgiven you.*" In a word, that the only true God and the promised Seed was the object of religious worship is certain. For idolatry was not established until long after, according to the Jews, who expound the 26th verse of this chapter, "*Then men began to call on the Name of the Lord,*" or, as our margin has it, to call themselves by the Name of the Lord, that is, in distinction from idolatry, which then received its first

---

[243] De Gols cites Samuel Parker (1681-1730), *Bibliotheca Biblica: Being A Commentary Upon All the Books of the Old and New Testament Gathered Out of the Genuine Writings of the Fathers and Ecclesiastical Historians, and Acts of Councils, Down to the year of our Lord 451* (Oxford: William and John Innys, 1720). The citations in what follows are from Volume 1: Genesis (Part I). See Gen 4:7, p. 160.

establishment, and which was, according to Mr. Perkins, *Anno Mundi* 235, more than 200 years after.

Enoch worshiped Christ as God.

That Enoch knew and worshiped Christ as God, is not only probable, as being a descendent from ancestors noted for being truly religious, but is very certain from Gen 5:24 where he has this grand character given him, *"and Enoch walked with God;"* that is, as the Targum of Jonathan explains that verse, "Enoch worshiped in truth before the Lord, and behold he is not numbered among the generations of the earth, for he was taken away from it, and ascended into heaven by the Word before the Lord." And the Jerusalem Targum says, "Enoch worshiped before the Lord in the Truth, and thus he was not! because he was translated by the Word of the Presence of the Lord."

An ancient Targumist (Pseudo-Jonathan) further says, "Enoch, ascended into Heaven by the Word of the Lord, and his Name is called Metatron, the great scribe." This is to say that he, being translated from the earth, by the power of the eternal Word and Son of God, has thereupon become a ministering spirit to the spirits of the prophets, and a great angelical prince under him in that order. According to this, the name of the angel who took him up at the command of the Lord should be Metatron, which is the Name commonly given by the learned Jews to the Angel of the Shekinah itself, when written with a yod.[244]

From these expositions of the Jews we may be very sure that Enoch not only believed in the promised Seed, the Man Jehovah, but worshiped him as Jehovah. And if their authority is not sufficient, I am very sure St. Paul's is, who numbers him among those heroes who were famous for their faith in Christ (Heb 11:5), and St. Jude the Apostle mentions this very man as a prophet of Christ, who spoke of Christ, and foretold his Coming to Judgment, *"Behold, the Lord comes with ten thousands of his holy ones, to execute judgment"* (Jude 1:14-15); which can pertain to no one but Christ, as that expression "the Lord comes," is frequently used concerning Christ, as we see in 1Th 4:15, 16 and elsewhere. Concerning that prophecy, I shall only observe that Drusius[245] says that it is to this day extant among the Ethiopians in the Abyssine language; but whether different from that which St. Augustine (*City of God* 15.23) has long since pronounced not genuine, I cannot say.[246]

---

[244] *Biblioth. Biblica*, Occasion. Annot. 11. P. 187.

[245] Johannes Drusius (1550-1616). Dutch scholar, Orientalist, Christian Hebraist and exegete. While De Gols does not cite a book, it is probable it comes from *Henoch; sive, De Patriarcha Henoch* (1612).

[246] While Drusius and others such as Nicolas-Claude Fabri de Peiresc (1580-1637) were speculating about the existence of what we now call 1 Enoch, it was not until 1773, 50 years after De Gols writes *A Vindication*, when James Bruce brought three Ethiopian copies of the book back to England, that it was confirmed that Jude was in fact quoting from 1 Enoch 1:9. As the writing of 1 Enoch clearly dates to

I shall only observe that St. Paul, when he speaks of Enoch, says that he had this testimony that he pleased God; wherein he followed not the original Hebrew, but the LXX translation, which has rendered, "*And Enoch walked with God,* by "Enoch pleased God" (*euērestēsen de Enoch tō Theō*); and the Syriac in the same manner, "he pleased God," which indeed is tantamount, because he could not please God without walking with God, and he could not walk with God without pleasing him. The LXX has rendered the same expression concerning Noah in the same words (Gen 6:9), so though the original has not the word of pleasing God, yet the sense is the same, the one being the exposition of the other, namely, that to walk with God is to please God.

Noah worshiped Christ as God.

That Noah worshiped God and lived in a pious obedience to the will of God is certain from that extraordinary character given him (Gen 6:9). "*Noah was a just man, and perfect in his generations, and Noah walked with God;*" which last is the same expression used of Enoch (Gen 5:24) and is explained in Gen 7:1, "*I have seen that you are righteous before me in this generation.*" That he knew and worshiped the Son of God is as plain, because the God that spoke to Noah is called the

the time before the NT and the Epistle of Jude was written, De Gols' argument is strengthened that Enoch in fact spoke of the Messiah.

Lord, the Jehovah (7:1), that Person of the sacred Trinity by whom all revelations were made and communications held with mankind. He is by the Targums called the "*Word of the Lord.*" This is confirmed by St. Paul, who numbers this great man among the ancient heroes, who are recorded for their faith in Christ the Son of God (Heb 11:7), and is further confirmed in that the very flood was an act of judgment executed by the Son of God, because all judgment is given to the Son.[247] St. Peter also tells us expressly that Christ preached repentance to the world in the days of Noah, while the Ark was preparing (1Pe 3:19-20; 2Pe 2:5), and that Noah was his servant and minister who is therefore, by St. Peter, called the preacher of righteousness. And when it is said, "*The Lord shut Noah in the Ark*" (Gen 7:16), this was the act and deed of the Son of God.[248] And at his delivery he built an altar to the LORD, to the Word of the LORD, in thanksgiving for his redemption, the figure and pledge of a far greater (1Pe 3:20).

The ancient Jews have a tradition that in the ark there was a "place of prayer," where there was an appearance of the Glory of the LORD, the divine Shekinah, which is the Son of God, as I shall now unfold for you. Before this Glory, Noah daily offered up prayers and intercessions. And the said tradition

---

[247] Hilary, Psalm 63, col. 160.
[248] Tertullian, *Against Praxeas* 16.

further adds that this chapel was at or about the center of the Ark, and that the body of Adam, enclosed in a shrine which had been preserved and handed down from father to son, was placed in this very chapel in the Ark at the very place where the Glory of God appeared. Every morning at day-break, as uncovered by the Zohar, or heavenly Light that was in the Ark,[249] Noah stood up towards the body of Adam and before the Lord, and the Shekinah appeared over it, and he and his sons made this prayer:

> O Lord, you are excellent in your truth and there is nothing great in comparison to you. Look upon us with the eye of mercy and compassion. Deliver us from this deluge of waters and set our feet in a larger room. By the sorrows of Adam, your first-made man; by the blood of Abel, your holy one; by the righteousness of Seth, in whom you are well pleased, number us not among those who have transgressed your statutes. But take us into your merciful care, for you are our Deliverer and to you is the praise for all the works of your hands forevermore.

And then all the sons of Noah cried, "Amen, Lord."[250]

Whatever may be thought of this prayer, the truth of the tradition seems liable to no objection, namely,

---

[249] *Biblioth. Bibl.* Occasion. Annot. 11. P. 202 in Gen.
[250] Mr. John Gregory's Notes on Heb 12:23.

That the sanctuary of God was within the Ark, and that Noah officiated as High-Priest from inside, making atonement by the blood of Christ, prefigured by that of Abel; and at the same time representing the miserable state of fallen man in Adam, and the happy deliverance out of it by the righteousness of that true Seth, or substitute, in whom God is well-pleased.

And so the Ark is to be considered as a consecrated place of worship of which the center was the body of the first Adam, overshadowed by the Glory of the body of the Second Adam. Thus, from the sacredness of the Ark and the appearance there of the Shekinah,[251] and the manner of Noah's worshiping, the Ark was anciently called *Haical*, the temple, or the church of God.

But further, that Noah worshiped the Son of God, is plain from the covenant of God with Noah after the Flood. For when God gave him a visible token of that covenant, not to destroy the world again by water, it is expressed, "*The covenant which I make between me and you ... between me and the earth*" (Gen 11:12-13). Now the Targums will tell us who the Person covenanting with Noah and the earth was, for they all unanimously interpret "between my Word and you," and "between my Word and the earth;" as if the divine Logos, or Christ, was made a party in the

---

[251] *Biblioth. Biblic.* Annot. on Gen 14, p. 241.

covenant. This is repeated no less than four times in vv. 15-16 from which it is eminently manifest that Noah worshiped Christ as God.

Melchizedek worshiped Christ as God.

That Melchizedek worshiped Christ as God, I think is beyond all doubt; for he was both a type of Christ and priest to Christ the Son of God. In Genesis 14:18 he is called "the priest of the Most High God," and in vs. 19 in his benediction he invokes the Most High God, possessor of heaven and earth. In this he invokes the holy Trinity, the great God essentially taken, and there is no doubt but Melchizedek knew God as such. But it is very likely that this man had received some peculiar revelation whereby he was appointed a priest to the Most High God, and that must be the Son, by whom all revelations were made. This is doubtless the reason. Hilary says this Most High God is our Lord Jesus Christ,"[252] Epiphanius says, the first person we find officiating in the priesthood of uncircumcision was Abel, the second was Noah, and the third was Melchizedek,[253] and as a priest, St. Paul largely speaks of him as the type of Christ (Heb 7:1ff). It would be very strange for him to be a type of Christ and at the same time a priest of a god different from Christ, and that the Most High God is the title of

---

[252] Hilary, *On the Trinity* 12.4.
[253] Epiphanius, *Against Melchizedekians* 55.3.1.

Christ, we have seen before. Though we know but little of this great man, and what is said of him beside what we find in the Scriptures, is conjecture only. We find from what is said of him that the Christian Fathers have believed him to have known and worshiped Christ as his priest,[254] and declared Christ to the Gentiles. For so Epiphanius,[255] and Gregory Nazianzen. "This Melchizedek was king, as well as priest, among the Gentiles; in which several capacities he was the type and representative of Christ, that great archetypal King and Priest, who offered himself a sacrifice for all mankind."[256]

I am not ignorant that several of the ancients[257] and moderns[258] are of opinion that this Melchizedek was not a man, but the Lord Jesus Christ himself, who appeared to Abraham in the way, and blessed him as the priest of the Most High God, the great Messenger (Angel) of Peace; and that thereupon Abraham offered to him tithes; and that both were figures, one of Christ's future office, the other of the Churches future submission and obedience; and that this priest offered bread and wine, a type of the Eucharist, to repast (a meal) the whole Christian Church,[259] as he did Abraham's army here. But this is beside my present purpose.

---

[254] Augustine, *City of God* 17.5.5.
[255] Epiphanius, *Against Melchizedekians* 55.3.1.
[256] Gregory Nazianzen, *Oration* 36.
[257] Ravanel. Bibliothec. Ver. Zelchiz. Suiceri Thesaur. Ver. Melchiz.
[258] Cunaei Rep. Hebr. 1.2.c.3. See Spanheim tom. 2. P. 189. Fol.
[259] *Biblioth. Bib*. In Gen 14:18. P. 348.

Abraham worshiped Christ as God.

I come now to that great instance of faith and piety, the father of the faithful, Abraham, of whom St. Paul gives a very large account both of his heroic faith and heroic obedience—his faith in Christ and his obedience to Christ (Heb 11:8-19).

That Abraham both knew and worshiped the Son of God, we shall find as clear as the day from the following particulars.

In Genesis 12:1 and 7 we find that the Lord appeared to Abram. This appearance language is the first that we read of where God is said to have explicitly made himself visible to any man, for it never unambiguously says he conversed visibly with Adam, Abel, Noah, or any other. That this Lord was Christ is not only asserted by the Christian writers,[260] but by the Jews themselves, who own that all the appearances of God were made by the (*mmr'*) Memra, the Word of the LORD, who is the Logos, the Son of God.

Thus, we find that, "*After these things the word of the LORD came to Abram in a vision: 'Fear not, Abram, I am your shield; your reward shall be very great'*" (Gen 15:1).[261] This is the first time that this expression of

---

[260] Tertullian, *Against Marcion*; *Against Praxeas*. Eusebius, *Demonstration of the Gospel*, and many others.

[261] De Gols inexplicably deletes the vital words, "in a vision," which is found in the KJV and all older English translations as well as the Hebrew and Greek. This surely would have bolstered his point even further, given that the Word is here expressly visible to the eye.

the Word of the Lord is found in Scripture; and if one text may explain another, as is agreed by all men, then it appears from John 1:1 that this Word of the Lord was Christ. And this is further explained in vs. 6 where it is said, "*He believed in the Lord, and it was counted to him as righteousness.*" What did he believe? Was his faith only concerning the number of his offspring or concerning the Messiah, "*That in your all the families of the earth shall be blessed*" (Gen 11:3)? If St. Paul understood it right, as he most certainly did, he tells us that this faith principally related to Christ. He believed indeed that God was able to make his offspring as numerous as the stars in the heavens (Rom 4:19), but he principally believed the promise of God, that the Savior, the Messiah, who is Christ, should be of his Seed (Gal 3:16) and was justified by his faith in the Savior.[262]

This is the second degree of the revelation of Christ. Thus far, the faithful only had the promise of the Seed of the woman to rely upon, but of whom that Seed was to come, or by what family, was yet a secret. But now God revealed to Abraham that it should be in his seed, and St. Paul says directly that this Seed was Christ (Gal 3:16).

To confirm that promise, God gave him the sacrament of circumcision, and promised to be his God and protector in this life and his Savior in the life to

---

[262] Irenaeus, *Against Heresies.*

come. For that sacrament was the seal of the covenant of God in Christ, and of Abraham's faith in Christ, as the Redeemer, for the gospel was preached to Abraham (Gal 3:8, 16-17) and the covenant was confirmed to Abraham in Christ (17).

Again, we find that Abraham worshiped the Son of God as God, and called him Lord and Judge of all the earth, in his intercession for Sodom (Gen 18:25).

From the account given us in that chapter, it is plain that the Lord appeared to Abraham, and that Abraham prayed to him and worshiped him. But how? With a civil worship? No, with a religious adoration, for he worshiped him as God, and as Lord of the whole earth. "For in this narration he is called God and Lord, which is a style," says Eusebius,[263] "too high for any angelical power, and therefore was the Logos, the Son of God, whom he adored." And Justin Martyr[264] proves largely against the Jews that the person who here appeared to Abraham was God the Son. And the Fathers of the Council of Antioch[265] in their excellent Epistle against Paul of Samosata, express themselves so fully and strongly, and yet so comprehensively upon this and the corresponding passages of the patriarchal history, that their argumentation deserves to appear in all its force.

---

[263] Eusebius, *Demonstration of the Gospel* 1.5.c.9.
[264] Justin, *Dialogue with Trypho*.
[265] De Gols refers to the Letter of Six Bishops in 268 AD. We have translated the entire letter in our book on the Angel of the LORD.

This Son of God, personally distinct from the Father, appeared to Abraham at the Oak of Mamre; he was that one of the three in human shape, with whom the Patriarch discoursed, *as with the universal Lord and Judge (hōs Kyriō kai kritē)*. He was the Lord that rained fire and brimstone upon Sodom and Gomorrah from the Lord out of Heaven; he was his holy Father's agent in his communications with the Patriarchs, and is the same Person under the several denominations of the Angel, of the divine counsel, of the Lord, and of God. Now certainly it must argue rank impiety and irreligion, to think that Moses would have called any angelic power "the God of the universe," of the whole creation; and yet he that is this LORD and God, is both the Son and the Angel, or Administrator of the Father.

If we compare this account of Moses with John 8:56 it will appear from Christ's own words that Abraham both saw him and worshiped him too.

That verse reads, "*Your father Abraham rejoiced to see my day. He saw it and was glad.*" Now the seeing of Christ's day must necessarily signify his real, actual, and proper sight of Christ himself; and so the Jews understood it, "*You are not yet fifty years old, and you have seen Abraham?*" (57) who has been dead many ages. And that they did understand Christ right is evident, because otherwise Christ would have corrected them, had they mistook or misapprehended him. But Christ allows their sense, and approves of their interpretation, and answers them in the same sense they put it to him by saying, "*Truly, truly, I say to you, before Abraham was, I am*" (John 8:58), thereby signifying his eternal existence. For I AM is one of the names of God, of his eternity, "*from everlasting to everlasting you are God*" (Ps 90:2). And so the text may be paraphrased, "It was no such difficult matter for Abraham to see my day, since I have a fixed, an eternal existence, and was in being before Abraham was born." And upon this foundation that the Council at Sirmium (351 A.D.), against Photinus, annexed this anathema to the creed,[266] "If any one shall affirm that it was not the Son which appeared to Abraham, but the ineffable Father, let him be accursed."

Further, we find that Abraham worshiped the Lord Christ as God and obeyed him as such in the sacrifice of his son Isaac.

We find when God tempted or tried Abraham's faith and obedience, he used the name of Elohim, which according to the Jewish doctors is the name of Judgment; but afterwards, when the sacrifice was accepted, the oblation was released by the Angel of the LORD (Gen 22:11-12). "*For the Angel of the LORD said, 'Do not lay your hand on the boy or do anything to him.'*" From this text St. Augustine proves that this

---

[266] Hilary, de Syn. col. 1176.

Angel was no creature, but God himself, the Son of God that accepted the intention and released the offering, for that God now appeared by the Name of Jehovah, which is the Name of Mercy, or of God covenanted with man; for which end the Angel or Messenger of the covenant is sent to preside over this great transaction (and to see it performed, and by substitution to redeem the sacrifice) who is called the Angel of the Lord.[267]

And that this Angel of the LORD was the Son of God is not only the exposition of the Christians,[268] but must necessarily be, because we find that Angel expressing himself in these words, "*'By myself I have sworn,' says the LORD*" (Gen 22:16), which none can say but God. Or, as the Targums[269] read it, "By my Word have I sworn," which is therefore necessarily God. That same Angel (vs. 17-18) expresses his benediction to Abraham in his posterity, and to all nations of the earth by his posterity, because of Abraham's obedience to his voice, in terms so lofty, and assuming a power which none but the eternal God enjoys.

I shall only add that we find Abraham built an altar to the LORD, and that the LORD was an Angel, which shows that the Angel was the eternal God; for

---

[267] Augustine, *Questions on Genesis* 59.
[268] St. Cyprian, Against the Jews 1.ii. § 5; Letter of the Six; Cyril of Alexandria, *cont. Julian* 1.9. p. 293. Who renders it, "By myself have I sworn," i.e. "By my eternal Son, of one Essence with myself."
[269] Onkelos and Jonathan.

had Abraham not known him as such, he would never have built an altar to him, for that was the highest act of the most solemn adoration. Had this Angel not been God, he would no more have permitted that worship than the Angel which forbade Manoah (Jdg 13:16)[270] or the other which hindered St. John (Rev 22:9). I cannot refrain from saying that Abraham's faith in Christ was so singularly great that he is not only called the father of the faithful (Rom 4:11) whose faith and obedience is set before all the world for imitation, but that even heaven itself, the purchase of the blood of Christ, is called by the name of Abraham's Bosom (Luke 16:22), that Harbor of Rest and Place of Honor which all the saints of God shall enjoy who follow the faith and imitate the obedience of faithful Abraham.

It is beside my present purpose to explain the reason of that expression; but we may be very sure that the Lord Jesus would never have called the state of rest "Abraham's Bosom," had not Abraham believed in him and obeyed him as the God and Savior of the World.

I have purposely omitted the opinion that the three Persons of the Holy Trinity, Father, Son, and Holy Ghost, appeared to Abraham at Mamre, and

---

[270] It is not certain that De Gols' interpretation of this verse with Manoah says that the Angel did not permit the worship of him. It could easily be interpreted that the Angel was telling Manoah that he is the LORD and that it is to the LORD, that is him rather than a mere creature, that he should offer his offering. This is actually De Gols' point later on.

were known by him as such, and yet confronted by him in the singular number, and adored in the unity of the divinity by him; because though many of the ancients, and some moderns are of that opinion, it seems not to be very well grounded, but liable to some exceptions, notwithstanding it has been largely defended by a late learned writer.[271]

Further, I have omitted the opinion of Cunæus,[272] that Christ appeared to Abraham in the very self-same form, features, and countenance as he afterwards had when in the flesh; and that this should be approved by John 8:56 because it is singular and stands in need of confirmation.

Hagar worshiped Christ as God.

That Hagar was instructed in the true religion, in the knowledge of the Triunal God, and the covenant of grace, and the expectation of a Savior, there is no room to doubt, being of Abraham's family; especially if we consider what God himself says of Abraham. *"For I have chosen him, that he may command his children and his household after him to keep the way of the LORD"* (Gen 18:19).

I have nothing to do at present with her perhaps too easy readiness to comply with her mistress's desire to receive her master's embraces. Though, I freely

---

[271] Witsius, *Economy of the Divine Covenants* 4.3.4.

[272] Petrus Cunæus (Peter van der Kun, 1586-1638). Dutch Christian Rabbinical scholar at the University of Leyden. The work is *The Hebrew Republic* (Amsterdam, 1682), 1.3. c. 3. P. 414.

own, I do not understand that surrogation whereby several of the Christian Fathers have excused the ancient Patriarchs.[273] My business is Hagar's religion, and I may venture to say that she knew, believed, and adored the Son of God.

Genesis 16:7. We find that the Angel of the LORD appeared to Hagar. Who that Angel was we find in vs. 10. He is the one who blessed in his own name and by his own authority. Then, in vs. 13, "*She called the name of the LORD who spoke to her, 'You God see me.*"[274] Thus, it is certain that the Angel who spoke to her was God.

The Targumists say that Hagar prayed in the name of the LORD, saying, "*You are a God seeing all things, because she said, 'I have begun to see since he appeared to me;' therefore she called the well, The Well Over Which Appeared the Angel of Life.*"

The Jews will have it that God was inclined in like manner to manifest himself to Sarah, as to a prophetess, by virtue of the relation she bore to Abraham; and that for his sake, this Angel was also sent to Hagar. The Jerusalem paraphrast describes this fully, "And Hagar gave thanks and prayed in the name of the Word of the LORD, who had appeared to her, saying, 'Blessed be you, O God, who are the enlivener of all worlds, in

---

[273] *Biblioth. Bib.* In Gen Occas. Annot. 33. Tecnopoeia, p. 649.
[274] This is my modern rendition of the KJV. Most translations say something like, "You are a God of seeing." The KJV makes De Gols' point a little more strongly.

that you have had regard to my affliction, for behold now to me also has God appeared after the same manner he was pleased to manifest himself to Sarah my lady." But Jonathan supposes that the very Shekinah, the Person of the Son of God, did appear to her; wherefore according to him, she gave thanks before the LORD whose Word has spoken to her, and spoke, "You are he who lives and makes alive, who beholds and are not beheld; for behold, here was the Glory of the Shekinah of the LORD revealed."

Lot worshiped Christ as God.

That Lot knew and worshiped Christ as God, I think is plain from the history of his deliverance from the judgment of Sodom.

For although we find that two angels came to him (Gen 19:1), which are expressly so called to let us know their natures, yet is seems from vs. 19 that the LORD, the Memra, the Logos, the Word had come to them. For there we find Lot praying to him. He confesses himself his servant and magnifies his mercy for sparing his life, which not the angel but God himself had spared. In vs. 21 the Angel says, *"I have accepted you,"* which no angel could say nor would have the power to do. And it is plain from vs. 24 that the LORD executed the judgment *"from the LORD out of heaven."* This proves that we have one LORD in Person distinct from the other LORD. Justin Martyr, St. Cyprian,[275] and others of the ancients assert that the LORD who executed this vengeance was God the Son, for all judgment was given to him by the Father (John 5:22).

Isaac worshiped Christ as God.

That Isaac worshiped Christ the Son of God as God is not only probable because he worshiped the God of his father Abraham, but it further appears from Genesis 26:2. Where *"The LORD appeared to Isaac"* and said, *"I will be with you,"* the Targums have rendered it, "My Word shall be with you, and be your defense."

This was the first time that God appeared to Isaac. That it was the Shekinah, the visible appearance of the Son of God, is plain from vv. 24-25 where we find that the LORD appeared to him a second time, and that Isaac built an altar there and called upon the Name of the Lord, or according to the Targums, he called upon the Word of the LORD. There, Isaac was installed in all the privileges of his father Abraham, in the special rights of the *segullah* (possession) and She-kinah (glory). And it is remarkable that this manifestation of God to Isaac was made in the same place which had been so solemnly dedicated to the Name of

---

[275] Justin Martyr, *Dialogue* 127; Cyprian, *Against the Jews* 3.33. See also Eusebius, *Ecclesiastical History* 1.2.9; Cyril of Alexandria, *Comments on 1Jn 1:2*; Tertullian, *Against Praxeas* 13; and many others.

the LORD, the Everlasting God (Gen 31:33). When he blessed his son Jacob, he called upon God by the Name of God Almighty (28:3), El Shaddai, the All-Sufficient; which is the same name (17:1) in which the covenant of grace was erected, and therefore has relation to the Son. Thus, the LXX has emphatically rendered it the God in covenant with me (*ha Theos mou*).

Jacob worshiped Christ as God.

That Jacob worshiped the Lord Christ appears from Genesis 28:12ff. where the ladder, the scale of providence, is described. In vs. 13 it said that the LORD stood above it, and said, "*I am the LORD God.*"

I purpose not to talk tediously at length upon this vision, but shall only observe that the Targums interpret this by the Glory of the LORD, which is none other than Christ, the Glory and Image of the invisible Father, or the Shekinah of the divine Word and Wisdom with an angelical retinue. "Neither may this unfitly be said to be a prefiguration of the deity uniting with the human nature; for this is still the same Angel, and God, and LORD, even the Lord Jesus Christ, whom Abraham beheld with a human shape—who stood above the mystic ladder, and with whom Jacob wrestled.[276] That this ladder was a symbol of

---

[276] Justin Martyr, *Dialogue* 58 in *Bibliotheca Biblica* on Gen 28:12 (p. 598).

Christ, Christ himself gave Nathanael to understand (John 1:51).

Further, we find that when God told Jacob to return to Bethel (Gen 31), that the Angel said, "*I am the God of Bethel*" (vs. 13). Novatius has these words, "If no Angel could be so presumptuous as to call himself God and to mention a vow made to him, then it is plain that this is Christ the Son of God, the great Angel."[277] And the ancient rabbis believed that the man who wrestled with Jacob was the Christ (Messiah), the Son of God.[278] And indeed, the several parts of the history compared together demonstrate that the Person who here appeared to and encountered Jacob was the only begotten Son of God, God of God, very God of God.[279] And the creed of the Sirmian Council (351 AD), against Photinus, has this anathema added to it, "If any one shall affirm that it was the ineffable Father, or part or portion of him, and not the Son, that wrestled as a man with Jacob, let him be Anathema.[280] And Eusebius delivers himself very exactly on this place in these words,

> Jacob did not see God the Father, the God over all, for he never exhibits himself visibly. He never appears in one and another place or form. He

---

[277] Novatian, *On The Trinity* 19.
[278] Ainsworth *in loc.* Gen 28.
[279] Theodoret, Q. in Genesis 93.
[280] Hilary, *On the Synod.* Col. 1176.

never joins himself to a human body, or shape, being supreme in being above all being. It was therefore another whom he saw. But if one now conceives that this "other" was a created angel, or any of those divine spirits in heaven who convey God's revelations to our senses, he is manifestly mistaken; for the Scripture expressly ascribes to him the style of "Lord" and "God;" even giving him that most sacred and peculiar designation of the four Letters [YHWH] which among the Jews denominate God himself.[281]

To put this matter beyond all doubt, the Holy Ghost has himself explained it by his prophet Hosea. *"In the womb he took his brother by the heel, and in his manhood he strove with God. He strove with the angel and prevailed; he wept and sought his favor. He met God at Bethel, and there God spoke with us—the LORD, the God of hosts, the LORD is his memorial Name"* (Hos 12:3-5).

Further, we find that God charged Jacob to go to Bethel (Gen 35:1) and there to erect an altar to the God who appeared to him when he fled from his brother thirty years earlier.

This place is remarkable, and the ancients took notice of it. Hilary disputes with irresistible force against the Arians, "Here, says he, God speaks, and he of whom he speaks is God; the divine character is here equally ascribed to both in the community of the

---

[281] Eusebius, *Demonstration of the Gospel* 1.5.c.11.

Name, and the subsistencies of both are as clearly distinguished."[282] Further, Jacob speaks of *"God who fed me"* and *"the Angel who redeemed me,"* as if they were one (Gen 48:15-16). It would be the greatest violence to grammatical construction and common sense to make the Angel in this verse one person and God in the former another; both being one and the same, in the nominative case to the verb bless. Nor can the God here, who is also called by the Name of Angel, be God the Father. He must be Christ, for Christ may truly be called both God and God's Angel or Agent.

Lastly, we find Jacob crying out, *"I have waited for your salvation, O LORD"* (Gen 49:18). In the Hebrew *Yeshuah* ("Salvation") expresses the very name of this desired Savior. When we find that Jacob erected altars to that God, that Angel, we must conclude that this Angel was the very eternal God. And this is confirmed by the Targum of Jerusalem, which introduces Jacob speaking to the twelve tribes in these words,

> Do you worship the idols that Terah the Father of Abraham worshiped? Or do you worship the idols that Laban the brother of my mother worshiped? Or do you worship the God of Jacob? The twelve tribes answered together, with a perfect heart, and said, 'Hear now, O Israel our Father, the Lord our God is One God: Jacob

---

[282] Hilary, *On the Trinity* 1.4. § 30.

answered and said, 'Let his great Name be blessed forever." (TDt 6:4)

Joseph worshiped Christ as God.

That Joseph knew and worshiped the God of his fathers is most certain; and that he worshiped the Son of God, we are assured by the authority of St. Paul, who numbers him among the heroes who were famous for their faith in, and reliance on, Jesus Christ the Son of God (Heb 11:22). He lived in the fear of God and his Savior (Gen 39:9), for it is said, "*The LORD was with him*" (21), which the Chaldee paraphrast renders, "The Word of the LORD was with him." That he died in the faith of Christ, or the Messiah, St. Paul tells us, "*By faith Joseph, at the end of his life, made mention of the exodus of the Israelites and gave directions concerning his bones*" (Heb 11:22). By this he testified his entire reliance on the promises of God made to his fore-fathers, and his belief of a resurrection from the dead, and the true rest in the Land of Promise above, typified by that here below.

CHAP. IX.

CHRIST WORSHIPED AS THE SUPREME GOD UNDER THE MOSAIC DISPENSATION

I come now to the second great epoch,

the Mosaic dispensation from Moses to Christ.

Moses worshiped Christ as God.

I come now to the great prophet Moses and declare that he knew and adored the Son of God, Jesus Christ as God and as the Savior of the world.

That Moses wrote of Christ is expressly declared by Christ himself, both before his death (John 5:46) and after his resurrection (Luke 24:27). That Moses was a faithful servant of Christ, St. Paul tells us (Heb 3:5). And that he believed in Christ, the same Apostle assures us (Heb 11:26). That he was a friend of God, we find in Exodus 33:11, and the greatest of the prophets; for he told the Jews even then, that God would raise them up a Prophet from among their brothers like him (Dt 18:18). And that this Prophet was Christ, we are assured by no less authority than that of St. John (John 1:45), St. Peter (Acts 3:22), and St. Stephen (Acts 7:37).

That the Son of God, as the God of the covenant, appeared to Moses, as he had done to the Patriarchs before, is beyond all contradiction; and that Moses worshiped him as the true and eternal God, will appear as evident, if we consult the history recorded in Exodus. Concerning this history, I shall make this observation only, that the account of the Exodus of Israel, and God's receiving them for his peculium,[283] and giving them the Law, is a most important history. For it regards that article of the divinity of the Logos or Word, the great Actor in this sacred transaction, against which the powers of hell have always exerted their utmost arts and violence and shown their fiercest rage and malice.

For here, the Angel of the LORD is not called the Angel of Elohim, as in Exodus 14:19, but the Angel of Jehovah (LORD), pointing completely to the gracious dispensation of that time. The Hebrew may be rendered not "the Angel of the LORD," but "the Angel, the LORD," or "the Jehovah," where the Angel of the LORD may reasonably be thought to be the Logos or Word. That is, the Lord the Messiah revealing himself to Moses as the Savior of his people Israel at that time,

---

[283] This interesting word is well chosen and there are no direct synonyms for it in English. It refers to property that a father or master allowed his child or slave to hold as his own. In other words, by definition, the word implies that the Son has received Israel as his own in that it was given to him by the Father. Therefore, in this sentence, "God's receiving them" has to mean "Christ."

in the same way that he was pleased afterwards in the days of his flesh, namely at his transfiguration, to reveal himself to this same Moses as the Savior of the world (Matt 17:3).

But let us consider the Person that is the prime Actor and the Legislator in this great affair.

This we find in Exodus 3:2, where the Person is called the Angel of the LORD, which is God the Son. For at the 4th verse he is called God, and he is called Angel, because he is the Angel of the great council, the mighty God, even Jesus Christ.[284] The Targums read it the Word of the LORD. At the 6th verse, this Angel styles himself, "*The God of Abraham, the God of Isaac, and the God of Jacob*," and there it is also said that, "*Moses hid his face because he was afraid to look upon God*." In vs. 14 he says his name is I AM THAT I AM. All of this demonstrates clearly that this Angel was God, truly and properly God, and yet not the Father, because the Father can in no sense be denominated as an Angel.[285] This was therefore God the Son, for no man has seen the Father and lived.[286]

And God the Son calls himself the God of Abraham, Isaac, and Jacob to let Moses know that he was the very God whom those great Patriarchs worshiped, the God who made the covenant with them, and the God who promised to be the deliverer of Israel. And that the

---

[284] Justin Martyr, *Dialogue* 60.
[285] Justin Martyr, *First Apology* 63.
[286] Tertullian, *An Answer to the Jews* 9.22-25.

name, *I am that I am*, is the proper name of Christ, and given to Christ, I have not only showed before, but is further confirmed by that of Tertullian. We assert, he says, that all the names of a true and proper divinity are common to the Son with the Father and that the Son came in these names, that he acted in these names, and manifested himself to mankind in these names.[287] What moved Moses to ask God for another name, when he had called himself the God of his Fathers, is not our present business to enquire, but it is remarkable that the final letters of Moses question "… what is his Name" (*li mah shemo mah*; vs. 13),[288] make up the most holy and incommunicable Name (YHWH), Jehovah (LORD). And the rabbis have made no small use of it to prove that this Angel of the LORD was the Angel Jehovah, the Memra, the Word.[289]

Job worshiped Christ as God.

That Job, whoever he was, worshiped the true God is most certain, and in no wise to be doubted, if he was a descendent of Abraham by Keturah; and it appears most evident from the LORD's speaking and revealing himself to him, as we find in Job 33:15 and

---

[287] Tertullian, *Against Praxeas*, 17.
[288] De Gols is arguing here that the last letter of each word in Hebrew form the divine name (ה ו ה י).
[289] B. Bibl. In Exodus Occas. Annot II. P. 45.

especially 42:5 and also from his being mentioned with Noah and Daniel by the prophet Ezekiel (Ezek 14:14) as a man that knew and feared God.

Some of the ancient Fathers have asserted that Job was a priest of the Most High God, as Abel, Noah, and Melchizedek,[290] and others that he knew God in Trinity and Unity, because he frequently mentions the Spirit of God,[291] and that he knew the Son of God, and worshiped him as such, is to me as plain as a demonstration.

Not to mention therefore what the Christian Fathers have written of him,[292] we have enough for our purpose in the sacred book that goes by his name, and is received in the canon of the Holy Scriptures; and there we find these very remarkable words, "*For I know that my Redeemer lives, and at the last he will stand upon the earth. And after my skin has been thus destroyed, yet in my flesh I shall see God*" (Job 19:25-26). In these few words he expresses his knowledge of, and his faith in his Redeemer. He acknowledges that Redeemer to be God. He owns that there will be a resurrection of the dead and an enjoyment of that God by whom he was redeemed. Very great things in few words, and that made one of the ancients say that no one had spoken so plainly of the resurrection since Christ, as Job had

---

[290] Jerome. Ep. Crit. Ad Evangel. Pr. Col. 571.

[291] Job 27:3; 26:13; 33:4.

[292] Augustine, *City of God* 1.18.c.47; Chrysostom, *Homily* 4. *De patient. Job*. See Spanheim's dissertation on Job. Edit. Ludg. Bar. 1703. Tom. 2.

before Christ.[293] And if we compare this with Genesis 49:18 it will agree exactly with Job's expression, "*I have waited for your salvation O LORD.*" And with the weighty truth of the resurrection our Savior tells us of, "*Do not marvel at this, for an hour is coming when all who are in the tombs will hear his voice and come out, those who have done good to the resurrection of life, and those who have done evil to the resurrection of judgment*" (John 5:28-29).

I must further observe that he calls his Savior by the Name of God, which signifies such a Savior as has paid a Price of Redemption (*lutron*); but of this I will say more later.

Job in a word affirms that his Redeemer lives and that he himself shall rise again; which is equivalent to that in the Gospel that "*Christ is the Resurrection and the Life.*" St. John could say no more than Job already had. It is Job's hope he is regenerate by it to a lively hope. St. Peter could say no more. He enters into such particulars as "*this flesh and these eyes*" which is as much as was or could be said by St. Paul himself. So that it is plain to a demonstration that Job believed and worshiped Christ as God.

---

[293] Jerome. Praef. In Job.

The Jewish Church in the Wilderness

Worshiped Christ as God.

I come now to the Jews as a people under a government, having a religion given to them by God himself, as being God's *Peculium*, his Church in the Wilderness.

That this Jewish church in the wilderness worshiped Christ as their God will appear when I shall have shown you,

> *First*, that Christ was the God of the Covenant with the Jews.
> *Second*, that Christ dwelt in the Tabernacle, as God and King of the Jewish church.
> *Third*, that Christ was the Guardian God of Israel in the Wilderness.
> *Fourth*, that they worshiped and adored Christ as their God.
> *Fifth*, that Christ Jesus was the true High-Priest of that church.

First, Christ was the God of the Covenant
with the Jewish Church.

That the God who entered into covenant with Abraham and his sons was the Son of God, I have already shown. Now we find Christ performing the promises made to the fathers and receiving them for his own people. He gives them his Law, instructs them in his religion, in that dispensation of it which was to last to the time of reformation; that is, to the time that he himself should *come to his temple* (Mal 3:1), that *God would be manifest in the flesh* (1Ti 3:16), whereupon the worship now erected in the wilderness was both a type and a pledge, shadows of *things to come, the body being Christ* (Col 2:17).

Exodus 19:6. We find the Person entering into this covenant is God, the God who said, "*All the earth is mine,*" or who, in St. Paul's words, "*is over all God blessed forever*" (Rom 9:5), and that is Christ.

Exodus 20. We find this God gave the Law with a majesty fitting the Almighty. Calling himself their God he said, "*I am the LORD your God, Jehovah Elohim, the God Almighty,*" the God of the covenant, the same God who called Moses (Ex 3). That this God was Christ, we have the authority of St. Stephen who says, "*This [Moses] is the one who was in the congregation in the wilderness with the angel who spoke to him at Mount Sinai*" (Acts 7:38).

What Angel was this? He was such a one who was counted worthy to represent the Person, and bear the name of God; for Moses says, "*God spoke all these words*" (Ex 20:1), and the Angel himself assumes that name, "*I am the LORD your God.*" And Moses says, "*Behold, the LORD our God has shown us his glory and greatness, and we have heard his voice out of the midst of the fire. This day we have seen God speak with man, and man still live"* (Deut 5:24). Thus, it is most evident that this Angel who delivered the Law was the Son of God, the Second Person of the Trinity, whose various appearances under the Old Testament were tokens and essays of his incarnation.

Here is a remarkable text. *"Behold, I send an angel before you to guard you on the way and to bring you to the place that I have prepared. Pay careful attention to him and obey his voice; do not rebel against him, for he will not pardon your transgression, for my name is in him"* (Ex 23:20-21). St. Augustine urges this text against Jews and Gentiles in these words,

> Let them diligently search and examine the Scriptures and see if they can find a parallel place where God has said this much of any angel, *"My name is in him."* No, this he only said of the one who brought the people into the Promised Land, and of him only in a view to the changing of his name (Num 13:16). He therefore that said my name is in that Joshua, or Jesus, was himself the true Jesus, governing and leading the people into the Heritage of eternal life, according to the new covenant, of which the old was a figure.[294]

---

[294] Augustine, *Against Faustus* 16:19. De Gols seems to take Augustine as saying God put his name into the Angel of the LORD *and also* into Joshua, son of Nun. It is clear from reading this passage in its context that Augustine is saying that the "angel" of Exodus 21 refers to Joshua.

The Jewish doctors say that this Angel was Metatron, the great scribe, the same one Isaiah calls the Counsellor (Isa 9:6), which the LXX call *the Angel of the Great Council*. And Rabbi Moses Nachmanides[295] understands here that Angel of the Covenant, which is spoken of by the prophet Malachi, that is the Messiah. And Maimonides renders this text, *"Behold I send my Word before you."*[296] Nothing can be plainer than that they themselves understood this to be the Son of God. And when we read that the elders saw the God of Israel (Ex 19:10), we must remember that the invisible Father never exhibited himself to human view and that Christ was therefore that Memra, that Word, which had all along appeared as the God of the covenant.

Let me add only here that Moses Gerund has these words relating to this angel,

> To speak the truth, that Angel is the Angel Redeemer of whom it is written, *"My Name is in him."* This, I say, is the same Angel who said to Jacob, *"I am the God of Bethel."* He is also the same Angel of whom it is said, *"and God called to Moses*

---

[295] Moses ben Nahman (1194-1270), was commonly called Nachmanides or Ramban. He was a leading medieval Jewish scholar, rabbi, philosopher, physician, kabbalist, and biblical commentator who lived in Spain but was an important figure in the re-establishment of the Jewish community in Jerusalem after the crusaders destroyed it in 1099.

[296] Maimonid. more Nevoch. P. 1.c.64.

out of the bush;" and he is called the Angel because he governs the Word. Therefore it is written, *"Jehovah the Lord God brought us out of Egypt;"* and elsewhere, *"he sent his Angel, and brought us out of Egypt."* Besides, it is written, *"and the Angel of his Face saved them."* Of this Angel it is also said, *"My Presence shall go before the camp of Israel and shall cause it to rest."* Lastly, this is the Angel of whom the prophet speaks, *"The Lord whom you seek shall suddenly come to his temple, the Angel of the covenant whom you desire."*[297]

The learned Jacobus Alting[298] tells us, from an ancient Jewish catechism,[299] the Hebrew masters say that in the giving of the Law more than one divine Person was concerned. For they say that in God is I, You, and He, which are three Names of three Persons, all which are invoked on the Feast of Tabernacles: "I, You, and He, O help us we beseech you." And that to the end of the Second Commandment the words run in the first person, and in the third and fourth, in the third person; from which they argue that the Most High Spirit spoke the first two commandments, but the rest were uttered by his Glory, which is the El Shaddai, the Lord God Almighty; who was known to the fathers,

---

[297] This is Moses ben Nachman. Cited by Masius, on Joshua 5. Could be Andreas Masius or the Lutheran Hector Gottfried Masius (1653-1709).

[298] Jacob Alting (1618-1679). A Dutch philologist and theologian, professor at the University of Groningen.

[299] Alting on Dt 5:6.

by whom the prophets spoke, who is called Jah, the Lord in whom the name of God is; who is the Beloved of God, who dwells in the temple; who is the Mouth of the LORD, the Face of the LORD, and the Rock, and that Goodness which Moses saw when he could not see God.

This they assert because they say that in God there are three Spirits united together. The lowest of these is the Holy Ghost. The Second is the Intermediate who is called Wisdom and Understanding, and this is the same Spirit who goes forth with water and fire from the middle of the most consummate Glory. The Supreme Spirit is absolutely in silence; and in him all the holy spirits, and in him all the lucid persons consist.

Second, Christ Dwells in the Tabernacle, as God and King of the Jewish Church.

The Person that had thus entered into covenant with the Jews, commanded Moses, his Prime Minister in State, to build him a tabernacle. "*And let them make me a sanctuary, that I may dwell in their midst*" (Ex 25:8); and "*I will dwell among the people of Israel and will be their God. And they shall know that I am the LORD their God, who brought them out of the land of Egypt that I might dwell among them. I am the LORD their God*" (Ex 29:45-46). When the tabernacle was finished, the same LORD entered it, with a glory and grandeur becoming the eternal majesty of the Son of God, the LORD of Glory. For so we read, "*Then the cloud covered the tent of meeting, and the glory of the LORD filled the tabernacle. And Moses was not able to enter the tent of meeting because the cloud settled on it, and the glory of the LORD filled the tabernacle*" (Ex 40:34-35). For the cloudy pillar which descended, and had previously stood before the door of Moses' tent (Ex 33:9), left now and again, and came here; not standing at the door of it in the form of a pillar, but spreading itself all over the tabernacle, so that it was covered with it (Num 9:15), and filled it within all over at the first consecration.

After this great day, the Glory of the LORD, the Shekinah, retired into the Most Holy Place, within the veil, and resided there over the Ark of the Testimony.[300]

Before I proceed, I must observe here that the Shekinah, the Glory of the LORD, did not only signify a symbol or token of the divine presence by a light or cloud or other glory, but that it signified a divine Person. Rittangel says that the ancient Jews believed the Shekinah not to be the divine Glory, but a divine Person; and that the Targum has frequently rendered it for a Person: and he produces ten places in

---

[300] See Manasse Ben Israel, Concil. Quaest. 44. In Exod.

evidence, and leaves, he says, many more to the reader's observation.[301]

If the Glory of the LORD therefore is a divine Person, and we compare this account with 2Co 6:15-16, it will appear that Christ is that God, that Glory, that divine Person, who dwelt among them. For there the Apostle says, "*What accord has Christ with Belial? Or what portion does a believer share with an unbeliever? What agreement has the temple of God with idols? For we are the temple of the living God; as God said, 'I will make my dwelling among them and walk among them, and I will be their God, and they shall be my people'*" (2Co 6:15-16). These are the very word of God from Leviticus 26:12, and therefore prove Christ to be that very God who dwelt among them. St. John also alludes to this when he says, "*The Word was made flesh and dwelt among us*," and tabernacled among us (John 1:14).

Further, that Christ presided in the Jewish church as their God and King is evident from these texts compared together:

Isa 60:1. *Arise, shine, for your light has come, and the glory of the LORD has risen upon you.*

Eph 5:14. *Therefore it says, "Awake, O sleeper, and arise from the dead, and Christ will shine on you.*

---

[301] Rittangel, p. 117.

Now if the LORD Jehovah is not Christ, the prophet is so far from saying that Christ shall give you light that he makes no mention at all of him; and yet St. Paul affirms that it is Christ who gives light. Therefore, that expression, "*The Glory of the Lord has risen upon you*," is identical with, "*Christ shall give you light.*" Christ is therefore that LORD Jehovah, because they are not two different Persons but one and the same here spoken of.

So again, God calls himself the King of Israel; and who that King of Israel is will appear from the description that King gives himself:

Isa 44:6. *Thus says the LORD, the King of Israel and his Redeemer, the LORD of hosts: "I am the first and I am the last; besides me there is no god."*	Rev 22:13. *Therefore* "*I am the Alpha and the Omega, the first and the last.*

Now there cannot be more than One who is the First and the Last, and the God who calls himself so calls himself the Redeemer, and the King of Israel, and Christ is that First and Last. It therefore follows that he is the God, and King, and Redeemer of Israel.

Again, the same King of Israel is described by the prophet Zechariah in a state of humiliation, as he was by Isaiah in Glory before:

Zech 9:9. *Rejoice greatly, O daughter of Zion! Shout aloud,*	Mt 21:4-5. *This took place to fulfill what was spoken by the*

O daughter of Jerusalem! Behold, your king is coming to you; righteous and having salvation is he, humble and mounted on a donkey, on a colt, the foal of a donkey.

prophet, saying, "Say to the daughter of Zion, 'Behold, your king is coming to you, humble, and mounted on a donkey, on a colt, the foal of a beast of burden.'"

From comparing these two texts together it appears that the Jewish church had a King, and that he was Christ. Thereupon, the prophet Malachi calls the temple, which was the palace of the divine King of Israel, the Temple of Christ, "*Behold, I send my messenger, and he will prepare the way before me. And the Lord whom you seek will suddenly come to his temple; and the messenger of the covenant in whom you delight, behold, he is coming, says the LORD of hosts*" (Mal 3:1). It therefore appears that Christ is the King of Israel, the LORD of Hosts, and is that God beside whom there is no other.

Third, Christ was the Guardian God of Israel in the Wilderness.

We have a very particular account of this in Exodus 33. In ch. 32, we find that God plagued Israelites (vs. 35), who had fallen into the sin of idolatry. Then we find that God refused to go any longer with them, but would leave them to the superintendence of an angel (33:2-3). Upon this melancholy news, the people mourned (vv. 4-6). In vs. 7 we find that God had removed his Presence from the camp. Upon this, Moses humbly interceded with God not to forsake them (12-13), and God was intreated (14). "*My Presence shall go with you.*" Moses rejoiced at this, and further begs that God will be pleased to perform that gracious promise (15-16). "*If your Presence will not go with me, do not bring us up from here.*" Then God assures Moses that he had heard him, "*This very thing that you have spoken I will do, for you have found favor in my sight, and I know you by name*" (Ex 33:17).

Upon the whole, therefore, we find that it was God who conducted Israel in the Wilderness, that God withdrew himself for the sin of the golden calf, that God threatened to leave them, that God promised to send an angel, that Moses prays that God would not give an angel the custody of the people, but that he himself would conduct them in person. God still assures him that an Angel shall accompany him; Moses persistently presses it, that he himself would go with them. Seeing then Moses declared himself so averse to the superintendence of an angel, yet that he who now and all along communed with him was the Person that consented at last to go with the host and govern them himself, it is plain that he must be God—the only begotten God, who called himself I AM, and who showed himself afterward to Moses, as the LORD, the LORD God (34:6), and to whom Moses prayed for pardon, and still interceded for his Presence (9).

We find the further expressed in the history of
Balaam (Num 22), where we see that he went to curse
the Israelites but was refrained by the Angel of the
LORD. Now that this Angel was no less than Jehovah
appears from vs. 32 where he tells Balaam, "*Behold, I
have come out to oppose you*," or to be an adversary to you
(22), "*because your way is perverse before me*," for Balaam
had done what was contrary to God's command (12).
There we find God said to Balaam, "*You shall not go
with them. You shall not curse the people, for they are
blessed.*" This is a plain evidence that this God and that
Angel were the same Person. But then we find that the
Angel of the LORD gave him to leave and go, yet under this constraint, "*Speak only the word that I tell you*"
(35). That it was God the Jehovah who put the words
in his mouth we find from the following, "*And God
met Balaam … and the LORD put a word in Balaam's
mouth*" (23:4-5).

That God Jehovah, and that Angel therefore are
one and the same Person is plain to a demonstration. Balaam acknowledges this himself when he says that the
appearance of this angel was "*the vision of the Almighty*"
(24:4), and further, that this Almighty was Jehovah
God, the King of Israel, the God who brought them out
of Egypt (23:21-22). These are the very words used by
God himself, "*I am the LORD your God who brought you
out of the land of Egypt*," and that is Christ.

Fourth, the Jewish Church Worshiped Christ as God.

I have shown before that Christ was the God of the covenant with the Jews. I have shown that Christ dwelt in the Tabernacle as God and King of the Jewish church. I have shown that Christ was the Guardian God of Israel in the wilderness. Now I will show that they worshiped this Christ as God. If I had not one word more to say on this Head, the very premise would produce this consequence, that they worshiped the God of the covenant, that they adored that God to whom they had built a Tabernacle, a moveable temple, and that by his own command, and that they worshiped their God, their Guardian and Defender, with the most solemn worship and adoration. I say, it is natural to believe they worshiped their God that had done such great things for them, and had made them his Peculium, his own people, according to that which God said, *"The people whom I formed for myself that they might declare my praise"* (Isa 43:21).

But however, St. Paul tells us that Christ was the divine Person who was always with the Jews in the wilderness and was both worshiped by them and provoked by them too. For in 1 Corinthians 10 he declares several parts of the divine dispensation such as the cloud, the passage through the Sea, manna, and the water from the Rock, which he says were all transacted by Jesus Christ. At vs. 4 he says expressly, *"And that Rock was Christ.*" Christ was the Supreme Agent, Christ preserved them by the cloud, Christ baptized them in the Sea, Christ led them with manna, Christ gave them drink from the rock. These were the figure and emblem of himself, "*of whose fulness we all receive grace after grace*" (John 1:16).

After that the Apostle relates the sins of the Jews against the very Christ their God. They committed idolatry, they murmured, they committed fornication, and they tempted Christ (vs. 9), they lusted, and received the reward of trespassing against Mercy. As they therefore sinned against him by idolatry, by murmuring, and by lust, so it appears that others who did not join with them in their sins did worship Christ as their God. And the Apostle warns us, from the punishment of those sinners, to worship that God, that Savior, that Jesus in sincerity, that we would not perish as they did who sinned against him. From this argument it is plain that Christ was the God worshiped by the Jews in the wilderness.

In a word, Christ was the end of the law (Rom 10:4). Christ was the body of the ceremonial shadows (Col 2:17). Christ was the center of the prophets (Acts 10:43). Christ is the key of knowledge (Luke 11:52). Christ is all the very spirit and soul of the Old Testament.

Fifth, Christ Jesus the True High-Priest Prefigured by Aaron.

As Jesus Christ was the God and King of the Jews, and dwelt in the tabernacle, and was worshiped as God by the Jews, so he was also prefigured as the *Thanthropos*, God and man, in Aaron the High-Priest.

So Philo the Jew says,[302] that the High-Priest was the type or figure of the only begotten Son of God, who is the eternal High Priest of the vast Temple of the Universe, as he is the Maker therefore.[303]

And when he speaks of his temple clothes, which he says represented the fabric of heaven and earth, he says particularly that the four letters on the front of Aaron's mitre answered to the eternal Being of God. He calls it "the name of the One who is" (*onoma tou ontos*); and says that by it was understood *Jehovah Filius*, God the Son.

Thus, Aaron in his priestly ornaments represented both the divine and human nature of Christ, for the riches of those vestments could signify no

---

[302] Philo. *de Somniis* (*On Dreams*). *Duo gar hiera theou, en men hode ho kosmos en ō kai archiereus ho prōtogonos autou, ho theois logos.* "For there are two temples of God, one [is] this world in which His Firstborn, the divine Word, is high priest." Thanks to Michael Emadi for the following translations.

[303] Ibid. *Logos de estin eikōn theou di' ou sympas ho kosmos edēmiourgeito.* "Now the Word is the image of God through whom the whole world was created."

clothing, but that of God. His Person as a man represented the antitype of this.

Because he was to sustain the Person of him who was truly God, some privileges were put upon him which supposed him in a manner elevated above the nature of man (Lev 21:10-12). On this, Philo breaks out in these words,

> The Law will have the High-Priest to partake of a nature greater than human, approaching nearer to the Divine; or to speak exactly, to be the confine of both; that men might propitiate God by a mediator partaking of both natures, and God by using his ministry may reach forth the supplies of grace to men.[304]

So clearly is the divinity of Christ prefigured in the Law of Moses; and thus was Aaron a figure of Christ. And thus we may say of him as Baruch said before, "This is our God, and none other shall be accounted of in comparison to him; he has found out all the ways of knowledge, and has given it to Jacob his servant, and to

---

[304] Philo. *de Monarch*. *Bouletai gar auton ho nomos meizoons memoipasthai phuseōs ē kat' anthrōpon, engyterō prosionta tēs theeas, methorion, ei dei talēthes legen, amphoin, hina dia mesou tinos anthrōpoi men hilaskōntai theon, theos de tas charitas anthrōpois hypodiakonō tini chrōmenos oregē kai chorēgē*. "For the law intends him to partake of a greater nature than what is customary with mankind being nearer to the divine, that is, on the boarder line. If it is necessary to speak accurately, it is both, so that men may, on the one hand, propitiate God through some mediator, and God, on the other hand, may offer and give his gifts to men by using some subordinate minister."

Israel his beloved. Afterward did he show himself upon earth and conversed with men" (Baruch 3:35-37).

It is admirable to consider with what exquisite reason the eternal Logos, who was the Framer of the World, and is as it were invested in his own work, should be the true High-Priest according to the type of Aaron. For who is so fit to be an intercessor with the Father for the offences of the world as he who made it and in whose breast is contained the whole platform? This is he who thoroughly understands the necessities of these and has a perfect knowledge of the frailties and miseries of his creatures. For it is necessary, says Philo, for those who would supplicate the Father of the world,[305] to make use of the Son, the Paraclete, and most consummate in goodness (or in other words, the most compassionate intercessor) for the forgiveness of sins, and the supplies of the most desirable pleasures.

This is very agreeable to what the prophet Zechariah and the Apostle St. Paul say concerning Christ. For the prophet says, "*Behold, the man whose name is the Branch: for he shall branch out from his place, and he shall build the temple of the LORD. It is he who shall build the temple of the LORD and shall bear royal honor and shall sit and rule on his throne. And there shall be*

---

[305] Paraklētō chrēsthai teleiotatō tēn aretēn huiō pros te amnēstian hamartēmatōn kai chorēhian aphthonōtatōn agathōn. "… to regard as *paraklete*, the most perfect Son, in excellence of virtue and that sins may be forgotten and good gifts supplied in abundance."

a priest on his throne, and the counsel of peace shall be between them both" (Zech 6:12-13). And St. Paul says, *"So also Christ did not exalt himself to be made a high priest, but was appointed by him who said to him, 'You are my Son, today I have begotten you'"* (Heb 5:5). And again, *"For it was indeed fitting that we should have such a high priest, holy, innocent, unstained, separated from sinners, and exalted above the heavens. He has no need, like those high priests, to offer sacrifices daily, first for his own sins and then for those of the people, since he did this once for all when he offered up himself"* (Heb 7:26-27). Thus, *"He is able to save to the uttermost those who draw near to God through him, since he always lives to make intercession for them"* (Heb 7:25).

Joshua worshiped Christ as God.

That Joshua the successor of Moses, and the type of the Messiah, worshiped Christ as God, is very plain from Joshua 5:14 where we find these words, *"'No; but I am the commander of the army of the LORD. Now I have come.' And Joshua fell on his face to the earth and worshiped and said to him, 'What does my lord say to his servant?'"* (Josh 5:14).

Now we find that the Person who commanded Moses the same excalceation[306] is there called both LORD, (Jehovah) and God; and by parity of reason,

---

[306] The act of depriving or divesting of shoes.

this Captain is that same LORD. As our marginal notes on this place says,[307] in that Joshua worshiped him, he acknowledged him to be God; and in that he calls himself the LORD's Captain, he declares himself to be Christ. For had this certainly not have allowed Joshua to worship him; and had Joshua not known him to be the eternal God, he would never have done it.

Christ the God of Israel in Canaan.

Moses had the promise that the Angel would go before the people to bring them into the place which God had prepared (Ex 23:21). This Angel was therefore the Guardian God of Israel in the wilderness, and we have seen before that God was Christ.

Now we find the same Angel, the God of Israel, in Canaan. For we read in Judges 2 that when the Jews were in the Promised Land and had transgressed the divine command, that the same Angel appeared to them and rebuked them at Bochim. Here he declares himself to be that same Angel that brought them from Egypt, and that Angel was God, for he speaks this way, "*Now the angel of the LORD went up from Gilgal to Bochim. And he said, "I brought you up from Egypt and brought you into the land that I swore to give to your fathers. I said, 'I will never break my covenant with you*" (Jdg 2:1). No one but the Almighty God could say this. Then,

---

[307] These *Notes on the Bible* refer to the Geneva Bible, printed at London (1599), by Christopher Barker (1529-1599).

after he had rebuked them for their sin, and declared to them the penalty (vs. 3), we find how the people were affected with it. *"As soon as the angel of the LORD spoke these words to all the people of Israel, the people lifted up their voices and wept"* (Jdg 2:4). In the next verse, *"They called the name of that place Bochim [that is Weepers] and they sacrificed there to the LORD,"* that Angel, that Christ against whom they had sinned.

Gideon worshiped Christ as God.

That Gideon worshiped Christ as God is so plain that anyone who reads Judges 6 must believe it, or else they must believe that Gideon was an idolater. At vs. 12 we find that, *"The angel of the LORD appeared to him and said to him, 'The LORD is with you, O mighty man of valor'"* (Jdg 6:12). From this is appears that Gideon thought it was a created angel (vs. 13). But when it says, *"Jehovah looked upon him"* (14), it convinced him that he was not a created angel and commissioned him to be a Judge and a Deliverer of Israel. Here we have still the same Person speaking first as an Angel, then as Jehovah, and assuring him of his Presence, *"I will be with you,"* in the same manner as he had done to the Patriarchs before. When Gideon had asked for a token of his Presence, and the Angel had produced a miracle and then departed from him, Gideon said, *"Alas, O LORD God!"* which was not an exclamation through fear or surprise, but was a recognition of his divinity and an act of adoration paid to the divine majesty.

I do freely acknowledge that men have always expressed a very terrible apprehension of present death whenever God decides to appear. Moses was afraid (Ex 3:6). The Israelites prayed that God would not speak to them or else they would die (Ex 20:19). And Manoah said to his wife, "*We shall surely die because we have seen God*" (Jdg 13:22). Even Isaiah said, "*Woe is me, for I am undone* [or cut off], *for my eyes have seen the King, the LORD of Hosts*" (Isa 6:5). If Gideon expressed the same fear, it must be because he has seen God rather than a mere angel.

If it is allowed that his exclamation, "*Alas, I LORD God!*" proceeds from fear, from surprise, and apprehension of present death, it must be allowed at the same time that the Angel was the very God; and this apprehension of death was so strong that God appeared again to remove it. "*Jehovah [The LORD] said to him, 'Peace be to you. Do not fear; you shall not die'*" (Jdg 6:23). This is a confirmation both that his fear was justified and that the Angel whom he had seen was Jehovah—the very God. And then Gideon built an altar there to the LORD, that very LORD who had appeared to him as an Angel, had commissioned him to be a Judge of Israel, and had promised to be with him. He built the altar to him and called it Jehovah Shalom, the

LORD Send Peace. This is certainly the highest act of divine worship that a creature can pay to God. That Gideon paid this to Christ is evident, not only because that Angel-Jehovah was the very Christ, but because St. Paul numbers him among the heroes that believed in Christ and worshiped him as the only true God (Heb 11:32).

Manoah worshiped Christ as God.

That Manoah worshiped the Son of God is evident from Judges 13 where we find an Angel appeared, first to his wife, and upon Manoah's prayer (Jdg 13:8-9), the Angel returned again to the woman and Manoah then went and communed with him. Manoah thought all this time that he had been a created angel, until he asked after his name. But that he then believed he was God is apparent, because he promised to worship him. He was confirmed in this opinion when the Angel refused to tell him his name, saying it was a secret, or rather, as in the margin, because it was "wonderful" (18). Upon that, Manoah offered a sacrifice, the Angel standing by who approved of it, *"doing wondrously,"* which is generally interpreted that this Angel Jehovah sent fire from heaven to consume the sacrifice and to confirm their faith his promise. In the flame the Angel ascended, and *"Then Manoah knew that he was the Angel of the LORD"* (Jdg 13:21). This may also be rendered, *"Then Manoah knew that he was the Angel Jehovah.*" That this is the right construction appears from vs. 22 where they expressed their dread, "*We shall surely die because we have seen God.*" From the whole, it spears that Manoah worshiped God, that this God was that Angel, and that this Angel was Christ. So the notes on this place (vs. 11) explain it, he calls him man because he so seemed, but he was Christ the eternal word.[308]

The Prophets worshiped Christ as God.

Our blessed Savior tells us that the things relating to himself were written in Moses, in the Prophets, and in the Psalms (Luke 24:44). St. Peter adds that the Spirit of Christ was in the prophets, who testified beforehand of the sufferings of Christ and of the Glory that should follow (1Pe 1:10-11). Now, can it possibly be conceived that these prophets should by the inspiration of the Holy Spirit of God, speak of all the particulars of the life and death, of the resurrection and ascension of Christ into heaven, and declare these things to the Jews, as the reason of their hope, and not at the same time themselves believe in him? Should they who believed the promise of God, of the Seed of the woman, that first Gospel given to Adam, enlarged to Abraham, and typified by Moses' Law, be ignorant of that Savior whom the Jews looked for and trusted

---

[308] Geneva Bible, Note on Jdg 13:11.

in? At the same time, would they then give and deliver particular revelations concerning him to the Jews, that after ages might know the Messiah by those very particulars which they related of him, and at the same time not believe in him themselves? This I say is inconceivable!

It has indeed been questioned by some men of learning whether the prophets had a distinct knowledge of every particular they foretold concerning the Messiah; and who can determine it? Who dares assert it? But that they knew and believed the chief, the principal things relating to the Messiah, this I am very sure of. This I dare boldly to assert and to prove.

They knew the Messiah to be the Son of God, and the Savior of the world. They knew he would appear in the flesh. They knew he would suffer, and that for the sins of mankind. They knew he was to die. They knew he would rise again from the dead. They knew that he by virtue of his death would overcome the Powers of Death, and the Grave. They knew that he would ascend into heaven and sit at the right hand of God. They knew that his Gospel would be preached all over the world, that idolatry would fall before him, and he alone should be adored as the LORD God Almighty, the God of heaven, and the Savior of men. They knew that the Messiah would judge the quick and the dead and that his Kingdom would be an everlasting Kingdom.

Now these are the principal articles of the Christian religion. If I can prove that the prophets knew and believed them, as I am very sure I can, then we may say with the ancients that the Jewish church was the Christian in promise, and the Christian the Jewish church accomplished.[309] Upon this the 7th Article of the Church of England (1571) is grounded which says,

> The Old Testament is not contrary to the New: for both in the Old and New Testament everlasting life is offered to Mankind by Christ, who is the only Mediator between God and Man, being both God and Man. Wherefore they are not to be heard, which feign that the old Fathers did look only for transitory promises.

They are not to be heard who profanely say that Christ was not worshiped by any recorded in the Scriptures.

Let St. Paul be a judge of this matter. *"For I do not want you to be unaware, brothers, that our fathers were all under the cloud, and all passed through the sea, and all were*

---

[309] De Gols cites a Greek text in *Answers to the Orthodox Faithful Concerning Some Necessary Questions* (*Quaestiones et Responsiones ad Orthodoxos*), Q. 101. Here is a translation: "Now nothing has separated the gospel from the law as to the manner of its teaching but as to promise and payment it has separated. For what is the law? The gospel announced beforehand. What is the gospel? The law fulfilled."

Older Christians like De Gols attributed this to Justin Martyr, but is almost certainly the work of a later Father, perhaps Theodoret (393 – c. 458/466). See Peter Toth, "New Questions on Old Answers: Towards a Critical Edition of the Answers to the Orthodox of Pseudo-Justin," *Journal of Theological Studies*, NS 65:2 (Oct 2014): 550-599.

baptized into Moses in the cloud and in the sea, and all ate the same spiritual food, and all drank the same spiritual drink. For they drank from the spiritual Rock that followed them, and the Rock was Christ" (1Co 10:1-4). Christ led them the entire forty years in the wilderness. Christ was their God, their King and Governor. Christ was all in all to them. And yet, for them not to know, nor worship him, who was their Jehovah, their Goel [Redeemer], their Shiloh [Peace], their Emmanuel [God With Us], their Messiah [Christ/Anointed], is a proposition as strange as it is false; so strange that none but such as are deluded by that Spirit of Error which possessed Socinus could have thought so.[310]

Give me leave to lay open their errors a little. The Racovian Catechism has spoken openly and asks this question. "Q. Were not the same promises that are made to us made by the Law of Moses? A. Not any of them; for neither eternal life, nor the Holy Ghost was promised to the obedient by Moses' Law."[311] And that we might know he understood the whole Mosaical dispensation he says in the answer to the 7th Question, that God has reserved the promise of eternal life to the days of the New Testament. And Question 6 he says that supposing any of the ancients were saved, they were saved not by virtue of any of God's promises,

---

[310] Socinians were nontrinitarian in their view of Christ and precursors to many forms of Unitarianism within Protestantism.
[311] *Racovian Catechism* (1605), Ch. 5: Of The Promise of Eternal Life.

but of his abundant goodness, which gave them more than he ever promised them.

Smalcius[312] doubts not to say it is an old wives fable to believe that any of the Fathers of the Old Testament were saved by faith in Christ as Mediator. And the Racovian Catechism says though none are saved but by faith, this pertains only to the dispensation of the Gospel.[313] To repeat such errors is to refute them, but the falseness has already appeared and will further appear in the following pages.

David worshiped Christ as God.

That David knew and worshiped Christ as God, I think is as plain as the light of the sun.

That he knew God to be Triunal is what several of the Christian writers have asserted,[314] especially from his words, *"By the word of the LORD the heavens were made, and by the breath of his mouth all their host"* (Ps 33:6). Indeed, if he did not mean the Three Persons of the Divinity, it is difficult to find out what he could mean.

---

[312] Smalcius, c. 4. De bon. oper.
[313] *Racovian Catechism*, Ch. 11: Of Justification.
[314] A large catalog of Fathers in Daniel Waterland, "Christ Properly Creator: or Christ's Divinity Proved from Creation, The Second Sermon Preached Oct. 7, 1719," in *The works of The Rev. Daniel Waterland, D. D.* 2nd ed. vol. 2, ed. William Van Mildert, D. D. (Oxford: University Press, 1843), 49-67. Daniel Cosgrove Waterland (1683 – 1740), was an English theologian, Chancellor of the Diocese of York and Archdeacon of Middlesex.

But however, he knew and worshiped the Son of God. "*Your throne, O God, is forever and ever. The scepter of your kingdom is a scepter of uprightness; you have loved righteousness and hated wickedness. Therefore God, your God, has anointed you with the oil of gladness beyond your companions*" (Ps 45:6-7); i.e. God has made your both Lord and Christ. And that this was spoken of Christ we have St. Paul's authority (Heb 1:8), and the Targum also, which perhaps may be of greater authority with our adversaries.[315]

Again, the same Psalmist says, "*The LORD* [Yahweh/Jehovah] *says to my Lord* [Adonai]: '*Sit at my right hand, until I make your enemies your footstool*'" (Ps 110:1). Our Savior himself produces this text as a proof of his Divinity and of David's knowing him to be God. This scene with Christ is of such importance that it is recorded by three Evangelists (Matt 22:44; Mark 12:36; Luke 20:42). The Apostles also have made use of this text as a testimony of Christ's Divinity and his ascension into heaven (Acts 2:34). Even some of the most learned Jews acknowledge that this Psalm is spoken of the Messiah.[316]

---

[315] It is difficult to know what De Gols means by including the Targum here, for he does not elaborate. It could be simply that the Targum calls this king "God." It could also be that some versions of the Targum refer to "the throne of your Glory, O LORD," where the Shekinah-Glory acts like the Memra and is therefore Christ.

[316] See Rabbi Saadia (882/892 – 942), cited by Grotius, Rel. Ch. 1.5. § 22. No. 1.

David not only worshiped Christ as God himself but called upon all true Israelites to join with him in the adoration. *"I will tell of the decree: The LORD said to me, 'You are my Son; today I have begotten you'"* (Ps 2:7). At vs. 8, he speaks of the glory of his kingdom, and talks of his power, and declares that he will be honored by all the kings and princes of the earth. Thereupon he says, *"Kiss the Son, lest he be angry"* (12). The adoration is not only required, but the reasons and motives are added. The reason is because he is the Son. St. Paul proves this in Hebrews 1 when he shows that he is the eternal Son of the eternal God. David calls him Jehovah, *"Serve the LORD with fear and rejoice with trembling"* (Psalm 2:11). Then he adds the motives. First, from the penalty, *"Lest you perish."* Next, from the benefit of his service, *"Blessed are all who put their trust in him."*

That divine worship and religious adoration is signified by *"kiss,"* will appear when I shall have shown you how a kiss was used as an act of divine worship and part of solemn adoration by almost all the nations of the world.

Of a kiss in religious worship.

That by the word "kiss" is understood an act of divine adoration, including all the acts of worship, of honor, prayer, thanksgiving, and service, will appear from the general use of that outward action, to declare all inward veneration and express all obedience.

So we find it: "*Yet I will leave seven thousand in Israel, all the knees that have not bowed to Baal, and every mouth that has not kissed him*" (1Kg 19:18). Also, "*And now they sin more and more, and make for themselves metal images ... It is said of them, 'Those who offer human sacrifice kiss calves!'*" (Hos 13:2).

Job tells us of the idolaters that worshiped the Sun and Moon, and that because they could not reach them, they lifted up their hands to them. They kissed their hands in demonstration of the most solemn worship and then held their hands up to them, as it were, to throw that kiss to them, which they would give them if they were within their reach. Thus, he says, "*If I have looked at the sun when it shone, or the moon moving in splendor, and my heart has been secretly enticed, and my mouth has kissed my hand*" (Job 31:26-27). And that Job understood by this kissing of the hand that the most solemn act of divine adoration and religious worship is evident from vs. 28, here he says it is open idolatry, "*This also would be an iniquity to be punished by the Judge, for I would have denied the God above*" (Job 31:28).

The word "adoration," which we use for the highest act of divine worship, signifies "to put the hand to the mouth." It is derived from this religious custom. Pliny says that in worship we put the right hand to the mouth.[317] Apuleius describes the manner of it among the Romans.[318] Lucian[319] among the Indians and Demosthenes for the Greeks say that except for when the idol or deity was out of their reach, they otherwise kissed the idol. Cicero tells us of a brazen statue of Hercules, whose jaws and chin were worn away by the worshipers who kissed it, because they were prone not only to pray to it, but to kiss it also.[320]

But let me now return to David. That he knew the Son of God would become flesh and appear in human nature is certain from Psalm 40:6-8. That this Psalm does pertain to Christ and speak of his incarnation for our redemption, St. Paul assures us, since he is certainly the best interpreter and in whose words we rind, *"Consequently, when Christ came into the world, he said, 'Sacrifices and offerings you have not desired, but a body have you prepared for me; in burnt offerings and sin offerings you have taken no pleasure. Then I said, 'Behold, I have come to do your will, O God, as it is written of me in the scroll of*

---

[317] Pliny, 1.20.c.2. *In adorando dextram ad osculum referimus.*
[318] Apuleius, 1.4. Asin. Aur.
[319] Lucian. 1. "When they arise in the morning they worship the sun, kissing their hand."
[320] For more see Pierre Danet, "Adorare," in *A Complete Dictionary of the Greek and Roman Antiquities Explaining the Obscure Places in Classic Authors and Ancient Historians Relating to the Religion, Mythology, History, Geography and Chronology of the Ancient Greeks and Romans, Their ... Rites and Customs, Laws, Polity, Arts and Engines of War: Also an Account of Their Navigations, Arts and Sciences and the Inventors of Them: With the Lives and Opinions of Their Philosophers / Compiled Originally in French ... by Monsieur Danet; Made English, with the Addition of Very Useful Mapps,* Early English Books Online (London: Printed for John Nicholson ... Tho. Newborough ... and John Bulford .., 1700).

*the book.'' When he said above, 'You have neither desired
nor taken pleasure in sacrifices and offerings and burnt offerings and sin offerings' (these are offered according to the law),
then he added, 'Behold, I have come to do your will.' He does
away with the first in order to establish the second. And by
that will we have been sanctified through the offering of the
body of Jesus Christ once for all''* (Heb 10:5-10). This is to
the point; God can assume a human body. This is not
only agreeable to his almighty power, and not contrary to our reason to believe, but is acknowledged
not only by the Talmud, but by Rabbi Solomon, as
Grotius tells us.[321]

Further, David believed that Christ, the Messiah,
was to suffer. In Psalm 22 he describes several particulars of his Passion. That they do pertain to Christ, we
must believe from the Evangelists. For,

Psalm 22	The NT
Vs. 1. *My God, my God, why have you forsaken me?*	Mt 27:46. *And about the ninth hour Jesus cried out with a loud voice, saying, "Eli, Eli, lema sabachthani?" that is, "My God, my God, why have you forsaken me?"*
Vv. 7-8. *All who see me mock me; they make mouths at me; they wag their heads;*	Mt 27:39. *And those who passed by derided him, wagging their heads.*

---

[321] Grotii Ver. Christ. Rel. 1. 5. § 21. no. 9.

"He trusts in the LORD; let him deliver him; let him rescue him, for he delights in him!"

Mt 27:43. *He trusts in God; let God deliver him now, if he desires him.*

Vs. 16. *They have pierced my hands and feet.*

Mt 27:35. *And when they had crucified him,*

Vs. 18. *They divide my garments among them, and for my clothing they cast lots.*

they divided his garments among them by casting lots. (see also Luke 23:34)

Vs. 22. *I will tell of your name to my brothers; in the midst of the congregation I will praise you.*

Heb 2:12. *I will tell of your name to my brothers; in the midst of the congregation I will sing your praise.*

From all these places it is evident that this Psalm relates to Christ, speaks of Christ, and was fulfilled in Christ. For to believe that all this was accidental only is to deny a providence. More, it is to deny the Evangelists themselves who acknowledge that these things were done that it might be fulfilled which was spoken by the prophet (Matt 27:35), and that the Scripture might be fulfilled (John 19:24, 37), which both refer to this very Psalm.

David believed and spoke of Christ's death and resurrection. *"For you will not abandon my soul to Sheol, or let your holy one see corruption"* (Ps 16:10). That the prophet spoke this of Christ, St. Peter assures us, *"Brothers, I may say to you with confidence about the patriarch David that he both died and was buried, and his tomb is with us to this day. Being therefore a prophet, and knowing that God had sworn with an oath to him that he would set one of his descendants on his throne, he foresaw and spoke about the resurrection of the Christ, that he was not abandoned to Hades, nor did his flesh see corruption"* (Acts 2:29-31).

David believed and spoke of Christ's ascension into heaven and the outpouring of the Holy Ghost, and that he was prepared a place in heaven for them that worship him here below. *"You ascended on high, leading a host of captives in your train and receiving gifts among men, even among the rebellious, that the LORD God may dwell there. Blessed be the Lord, who daily bears us up; God is our salvation. Selah. Our God is a God of salvation, and to GOD, the Lord, belong deliverances from death"* (Ps 68:18-20). What could any Christian add to this or profess more plainly? And how St. Paul applies this to Christ, we find in Ephesians 4:8. That it does belong to Christ is certain; for either Christ must be the Person of whom the Psalmist speaks, or St. Paul must grossly misquote and misapply him. If he is the same Person, then from that Psalm it is evident:

- That Christ went before the people and marched with them through the wilderness (Ps 68:7-15).
- That it was Christ who was among the thousands of angels in Sinai, in the holy place, and by their ministry gave the Law (vs. 17).
- That Christ was the God and King, whose goings were seen in the sanctuary (vs. 24).

- That it was Christ who was the God of the temple at Jerusalem (vs. 29).

All these things are expressly spoken of him who ascended on high, and led captivity captive, and received gifts for men; and the Apostle says that this was Christ.

Lastly, David believed Christ to be the Judge of all the world. This appears in his excellent prayer, *"May God be gracious to us and bless us and make his face to shine upon us, Selah. That your way may be known on earth, your saving power among all nations. Let the peoples praise you, O God; let all the peoples praise you! Let the nations be glad and sing for joy, for you judge the peoples with equity and guide the nations upon earth"* (Ps 67:1-4). What Christian could have made a more excellent prayer or more agreeable to what our Savior taught us, *"Hallowed be your Name, your Kingdom come?"* What Christian could have made a truer confession of faith in Christ than this one from David? And therefore, to assert that David knew nothing of Christ, and never worshiped him, is a piece of amazing impudence.

Solomon worshiped Christ as God.

That Solomon worshiped Christ as God is certain, for he was instructed in the religion of his father David; and he has given us such descriptions of the

Son of God as must convince us that he both knew and adored him as God.

As soon as Solomon was born, "*The LORD loved him*" (2Sa 12:24). In demonstration of that love, God sent Nathan the prophet to call him Jedidia, i.e. Beloved of God, or beloved because of God, or beloved for the sake of God, for Christ's sake, in whom he was acceptable to God, and of whose Glory and Kingdom he was a type and figure.[322] Indeed, he was so beloved of God that God said, "*He shall be my son, and I will be his Father*" (1Ch 22:9).

This man, according to God's own appointment, built a temple to God and consecrated it with a most excellent prayer, even to that God who was the God of the covenant—Christ Jesus. Christ's Ark, the visible token of the covenant, and figure of the body of Christ, was placed inside. How acceptable both the temple and consecration was appears from the gracious answer God gave. "*Now my eyes will be open and my ears attentive to the prayer that is made in this place. For now I have chosen and consecrated this house that my name may be there forever. My eyes and my heart will be there for all time*" (2Ch 7:15-16). Then the Shekinah, the Glory of the LORD, which is Christ, he himself dwelt there and filled the house with a cloud. He took possession of it as his palace, with a pomp and magnificence

---

[322] Junius-Tremellius Bible (1575), in the place cited.

becoming the God and King of the Jews (1Kg 8:10), as he had done to the tabernacle before.

This Solomon speaks of the Son of God, and of his eternal Generation before the creation of the world (Prov 8:22-32), and then closes that description with these words, "*And now, O sons, listen to me: blessed are those who keep my ways*" (Prov 8:32), which Christ Jesus, his Antitype, expressed when he said, "*Blessed rather are those who hear the word of God and keep it!*" (Luke 11:28).

For that the Wisdom of God, so often mentioned, and so much celebrated by Solomon, does not signify the essential property of the divine Nature, his knowledge and understanding, but the Person of the Son of God, the Lord Jesus Christ, is beyond all doubt. This is because Christ is called the Wisdom of God (Luke 11:49). That Christ must be understood there, is plain in the parallel when it says, "*I will send to you prophets and wise men*" (Matt 23:34), which the Wisdom of God in the other place is said to send. St. Paul gives us the reason why he is called the Wisdom of God. "*In him are hidden all the treasures of wisdom and knowledge*" (Col 2:3).

This text of Solomon's is a strong argument for the divinity of this personal Wisdom, though Arius made use of it against Christ, because the LXX had rendered the Hebrew "possessed me" (*qanani*), with "created me" (*ektisen me*), instead of "possessed me" (*ektēse me*). But the original is to be our guide, and that has it from the root "to possess, to enjoy in possession" (*qanah*). Aquila has rendered it with the affix, as it is in the Hebrew "he possessed me" (*ektēsato me*); although the other word might bear a good construction with those who are not heretically minded.[323]

And of this Wisdom he says that he is eternal, is equal with God, is of God, is the Creator of all things, always was, and always is with the Father; and that he is the Blessing of God to mankind, is their God and Guide here, and their Glory and Salvation hereafter.

Further, at vs. 31 Solomon speaks of his incarnation, "*Rejoicing in his inhabited world and delighting with the children of man*" (Prov 8:31), which Baruch, speaking of the same Wisdom, explains, "Afterward he showed himself upon earth, and conversed with men" (Baruch 3:37).

Proverbs 30:4 speaks of the Son of God in these words, "*Who has ascended to heaven and come down? Who has gathered the wind in his fists? Who has wrapped up the waters in a garment? Who has established all the ends of the earth? What is his name, and what is his son's name? Surely you know!*" In these words Solomon asserts the omnipotence both of God the Father and God the Son; and plainly acquaints us that he knew the Son of God and adored him too.[324] This is so evident that the Jewish

---

[323] See Zanch. Trib. Elohim 1. 3. C. 8. P. 470.
[324] Remus in Proverbs 30. De Gols seems to refer to Georg Remus (1561-1625).

masters of old believed that Wisdom and this Son were the same—either the Word or the Spirit, but generally the former.[325]

Even more, Solomon made his prayers to the Son of God, to Christ. This appears in Proverbs 30:1. The prayer we have is in vv. 7-9, but the object of that invocation is in vs. 1, "*The man spoke to Ithiel and Ucal.*"[326] These are two names given to the Son of God, answering to Emmanuel. For Ithiel signifies "*My Strong God,*" or The Powerful God is With Me; and Ucal, a word which signifies ability, is, my God Who is Able to Save Me. This is explained by Isaiah 9:6, "*The Mighty God.*" And what that mighty God is to mankind we find in St. Paul. "*Because of him you are in Christ Jesus, who became to us Wisdom from God, Righteousness and Sanctification and Redemption*" (1Co 1:30).

Lastly, this very Solomon confessed his belief of a future judgment and warned others of it (Ecc 11:9). Therefore, for the Socinians to say that he knew not the Son of God is as false as it was rash for Cardinal Bellarmine to say that Solomon was forsaken of God and reprobated.[327] For though Solomon sinned greatly, yet there is reason to believe he repented sincerely, from his book of Ecclesiastes, and that this very

---

[325] Peter Allix, *Judgment of the Jewish Church.*
[326] The ESV translates this as, "*The man declares, I am weary, O God; I am weary, O God, and worn out.*" The NAS follows the KJV, however, choosing to interpret these words as names.
[327] Bellarm. De verb. Dei, 1. 1. C. 5.

book was a demonstration of it (Ecc 7:23, etc.). Neither can it be deemed otherwise. Rather, it is exceedingly rash to judge such a person, whom God had made a type of his Son and an author of such books as are the canon of Salvation to others, to judge such a person a cast-away. God had promised, *"When he commits iniquity, I will discipline him with the rod of men, with the stripes of the sons of men, but my steadfast love will not depart from him"* (2Sa 7:14-15). From this text and 2 Chronicles 11:17, where the way of David and Solomon are mentioned with honor, the ancient Jews have concluded and asserted that he did repent.[328]

Isaiah worshiped Christ as God.

I come now to the prophet Isaiah, whom Jesu Sirach calls the Great Prophet (Ecclesiasticus 48:22). He was a great prophet indeed, in every respect, but more especially in regard to his knowledge and description of the Messiah, the Son of God, and the Savior of the world; whose life and death he described not as a prophet but an historian, not as a prophecy to come, but as a fact already past. Thus, St. Jerome[329] does not doubt to call this Isaiah both an Evangelist and Apostle; and St. Athanasius[330] says that the greatest part of his prophecy is the Gospel concerning the coming of

---

[328] Ravanel. Bibl. P. 637.
[329] Jerome, in Proaem. In If.
[330] Athanasius, in Synopsi.

the Word of God in the flesh, and of the sufferings he underwent for our sakes.

This Isaiah is the great morning-star, shining through the veil of Moses' types, and foreshadowing the rising of the Sun of Righteousness. To mention all that he knew and believed of the Son of God, and how he worshiped him as God and Savior, would be to transcribe him. I shall mention only a few particulars.

That Isaiah knew the Trinity of Persons in the Unity of the Divine Nature is more than probable because he names them most distinctly and ascribes personal attributes and operations to them. He says, "*I will recount the steadfast love of the LORD, the praises of the LORD, according to all that the LORD has granted us*" (Isa 63:7). Whether there is any force in the three-fold repeating of the word Jehovah, I take not upon me to determine. But I am very sure there is just two verses later. "*In all their affliction he was afflicted, and the angel of his presence saved them; in his love and in his pity he redeemed them; he lifted them up and carried them all the days of old. But they rebelled and grieved his Holy Spirit*" (Isa 63:9-10). Here, the Son and Spirit are distinctly named, and both act as Persons distinct from the Father.

But however that is, it is certain that Isaiah knew the Messiah to be God, to be the Son of God, and adored him as such. For so we find from his own words, "*I saw the Lord sitting upon a throne, high and lifted up; and the train of his robe filled the temple. Above him stood the seraphim ... And one called to another and said: 'Holy, holy, holy is the LORD of hosts; the whole earth is full of his glory!' ... And I said: 'Woe is me! For I am lost; for I am a man of unclean lips ... for my eyes have seen the King, the LORD of hosts!"* (Isa 6:1-5).

Now who this LORD of Hosts was, whom Isaiah saw, St. John tells us; it is Christ. For he says, *"Isaiah said these things because he saw his glory and spoke of him"* (John 12:41). And what St. John quotes from the prophet of the judicial hardness that should befall the Jews is taken from vv. 9-10 of that chapter of Isaiah.

If we compare this text with Revelation 4:8, we find this same Glory given to God the Father. From this it necessarily follows that Christ is of the same nature, honor, and glory with the Father, the same LORD of Hosts, the same eternal God. Or, we must believe that Isaiah and the Evangelist have robbed the Father of his Honor and given it to another, to whom it was not due. And here I am further to observe that the seraphim, by crying to each other, did not only declare the nature of God, and recognize his authority over all the world, but did solemnly invoke and worship him as that God , who is most holy, and by whom they are and were created.

Again, Isaiah calls Christ the Immanuel, which is the chief name of the Messiah, having relation to the divine and human natures in the hypostatic union,

Christ, God and man (Isa 7:14 and 8:8), which was the name given by the angel. "*They shall call his name Immanuel, which means, 'God with us'*" (Matt 1:23).

Again, Isaiah calls Christ by the name of Goel, the Redeemer, "*And the Redeemer shall come to Zion*" (Isa 59:20).

Goel, Redeemer.

Here I find myself obliged to explain the word, because I find there is very great stress laid upon it in the holy Scriptures, and because it has been observed[331] that this word is used more than six hundred times in the Old Testament, for such a Redeemer as the New Testament describes Jesus Christ to be.

The word *goel* signifies one allied or related in blood. Thus, it is rendered "a relation" (*propinquus*). Thus, Christ, who took upon him the Seed of Abraham, is not ashamed to call us brothers, so the Apostle tells us, "*For he who sanctifies and those who are sanctified all have one source. That is why he is not ashamed to call them brothers*" (Heb 2:11). The Apostle confirms this with a prophecy of David's (Ps 22:22), that the Savior should call his redeemed "brothers."

Again, Goel signifies a person who has the right of inheritance (Lev 25:25), and not a right only, but a power also, to vindicate his right. Thus, Christ is so

---

[331] Fredrick Spanheim. Dissert. De Jobo, p. 108. Tom. Ii. Lug. Bat. 1703.

called, because he has a right to have the heathen for his inheritance, and the utmost parts of the earth for his possession (Ps 2:8).

And again, Goel is such a redeemer as has paid a ransom, a price of redemption.

That a ransom, a *lutron*, was necessary for our redemption, Job was not ignorant of; for these are his words, "*If there be for him an angel, a mediator, one of the thousand, to declare to man what is right for him, and he is merciful to him, and says, 'Deliver him from going down into the pit; I have found a ransom'*" (Job 33:23-24), or an atonement, as it is in the margin note. And David says, "*Truly no man can ransom another, or give to God the price of his life, for the ransom of their life is costly and can never suffice*" (Ps 49:7-8). It also seems that Jacob, before them both, knew and understood the redemption by a ransom; for he uses this very word when he calls the Son of God, "*The Angel who redeemed me*" (Gen 48:16). And Aben Ezra, expounding Isaiah 59:20. "*And the Redeemer shall come to Zion,*" acknowledges this Redeemer to be one who must pay the price of redemption.

And so, the New Testament describes Christ as that Redeemer who has paid for our redemption. "*Christ gave his life a ransom for many*" (Matt 20:28). "*God has purchased his Church with his own blood*" (Acts 20:28). "*For there is one God, and one Mediator between God and man, the Man Christ Jesus, who gave himself a ransom for all"* (1Ti 2:5-6). *"For you are bought with a price"* (1Co 6:20). *"For as much as you know that you were not redeemed with corruptible things, like silver and gold ... but with the precious blood of Christ, the Lamb without blemish or spot"* (1Pe 1:18-19).

To return to Isaiah, as he knew the Messiah the Son of God to be the Redeemer, so he has given a most particular account of the sufferings he underwent to perfect that redemption, in the fifty-third chapter of his prophecy, where he describes the Messiah in the state of humiliation, his sorrows, sufferings, death, and burial; and also the state of his glorification. The particulars are so lively and so perfect that whosoever reads that chapter attentively must think it to be something a Gospel writer described rather than a prophet predicting the suffering of a Person to come. Thus, several of the greatest masters of the Jews have acknowledged that this chapter related entirely to the Messiah.[332]

What Isaiah believed and wrote of Christ the Son of God we have seen before. What the other prophets knew and believed, this would take a whole volume to describe. Thus, I could say much. Whatever the Gospel of Christ has taught us, One or another of the prophets have known, revealed, and believed. Whatever the Apostles preached of Jesus Christ and the

---

[332] See the Targum and Gemara of Babylon. Grotius, Rel. Ch. Verit. 1. 5. § 19. And Rivet. In Isa 53:4.

power of his resurrection, the prophets have known and revealed, not all at once, as it is delivered to us, but by degrees, plainer and clearer, as Christ the Sun of Righteousness drew nearer and nearer to his rising to this world (Acts 3:24).

Glossary of Works & Authors Cited

There are many obscure and long since forgotten authors and works cited in Owen's discussion on the Angel. This Glossary is provided to acquaint you with some of them.

ABRAHAM SABA (1440-1509). Seba or Sabaa. Portuguese rabbi who wrote a commentary on the Pentateuch called *Tseror Hammor* (*Bundle of Myrrh*; Venice, 1523).

ARBANEL. Portuguese Jewish statemen, religious Jew, scholar, Bible commentator and philosopher of the "Spanish Golden Age."

ABEN SUEB (15th cent.). Joel ibn Shu'aib. Spanish rabbi, preaching, commentator.

ABENEZRA. Abraham ben Meir Ibn Ezra (1089-1167). One of the most distinguished Jewish biblical commentators and philosophers of the Middle Ages.

AGRIPPA HENRY, CORNELIUS (1486-1535). German polymath, physician, legal scholar, soldier, theologian, and occult writer. Later rejected his book *Occult Philosophy*.

AINSWORTH, HENRY (1571-1622). English Nonconformist clergyman and scholar.

AKIBA (50-135). Akiva. A leading Jewish scholar and sage, a tanna of the latter part of the first century. He was a leading contributor to the Mishnah.

ALSHEK (1508-1593). Moshe Alshich. Prominent rabbi, preacher, commentator. Legend says his son was kidnapped as a child and became a Muslim and that a special prayer was written for his return.

ALTING, JACOBUS (1618-1679). A Dutch philologist and theologian, professor at the University of Groningen.

AMBROSE OF MILAN (333–397). Bishop of Milan and teacher of Augustine who defended the divinity of the Holy Spirit and the perpetual virginity of Mary.

ARETHAS OF CAESAREA (c. 860–940). Byzantine scholar and disciple of Photius. He was a deacon in Constantinople, then archbishop of Caesarea from 901.

ARISTOBULUS OF ALEXANDRIA (181-124 B.C.). A Hellenistic Jewish philosopher, was the predecessor of Philo and tried to fuse Hebrew Scriptures with Greek thought.

ATHANASIUS OF ALEXANDRIA (c. 295–373; fl. 325–373). Bishop of Alexandria from 328, though often in exile. He wrote his classic polemics against the Arians while most of the eastern bishops were against him.

ATHENAGORAS (fl. 176–180). Early Christian philosopher and apologist from Athens, whose only authenticated writing, *A Plea Regarding Christians*, is addressed to the emperors Marcus Aurelius and Commodus, and defends Christians from the common accusations of atheism, incest and cannibalism.

ATHIAS. (16th cent.). Yom-Tov Ben Levi Athias or Jerónimo de Vargas, he produced and paid for a Spanish translation of the Bible called **The Ferrara Bible** (1553).

AUGUSTINE (354–430). Bishop of Hippo and a voluminous writer on philosophical, exegetical, theological and ecclesiological topics. In the West, he towers over all others.

AUTPERT AMBROSE (730-784). Frankish Benedictine monk who wrote commentaries on the Apocalypse, Psalms, and Song of Solomon.

BARKER, CHRISTOPHER (1529-1599). Printer to Queen Elizabeth. Printed the Geneva Bible and its notes.

BASIL THE GREAT (329-79). One of the Cappadocian fathers, bishop of Caesarea and champion of the teaching on the Trinity propounded at Nicaea in 325. He was a great administrator and founded a monastic rule.

BECHAI (1255-1340). Bahya ben Asher ibn Halawa. Distinguished Spanish rabbi who wrote a commentary on the Hebrew Bible.

BEDE THE VENERABLE (672–735). Born in Northumbria, at the age of seven he was put under the care of the Benedictine monks of Saints Peter and Paul at Jarrow and given a broad classical education in the monastic tradition.

BELLARMINE, ROBERT (1542 –1621). Italian Jesuit and Cardinal. He was an important figure in the Counter-Reformation and a proponent of the Council of Trent.

BEN UZZIEL (first cent. BC – AD). Pupil of the famed Hillel the Elder, he is authored some of the Targums.

BERIT MENUCHAH is a work of practical Kabbalah written down in the 14th century by Rabbi Abraham ben Isaac of Granada. It contains a system of theurgy which uses secret names of God and his emanations for spiritual and magical purposes.

BEZA, THEODORE (1519-1605). French Reformed Protestant theologian, disciple of John Calvin, successor to Calvin as the spiritual leader of Geneva.

BULL, GEORGE (1634-1710). English theologian, Bishop of St. David's. Wrote a work on the Creed and defended the Trinity against heretics.

BUXTORF (1564-1629). Johannes Bustorf. Hebraist, professor of Hebrew at Basel (Switzerland), known as "Master of the Rabbis." (PA)

CELSUS (2nd Cent. AD). Greek philosopher and opponent of Christianity.

CHRYSOSTOM, JOHN (344/354–407; fl. 386–407). Bishop of Constantinople who was noted for his orthodoxy, his eloquence and his attacks on Christian laxity in high places.

CLARK, SAMUEL (1626-1701). English Nonconformist, rector at Grendon Underwood, Buckinghamshire, and annotator of the Bible. He was a friend of John Owen, Richard Baxter, and George Whitefield.

CLARKE, SAMUEL (1675-1729). Socinian and anti-Trinitarian leader of the Enlightenment. He believed that Christ was merely a man.

CLEMENT OF ALEXANDRIA (c. 150–215). A highly educated Christian convert from paganism, head of the catechetical school in Alexandria and pioneer of Christian scholarship.

CUNÆUS, PETRUS (1586-1638). Peter van der Kun. Dutch Christian Rabbinical scholar at the University of Leyden.

CYPRIAN (200-258). Martyred bishop of Carthage who maintained that those baptized by schismatics and heretics had no share in the blessings of the church.

CYRIL OF ALEXANDRIA (375–444). Patriarch of Alexandria whose extensive exegesis and strong view of the unity of Christ led to the condemnation of Nestorius in 431.

DAVID THE LESS. Probably David ben Yom Tov ibn Bilia (c. 1300-1361). Portuguese Hebrew scholar, translator, philosopher, exegete, and poet who wrote *Me'or Enayim*, a commentary on the Pentateuch.

DRUSIUS (1550-1616). Johannes van den Driesche. Flemish Protestant divine, Orientalist, Christian Hebraist, and exegete; speculated about the existence of 1 Enoch.

ELIEZER (1st-2nd cent.). Eliezer ben Hurcanus, one of the most prominent sages of the 1st and 2nd centuries in Judea. He is the sixth most frequently mentioned sage in the Mishnah.

ELIJAH LEVITA (1469-1549). Renaissance Hebrew grammarian, scholar, and poet. Wrote a diction called Tishbi on the Talmud, Midrash, and Targums.

EPIPHANIUS OF SALAMIS (310-403 A.D). Bishop of Salamis, Cyprus, defender of the orthodox faith against various heresies.

ERASMUS, DESIDERIUS (1466-1536). Dutch Catholic "Prince of the Humanists," his work in the New Testament raised important questions for the Reformers, but he himself remained loyal to Rome.

EUSEBIUS OF CAESAREA (c. 260/263–340). Bishop of Caesarea, partisan of the Emperor Constantine and first historian of the Christian church.

FAGIUS, PAUL (1504-49). Renaissance scholar of Biblical Hebrew and Protestant Reformer.

THE FERRARA BIBLE (1553). Made and paid for by Yom-Tov Ben Levi Athias (typographer) and Abraham ben Salomon Usque (translator) and dedicated to the Duke of Ferrara. It was a translation of an older circulating Spanish translation.

GALE, THEOPHILUS (1628-1678). English Puritan educationalist, nonconformist, and theologian of dissent.

GEKATILIA, JOSEPH (1248-1305). Joseph ben Abraham Gikatilla. Spanish kabbalist.

GOSLAVIUS, ADAM (1577-1642). 17th century Socinian pupil of Nicholas Taurelli. He was a Polish Knight from Bebeln, Germany and had a brother named Andrew who was also a Socinian.

GREGORY, JOHN (1607-1646). English orientalist, he wrote *Notes and Observations upon some Passages of Scripture* (1646).

GREGORY OF ELVIRA (fl. 359–385). Bishop of Elvira who wrote allegorical treatises in the style of Origen and defended the Nicene faith against the Arians.

GREGORY OF NAZIANZUS (b. 329/330; fl. 372–389). Cappadocian father, bishop of Constantinople, friend of Basil the Great and Gregory of Nyssa, and author of theological orations, sermons and poetry.

GREGORY OF NYSSA (c. 335–394). Bishop of Nyssa and brother of Basil the Great. A Cappadocian father and author of catechetical orations, he was a philosophical theologian of great originality.

GROTIUS, HUGO (1583-1645). Dutch Jurist and Arminian theologian, he is noted for his "governmental" or "moral government" theory of the atonement and for being imprisoned for his views.

HAYMO. At least three prominent Christians bear this name and Allix does not tell us which one he has in mind. These are Haymo of Halberstadt (d. 835) a German Benedictine monk, Haymo of Auxerre (d. 865) another German Benedictine, and Haymo of Faversham (d. 1243) an English Franciscan. The most likely candidate is Haymo of Halberstadt.

HEYLIN, PETER (1599-1662) English ecclesiastic and author of many works, including one on the Apostle's Creed.

HILARY OF POITIERS (c. 315–367). Bishop of Poitiers and called the "Athanasius of the West" because of his defense (against the Arians) of the common nature of Father and Son.

HOORNBECK, JOHANNES (1617-1666). Dutch Reformed theologian, pupil of Voetius; moved to Germany to pastor a refugee Reformed church in Mulheim. Later became professor at Leiden. Wrote important works on missions.

IRENAEUS OF LYONS (c. 135–c. 202). Bishop of Lyons who published the most famous and influential refutation of Gnostic thought.

JAKULT (13th cent.). A collection of commentaries from various ancient books by **R. Shimeon of Frankfurt**.

JARKI (1040-1105). Shlomo Yitzchaki, also called Rashi, he was a medieval French rabbi and author of a commentary on the Tanakh.

JELAMMEDENU (8th cent.). A popular Homily-Midrash originating in Israel that bears **Tanchuma**'s name but was not written by him.

JEROME (c. 347–420). Gifted exegete and exponent of a classical Latin style, now best known as the translator of the Latin Vulgate. He defended the perpetual virginity of Mary, attacked Origen and Pelagius and supported extreme ascetic practices.

JOCHANAN (30-90 A.D.). R. Yohanan ben Zeccai. A primary contributor to the core text of the Mishnah.

JONAH (4th century). Palestinian amora rabbi who was the leading rabbinical authority in the 4th amoraic generation.

JUNIUS-TREMELLIUS BIBLE (1575). Immanuel Tremellius (1510-80) was an Italian Jewish convert to Christianity, a leading Hebraist and Bible translator. Franciscus Junius was his son-in-law and together they worked on a Latin translation of the Bible from the Hebrew and Syriac.

JUSTIN MARTYR (100/110–165). Palestinian philosopher who was converted to Christianity. He traveled to Rome and wrote several apologies (defenses of the faith) against both pagans and Jews; he was eventually martyred.

KABBALAH. Esoteric method, discipline, and school of thought of Judaism. The **Zohar** (13th cent. but with oral tradition dating back to untold primordial time) is one of the main texts of Kabbalah.

KIRCHER, CONRAD (d. 1622). German philologian of Augsburg, Lutheran pastor first at Donauwerth and later at Jaxtdorf. He published a concordance of the LXX in 1607 called *Concordic veteris Testamenti Gracace Ebreis vocibus respondents*.

LEO THE GREAT (regn. 440–461). Bishop of Rome whose *Tome to Flavian* helped to strike a balance between Nestorian and Cyrilline positions at the Council of Chalcedon in 451.

LETTER OF SIX BISHOPS (268 AD). Or *Letter of Hymenaeus*. Letter elaborating the received catechetical tradition of Christ in the Old Testament, directed at the heretic Paul of Samosata. Soon led to the synod of seventy elders.

LEVI BEN GERSOM (1288-1344). Best known as Gersonides or Magister Leo Hebraeus. French Jewish philosopher, Talmudist, Mathematician, physician, astronomer. Wrote several commentaries on Scripture.

Lightfoot, John (1602-1675). English churchman, rabbinical scholar, Vice-Chancellor at the University of Cambridge. Wrote the important work *A Commentary on the New Testament from the Talmud and Hebraica*.

LORINUS OF AVIGNON (1559-1634). Jesuit who published a commentary on Scripture.

MAIMONIDES (1135-1204). Moses ben Maimon. Spanish born rabbi who become one of the most influential of all medieval Torah scholars.

MANASSEH BEN ISRAEL (1604-1657). Manoel Dias Soeiro. Portuguese rabbi, kabbalist, printer and publisher.

MARCKII, JOHANNIS (1656-1731). Johannes a Marck. Dutch Reformed theologian and church historian who the book *Compendium theologiæ Christianæ*.

MASIUS, ANDREAS (1514-73). Catholic priest, humanist, and one of the first Europeans to specialize in the Syriac language.

MENAHEM BEN BENJAMIN RECANATI (1223-1290). Italian rabbi who wrote a commentary on the Torah.

MENASSEH BEN ISRAEL (1604-1657). Manoel Dias Soeiro. Portuguese rabbi, kabbalist, writer, diplomat, and founded the first Hebrew printing press in Amsterdam in 1626. The book cited seems to be *Primo Questionum in Genesis*, previously published as *The Conciliator*.

MILL, JOHN (1645-1707). English theologian who wrote a critical edition of the Greek New Testament with notes on over thirty-thousand variants.

MORE, HENRY (1614-1687). English philosopher and Rationalist of the Cambridge Platonist school.

MOSES BEN MAIMON. See **Maimonides**.

MOSES BEN NAHMAN (1194-1270). Commonly called Nachmanides or Ramban or Moses ben Nachman Gerondi (Moses Gerundensis). Leading medieval Jewish scholar, rabbi, philosopher, physician, kabbalist, and biblical commentator. He lived most of his life in Girona, Catalonia (Spain).

MOSES GERUND. See **Moses Ben Nachman**.

MUNSTERUS (1488-1552). Sebastian Münster. German cartographer, cosmographer, and Christian Hebraist scholar. Early on he was a Franciscan, then became Lutheran to accept a chair at the University of Basel.

Noetus (fl. 230 AD). Presbyter in Asia Minor and proponent of the heresy called modalistic Monarchianism or Patripassianism.

NOVATIAN OF ROME (fl. 235–258). Roman theologian, otherwise orthodox, who formed a schismatic church after failing to become pope. His treatise on the Trinity states the classic Western doctrine.

ORIGEN (b. 185; fl. c. 200–254). Influential exegete and systematic theologian from Alexandria, Egypt. He was condemned (perhaps unfairly) for maintaining the preexistence of souls while purportedly denying the resurrection of the body. His extensive works of exegesis focus on the spiritual meaning of the text.

PARKER, SAMUEL (1681-1730). Nonjuror (declined oaths of allegiance) and theological writer, bishop of Oxford, wrote *Bibliotheca Biblica*, a *Patristic Commentary on the Scriptures* (1720-35). It only covered the Pentateuch.

PEARSON, JOHN (1613-1686). English theologian and scholar. Wrote a work in the Creed that mined the Church Fathers.

PERKINS, WILLIAM (1558-1602). English Puritan theologian and leader of the Puritan movement in the Church of England during Elizabeth's reign.

PHILO (20 BC – 50 AD). Alexandrians Jewish Hellenistic philosopher who lived during the time of Christ, he is one of the best monotheistic proponents who believed in a "second God" called the Logos, which lends itself nicely towards an understanding of Christ in the OT.

PROCOPIUS OF GAZA (c. 465–c. 530). A Christian exegete educated in Alexandria. He wrote numerous theological works and commentaries on Scripture (particularly the Hebrew Bible), the latter marked by the allegorical exegesis for which the Alexandrian school was known.

RACOVIAN CATECHISM (1605). A Socinian catechism meant to destroy the Gospel.

RAVANELLUS, PETRUS (d. 1680). Published *Bibliothica Sacra, seu Thesaurus Scripturea*. Geneva, 1654.

REMUS, GEORG (1561-1625). German lawyer, philologe, historian, poet. Vice Chancellor at the University of Jena.

REUCHLIN, JOHANN (1455-1522). German humanist and Greek and Hebrew scholar. He wrote a treatise *On the Art of Kabbalah* (1517).

RIDDERUS, FRANCISCUS (1618-1683). Dutch Reformed minister who served at Schermorhorn, Brielle, and Rotterdam. He wrote religious poems and devotional books.

RITTANGEL, JOHANN STEPHAN (1602-1652). German Jew who converted to Roman Catholicism, then became a Calvinist, and later a Lutheran. He was professor of Oriental languages at Königsberg.

RUPERTUS. Allix probably has in mind Rupert of Deutz (1075-1129) an influential Benedictine from Belgium.

SAADIA (882/892 – 942). Saadia Gaon, rabbi, philosopher, exegete who wrote extensively in Arabic.

SANCTIUS (1553-1628). Gaspar Sanchez. Spanish Jesuit. Taught at Oropesa in Madrid. Spent thirteen years writing commentaries on Scripture.

SAMUEL (165-254). Samuel of Nehardea or Samuel bar Abba. One of the early rabbinical authorities cited in Genesis Rabbah.

SCHLICHTINGIUS, JONAS (1592-1661). Polish nobleman, this Socinian wrote commentaries on the New Testament.

SERRANO, JOSEPH FRANCO (1652-1695). Rabbi, teacher of Hebrew at the Portuguese synagogue in Amsterdam. He provided a Spanish translation of the books of Moses with marginal notes from the Talmud and the Rabbis who commented on them.

SHIMEON OF FRANKFURT (13th cent.). Rabbi who wrote the **Jalkut**.

SMALCIUS, VALENTINUS (1572-1622). German Socinian.

SOCINIANISM. Named for Italian theologian Fausto Sozzini (Lat: **Faustus Socinus**). It is nontrinitarian in its view of Christ and precursor to many forms of Unitarianism within Protestantism.

SOCINUS, (FAUSTUS 1539-1604). Fausto Paolo Sozzini. Italian theologian and founder of Socinianism, precursor to many forms of Unitarianism within Protestantism.

SOLOMON BEN MELEK (16th cent.) From Fez, Morocco. He published his Bible commentary *Michlol Jophi* (*Perfection of Beauty*) in 1549 through a press in Constantinople.

SPANHEIM, FREDRICK (1600-1649). Calvinist professor at Leiden.

STAUNTON, WILLIAM (17th-18th cent.). Clerk in Chancery, Socinian who denied the deity of Christ.

STRABO, WALAFRID (808-849). Alemannic Benedictine monk and theological writer who lived in southern Germany. He wrote on the Psalms and Leviticus.

TANCHUMA (350-71). Tanchuma bar Abba. Jewish Rabbi of the 5th generation amora (Jewish scholars of the period from 200-500 AD).

TARGUM. A Targum is a paraphrastic rendition of the Hebrew Scripture into Aramaic for Jews who did not speak Hebrew. They contain both oral tradition and interpretation of the Scripture and were probably first written down around the first century by the Jews.

TATIAN (second century). Christian apologist from the East. Famous for his Gospel harmony, the *Diatessaron*, he also wrote *Address to the Greeks*, a defense of Christianity addressed to the pagan world.

TERTULLIAN (c. 155/160–225/250). Carthaginian apologist and polemicist who laid the foundations of Christology and Trinitarian Orthodoxy in the West, though he himself was later estranged from the catholic tradition.

THEODORET OF CYR (c. 393–466). Bishop of Cyr (Cyrrhus), he was an opponent of Cyril who commented extensively on Old Testament texts as a lucid exponent of Antiochene exegesis.

USQUE, ABRAHAM (16ᵗʰ cent.). Also known as Duarte Pinel (Pinhel). Marrano printer. Born in Portugal but fled from the Inquisition shortly after 1543, established himself at Ferrara, and became associated with the press established by the Spanish ex-Marrano, **Yom-Tov ben Levi Athias** (Jerónimo de Vargas). He followed Athias' plan of publishing Jewish liturgies in the vernacular, as well as other texts intended to facilitate the Marranos' return to Judaism. Usque's name first appears in connection with the famous Bible translation of 1553, the so-called *Ferrara Bible*.

VATABLE, FRANÇOIS (d. 1547). French humanist scholar, a Hellenist, and a Hebraist.

VECHNER, DANIEL (1572-1632). Taught at the Gymnasium at Goldberg (Germany). Wrote several works in Latin. (PÁ)

VICTORINUS OF PETOVIUM (d. c. 304). Latin biblical exegete. With multiple works attributed to him, his sole surviving work is the *Commentary on the Apocalypse* and perhaps some fragments from *Commentary on Matthew*. a spiritual disciple of Origen. Victorinus died during the first year of Diocletian's persecution, probably in 304.

WATERLAND, DANIEL (1683-1740), an English theologian who became Master of Magdalene College, Cambridge in 1714, Chancellor of the Diocese of York in 1722, and Archdeacon of Middlesex in 1730.

WHISTON, WILLIAM (1667-1752). English theologian, historian, and mathematician, a leading figure in the popularization of the ideas of Isaac Newton, including Newton's Arianism. Worked on important translations of the Antiquities of the Jews by Josephus.

Witsius, Herman (1636-1708). Dutch Calvinist who wrote an important work on the divine covenants.

ZANCHI, JEROME (1516-1590). Italian Protestant Reformer, very influential after Calvin's death.

Zohar (13ᵗʰ cent.). The foundational text of Kabbalah. It first appeared in Spain in the 13ᵗʰ century and was published by Moses de León who ascribed it to Shimon bar Yochai (Rashbi), a rabbi of the 2ⁿᵈ century.

Author Index

A

Abarbanel 76
Aben Ezra 30, 32, 136
Abraham ben Salomon Usque 62
Abraham Saba 25
Abravanel, Don Isaac 72
Agrippa, Henry 287
Ainsworth 326
Akiba 157
Allix, Peter 26, 287, 375
Alshich, Moshe 72
Alting, Jacob. 341
Ambrose . 95, 233
Amelius 294
Apostolic Constitutions 68
Apuleius 367
Aquila a Jew . 111
Aquinas, Thomas 95
Arethas of Caesarea 95
Aristobulus .. 112, 293
Athanasius 376

Athias ...*See* Yom-Tov Ben Levi Athias
Augustine 92, 274, 307, 313, 319, 335, 339
Autpert Ambrose 95

B

Bahya ben Asher ibn Halawa . 80
Barker, Margaret 9
Bauckham, Richard 9
Bede 95
Bellarmine, Robert 84, 375
Beza, Theodore . 217, 221, 266
Bomberg, Daniel 139
Boyarin, Daniel 9
Bruce, James . 307
Bull, George 223, 248
Buxtorf, Johannes ... 89, 138, 208, 211, 212, 220, 281

C

Cælius of Pannonia 95

Celsus 287
Chrysostom ... 68, 335
Clark, Samuel 160, 216
Clarke, Samuel . 209, 215, 251
Clement of Alexandria. 68, 69, 288
Clifford, Hywel 7
Council at Sirmium .. 318
Council of Antioch 316
Cyprian . 68, 221, 319, 324
Cyril of Alexandria. 68, 92, 292, 319, 324

D

Danet, Pierre 367
David ben Yom Tov ibn Bilia 82
De Gols, Gerard 26, 110
de Peiresc, Nicolas 307
Dionysius the Areopagite . 70
Drusius 111

see Abraham
ben
Salonom 62
Drusius,
Johannes .. 307

E

Elijah Levita ... 54
Emadi, Michael
.... 351
Epiphanius of
Salamis.... 221,
231, 298, 312,
313
Erasmus........ 221
Eusebius 68, 112,
138, 293, 295,
297, 316, 324,
327

F

Fagius, Paul.. 300
Fossum, Jarl E.. 9

G

Gathercole,
Simon 10
Gordon, Cyrus
.... 226
Goslavius, Adam
.... 252
Gregory
Nazianzen 313
Gregory of Elvira
.... 69
Gregory of
Nyssa 231
Gregory, John
.... 310
Grotius, Hugo 60,
112, 130, 140,
255, 284, 368,
381

H

Hannah, Darrell
D............... 10

Haylin, Peter 260
Haymo of
Halberstadt 95
Heiser, Michael
S. 10
Heraclitus 295
Heylin, Peter 302
Hilary of Poitiers
221, 312, 318,
326, 327, 328
Hillary of
Poitiers..... 309
Hoornbeck,
Johannes ..219
Hurtado, Larry
W............... 10

I

Irenaeus 298, 315

J

Jarki
also called
Rashi 35, 37
Jerome 63, 90,
111, 218, 233,
236, 335, 336,
376
Joel ibn Shu'aib
.... 81
Johannes van den
Driesche..... 62
Jonah (rabbi) ..30
Joseph ben
Abraham
Gikatilla 81,
140
Josephus 147
Justin Martyr .49,
68, 69, 92, 98,
99, 287, 298,
316, 324, 325,
333, 361

K

Kircher, Conrad
.... 63

L

Lee, Aquila H. I.
.... 10
Leo the Great 69,
295
*Letter of Six
Bishops*......316,
319
Lightfoot, John
........248, 300
Lorinus of
Avignon 70
Lucian...........367

M

Maimonides ...77,
83, 173, 228,
340
Manasse Ben
Israel.........343
Manoel Dias
Soeiro.........81
Marckii,
Johannis ..227,
298
Masius, Andreas
...........85, 178
Menachem......50
Menahem ben
Benjamin
Recanati 69
Metatron..54, 55,
88, 89, 90, 91,
306, 340
Metzger, Bruce
M..3, 204, 221
Mill, John 221
More, Henry 237
Moses ben
Maimon 83,
213
Moses ben
Nachman ..50,
79, 178, 340,
341

called
   Nachmanid
   es 52
Münster,
   Sebastian.... 72

N

Neusner, Jacob
   67
Noetus.......... 221
Novatian. 69, 326
Numenius the
   Pythagorean
   288

O

Origen 68
Orlov, Andrei A.
   55

P

Parker, Samuel
   305, 307, 310,
   311, 313, 322,
   334
Paul of Samosata
   316
Pearson, John
   223
Perkins, William
   .... 217, 306
Philo .. 26, 69, 78,
   118, 119, 124,
   128, 129, 131,
   132, 133, 137,
   138, 141, 142,
   147, 150, 151,
   163, 172, 197,
   284, 288, 289,
   290, 293, 351,
   352, 353
Photinus 318
Plato 28, 292
Pliny 367
Plotinus 237, 288,
   292, 293
Porphryr 292

Procopius of
   Gaza 69

R

R. Eliezer........ 91
R. Gekatalia 82
R. Johanan 67
R. Levi ben
   Gersom 82
R. Menachem de
   Rekanah 87
R. Menachem of
   Rekan 80
R. Menasseh ... 82
R. Shimeon of
   Frankfurt.... 74
R. Solomon 79
R. Yohanan ben
   Zeccai 73
Rabbi Saadia . 364
Racovian
   Catechism 362
Ravanellus,
   Petrus 264,
   313, 376
Remus, Georg
   374
Reuchlin, Johann
   .... 54, 90
Ridderus,
   Franciscus 248
Rittangel, Johann
   .... 286, 344
Rodkinson,
   Michael L. . 67
Rupert of Deutz
   95

S

Sanchez, Gaspar
   70
Schlichtingius,
   Jonas......... 252
Segal, Alan F. . 10
Serrano, Joseph
   Franco 76

Sirmian Council
   326
Smalcius,
   Valentinus
   .... 273, 363
Socinus 196, 209,
   241
Solomon ben
   Melek 66
Spanheim,
   Fredrick.. 313,
   335, 379
Staunton,
   William ... 222
Stuckenbruck,
   Loren T. ... 10

T

Tanchuma bar
   Abba 79
Tertullian 49, 68,
   92, 274, 288,
   298, 309, 314,
   324, 333, 334
The Council of
   Sirmium 68
Theodoret of
   Cyrus 69, 326,
   361
Toth, Peter .. 361
Tremellius,
   Immanuel 259

U

Usquez .... *See*
   Abraham ben
   Salonon
   Usque

V

van der Kun,
   Peter 321
Vatable, François
   237
Vechner, Daniel
   129

Victorinus of
  Pettau......... 95
Vreugdenhil,
  Arjen 70

W

Walafrid Strabo
  95
Walker, Luke ... 5

Waterland,
  Daniel 218,
  240, 363
Witsius, Herman
  .298, 301, 321

Y

Yitzchaki,
  Shlomo 90

Yom-Tov Ben
  Levi Athias .62

Z

Zanchi, Jerome
  ....298, 374
Zohar 79

Scripture Index

Genesis

Gen 1 117
Gen 1:1 .. 235, 236
Gen 1:1-3 203
Gen 1:2 248
Gen 1:26 101, 119, 203
Gen 1:27 144, 285
Gen 1:28 144
Gen 3:8 ... 24, 145, 285
Gen 3:9 .... 25, 145
Gen 3:10 145
Gen 3:15 299
Gen 3:20 301
Gen 3:22 285
Gen 4:7 304
Gen 4:23 34
Gen 4:26 305
Gen 5:22 66
Gen 5:24 306, 308
Gen 6:6 29
Gen 6:9 308
Gen 7:1 308
Gen 7:16 309
Gen 11:3 315

Gen 11:12-13 . 311
Gen 11:15-16 . 312
Gen 12:1, 7 314
Gen 13:13 326
Gen 14:18 312
Gen 14:19 312
Gen 15:1 314
Gen 15:6 78
Gen 16:7 149, 322
Gen 16:9 149
Gen 16:10 149
Gen 16:13 ..... 149, 322
Gen 17:1 ...... 203, 231, 325
Gen 18:1 142
Gen 18:1–3 30
Gen 18:15-16 . 153
Gen 18:19 321
Gen 18:25 316
Gen 18:27 275
Gen 19:1 .. 33, 323
Gen 19:21 323
Gen 19:24 . 33, 34, 139, 323
Gen 20 149
Gen 21:16 150

Gen 21:18 150
Gen 22:2 147
Gen 22:11-12 . 318
Gen 22:16 319
Gen 22:17-18 . 319
Gen 26:2 150, 324
Gen 26:3 150
Gen 26:24 150
Gen 26:24-25 . 324
Gen 28:3 325
Gen 28:10–22 ... 39
Gen 28:12ff 325
Gen 28:13 ..... 151, 325
Gen 28:13-16 . 151
Gen 28:20-21 ... 74, 285
Gen 31 326
Gen 31:11 152
Gen 31:13 152
Gen 31:33 325
Gen 32:1-2 34
Gen 32:9 275
Gen 32:9, 10, 11. 75
Gen 32:11 37
Gen 32:24 36

Gen 32:24, 26–30
.... 36
Gen 32:26 38
Gen 32:29 110
Gen 35:1 .. 39, 327
Gen 35:9144, 151,
152
Gen 39:9 329
Gen 39:21 329
Gen 48:3-465, 151
Gen 48:15... 66, 87
Gen 48:15-16 7,
36, 61, 109,
328
Gen 48:16 . 37, 38,
39, 75, 79, 80,
84, 86, 108,
380
Gen 49:3 236
Gen 49 75
Gen 49:18 290,
328, 336
Gen 49:24 87
Gen 49:25... 76, 81

Exodus

Ex 3 . 89, 136, 338
Ex 3:1 187
Ex 3:1–6 40
Ex 3:2 ..... 41, 155,
333
Ex 3:2-3 177
Ex 3:4 ..... 40, 155,
333
Ex 3:5 48
Ex 3:640, 41, 155,
187, 333, 357
Ex 3:13 334
Ex 3:14 .... 40, 209
Ex 3:15 209

Ex 3:16 155
Ex 12:12......... 208
Ex 13:21. 136, 163
Ex 14:19.. 81, 136,
163, 332
Ex 14:24 163
Ex 15:2 209
Ex 15:3 .... 46, 106
Ex 15:3, 11 110
Ex 15:11 110
Ex 15:25 163
Ex 16:7, 10..... 164
Ex 17:8ff. 164
Ex 17:14 164
Ex 17:15 164
Ex 17:16 209
Ex 19:6 338
Ex 19:10 340
Ex 19:18–20 41
Ex 19:19........... 29
Ex 20............. 338
Ex 20:1 .. 285, 338
Ex 20:2 203
Ex 20:11 235
Ex 20:19 357
Ex 20:22........... 42
Ex 23 .... 90, 143
Ex 23:18........... 45
Ex 23:20.... 43, 44,
53
Ex 23:20-21 ... 339
Ex 23:20-22 43,
270
Ex 23:21.... 44, 53,
355
Ex 23:22........... 45
Ex 23:23..... 43, 44
Ex 23:31......... 107
Ex 24.............. 143
Ex 24:6 45

Ex 25:8 342
Ex 25:40......... 166
Ex 27:31......... 166
Ex 27:33......... 166
Ex 29:45-46 ...342
Ex 33 79
Ex 33:2............43
Ex 33:3............44
Ex 33:4............44
Ex 33:4-6 346
Ex 34:6... 211, 347
Ex 34:6-7 246
Ex 33:7...........346
Ex 33:9 343
Ex 34:9...275, 347
Ex 33:2-3 .43, 346
Ex 33:10.........163
Ex 33:11.........331
Ex 33:12-13 ...347
Ex 33:13...........44
Ex 33:13-16 43
Ex 33:14... 44, 347
Ex 33:15-163..347
Ex 33:17.........347
Ex 33:20.........282
Ex 33:35.........346
Ex 37:9...........166
Ex 40:34-35 ...343

Leviticus

Lev 7:15 183
Lev 25:25 379
Lev 26:12 344

Numbers

Num 6:22ff.......84
Num 6:24 275
Num 6:24-26 .203
Num 7:89.......157
Num 9:15 343

Num 10:35 136
Num 11:20 285
Num 12:5 163
Num 13:16 339
Num 14 143
Num 14:35 ... 203
Num 22:12 348
Num 22:22 348
Num 22:32 348
Num 22:35 ... 174, 348
Num 23:21-22 348
Num 23:4-5 ... 348
Num 24:20 ... 236
Num 24:4 348

Deuteronomy

Dt 1:30, 32 .... 285, 286
Dt 5:6 341
Dt 5:24 339
Dt 6:4 202
Dt 6:5 .... 263, 273
Dt 6:13 274
Dt 12:5, 11 185
Dt 13:4 270
Dt 18:18 331
Dt 27:10 270
Dt 32:9 105
Dt 32:39 291
Dt 32:40 225
Dt 32:43 281
Dt 32:48-49 ... 172
Dt 33:1 172
Dt 33:16 .... 41, 46
Dt 34:1 172

Joshua

Josh 5:13 .. 46, 178
Josh 5:13-14 ... 176

Josh 5:13-15 .... 46, 104
Josh 5:14 176, 354
Josh 5:15 177
Josh 6:2 177
Josh 24:19 45

Judges

Jdg 2:1 355
Jdg 2:3 356
Jdg 2:4 356
Jdg 13 179
Jdg 13:8-9 358
Jdg 13:11 359
Jdg 13:16 320
Jdg 13:18 110, 358
Jdg 13:21 358
Jdg 13:22 357, 359
Jdg 5:31 263
Jdg 6:11-12 178
Jdg 6:12 356
Jdg 6:13 356
Jdg 6:14 . 178, 356
Jdg 6:15 136
Jdg 6:16 178
Jdg 6:20-22 178
Jdg 6:23 357
Jdg 6:23-25 178
Jdg 6:27 178
Jdg 7:18, 20.... 179

Ruth

Ruth 3:8 29
Ruth 4:8 63

1 Samuel

1Sa 3:3-4........ 179
1Sa 3:21 . 179, 180
1Sa 8:16 107

2 Samuel

2Sa 6:18 107
2Sa 7:14-15 376
2Sa 12:24 372
2Sa 24:14 182
2Sa 24:15 180
2Sa 24:16 181
2Sa 24:16-17 .. 181
2Sa 24:17 181

1 Kings

1Kg 1:33 34
1Kg 3:5 183
1Kg 3:15 183
1Kg 8 275
1Kg 8:6 185
1Kg 8:10 373
1Kg 8:10-11 .. 185, 189
1Kg 8:11 191
1Kg 8:12-61 ... 185
1Kg 8:15 182
1Kg 8:39 232
1Kg 9:1 185
1Kg 9:2 .. 183, 185
1Kg 9:3 185
1Kg 19 186
1Kg 19:5, 7 188
1Kg 19:8 187
1Kg 19:13 187
1Kg 19:18 366
1Kg 22:19-23 110
1Kg 22:19ff. ... 188

2 Kings

2Kg 1 188
2Kg 6:17 34
2Kg 19:15 235
2Kg 19:34 182

2Kg 19:35 188
2Kg 20:6 182

1 Chronicles

1Ch 7:12 185
1Ch 21:13 180
1Ch 21:16 181
1Ch 22:9 372

2 Chronicles

2Ch 1:2-4 184
2Ch 1:6 184
2Ch 1:7 184
2Ch 6:4 186
2Ch 7:15-16 ... 372
2Ch 11:17 376

Ezra

Ezra 3:11 275
Ezra 9 275

Nehemiah

Neh 9:6 242

Esther

Est 8:8 34

Job

Job 12:7-9 240
Job 19:25 225
Job 19:25-26 ... 335
Job 26:13 335
Job 27:3 335
Job 31:26-27 .. 366
Job 31:28 366
Job 33:4 335
Job 33:15 334
Job 33:23-24 .. 380
Job 40:19 236
Job 42:5 335

Psalms

Ps 2 103
Ps 2:12 ... 277, 365
Ps 2:7 365
Ps 2:8 380
Ps 2:11 365
Ps 5:11 263
Ps 16:10 369
Ps 18:46 269
Ps 19:14 75
Ps 22:1 368
Ps 22:7-8 368
Ps 22:16 368
Ps 22:18 368
Ps 22:22 . 368, 379
Ps 23:1 119
Ps 24:8 224
Ps 29:3–9 24
Ps 33:6 .... 27, 101,
    113, 203, 363
Ps 33:9 27
Ps 34:19 75
Ps 36:6 242
Ps 45:6 203
Ps 45:6-7 364
Ps 45:11 277
Ps 48:8-10 219
Ps 49:7-8 380
Ps 50:1 .... 220, 250
Ps 50:15 274
Ps 67:1-4 371
Ps 68 167
Ps 68:7-15 370
Ps 68:17 ... 42, 370
Ps 68:18-20 370
Ps 68:24 370
Ps 68:29 371
Ps 72. 110
Ps 72:18 243

Ps 77:14 110
Ps 82:8 220
Ps 83:18 209
Ps 86:9-10, 12 . 265
Ps 86:10 243
Ps 89:35 205
Ps 92 275
Ps 90:2 318
Ps 96:5 219
Ps 96:7-8 265
Ps 96:13 250
Ps 97:7 281
Ps 97:9 267
Ps 98 275
Ps 98:9 250
Ps 102 ..... 229, 275
Ps 102:25-27 .. 229
Ps 105:15 297
Ps 110 103
Ps 110:1 114, 203,
    364
Ps 110:4 195
Ps 128:28 269
Ps 136:4 243
Ps 145:15 242

Proverbs

Prov 3 103
Prov 8:22–26 25
Prov 8:22 103,
    111, 236
Prov 8:22-23 .. 227
Prov 8:22-32 .. 373
Prov 8:25 103
Prov 8:31 374
Prov 8:32 373
Prov 30:1 375
Prov 30:4 374
Prov 30:7 275
Prov 30:7-9 375

Ecclesiastes

Ecc 7:23 376
Ecc 8:17 28
Ecc 11:9 375

Song of Solomon

SS 8:6 209

Isaiah

Isa 6:1 189
Isa 6:1-5 378
Isa 6:1ff. 189
Isa 6:3 233
Isa 6:3, 8 203
Isa 6:5 .... 233, 357
Isa 6:8 189
Isa 6:9-10 189
Isa 7:14 379
Isa 8:8 379
Isa 9:6 ... 179, 217, 218, 259, 340, 375
Isa 9:7 110
Isa 10:21 218
Isa 11:2-3 94
Isa 23:14 75
Isa 25:9 245
Isa 33:22 203
Isa 38:11 209
Isa 40:26 240
Isa 42:8 .. 205, 208
Isa 43:10 227
Isa 43:21 349
Isa 43:25 246
Isa 44:6 . 209, 212, 345
Isa 44:6-8 213
Isa 45:12 27
Isa 45:17 285
Isa 45:21-25 ... 209

Isa 46:8 202
Isa 47:4 75
Isa 48:13 27
Isa 55:6 274
Isa 56:7 274
Isa 59:20 . 38, 379, 380
Isa 60:1 344
Isa 61:1 203
Isa 63:7 377
Isa 63:8 179
Isa 63:8-10........ 78
Isa 63:9..... 88, 110
Isa 63:9,10, 11, 14 203
Isa 63:9-10 377
Isa 63:16... 75, 245

Jeremiah

Jer 10:10 225
Jer 17:10 232
Jer 17:5 261
Jer 17:7 261
Jer 23:23 217
Jer 23:23-24 ... 228
Jer 23:6 210
Jer 31:34 246
Jer 32 275
Jer 32:27 208
Jer 46:22 29

Ezekiel

Ezek 1:6 190
Ezek 1:21 190
Ezek 1:24 ... 28, 90
Ezek 1:26, 28 . 190
Ezek 3:12 190
Ezek 6:13 290
Ezek 9:3 190
Ezek 9:5-7 191

Ezek 10:1 190
Ezek 10:4 191
Ezek 10:18-19 191
Ezek 11:23 191
Ezek 14:14 335
Ezek 33:21ff... 191
Ezek 40:3-5 193
Ezek 41:19 190
Ezek 42-43 191
Ezek 43:2 191
Ezek 43:4 191
Ezek 43:5 191
Ezek 44:4 191

Daniel

Dan 3:25 110
Dan 4:4, 18, 20 203
Dan 4:17 110
Dan 5:14 203
Dan 6:26 203
Dan 7:8 94
Dan 7:9ff. 110
Dan 9:17 275, 277

Hosea

Hos 1:7.... 27, 219, 245
Hos 12:3, 5 37
Hos 12:3-4 153
Hos 12:3-5 36, 327
Hos 12:4 38
Hos 12:5 .. 39, 208
Hos 13:2 366

Joel

Joel 2 275

Micah

Mic 5:2 227

Habakkuk

Hab 3 275

Zechariah

Zech 1:8, 10 ... 193
Zech 1:9 193
Zech 1:13-14 . 193
Zech 1:19 193
Zech 2:1 193
Zech 2:3. 193, 196
Zech 2:4. 193, 196
Zech 2:5 196
Zech 2:8-9 193
Zech 2:10 196
Zech 2:10-11. 196, 197
Zech 2:11 193
Zech 3:1 195
Zech 3:2. 195, 196
Zech 3:3-4 195
Zech 3:4 196
Zech 3:4-5 196
Zech 3:9 92
Zech 5:5-6 193
Zech 6:4 193
Zech 6:12-13 . 354
Zech 9:9. 3451 Esd
1:50-51 108
Zech 12:5, 10 . 233
Zech 14:4 191

Malachi

Mal 1:6 265
Mal 3:1 ..... 51, 88, 220, 338, 346
Mal 3:6 229

Matthew

Matt 1:23 379
Matt 3:16-17.. 203

Matt 4:7 258
Matt 4:10 258
Matt 5:16 258
Matt 6:4 258
Matt 8:27 271
Matt 9:2-3 195
Matt 9:2, 6 246
Mat 10:37 263
Matt 11:5 243
Matt 17:3 333
Matt 17:5 271
Matt 18:20 228
Matt 20:28 380
Matt 21:4-5 345
Matt 22:37 263
Matt 22:44 364
Matt 23:34 373
Matt 26:28 246
Matt 27:35 369
Matt 27:39 368
Matt 27:43 369
Matt 27:46 368
Matt 28:19 203
Matt 28:20 228

Mark

Mark 1:27 271
Mark 12:29 202
Mark 12:36 364

Luke

Luke 1:16-17... 220
Luke 1:68 245
Luke 3:4 220
Luke 5:21 246
Luke 6:19 243
Luke 10:19 243
Luke 11:28 373
Luke 11:49 373
Luke 11:52 350

Luke 16:22 320
Luke 20:42 364
Luke 23:34 369
Luke 24:44 359

John

John 1:1 ... 27, 251, 282, 292, 315
John 1:1, 2 25
John 1:2 292
John 1:3 ..... 25, 27, 292
John 1:3, 10 235
John 1:4 225, 292, 302
John 1:9 .. 292, 350
John 1:14 292, 344
John 1:16. 245, 350
John 1:18 283, 292
John 1:45 332
John 1:51 326
John 3:16 244
John 3:31 247
John 3:36 262
John 4:24 258
John 5:17 242
John 5:19 234
John 5:22 220, 249, 250, 324
John 5:22, 2 207
John 5:23 254, 265
John 5:26 225, 231
John 5:27 249
John 5:28-29 ... 336
John 5:37 283, 296
John 6:33, 35 .. 289
John 6:35, 36, 38 262
John 6:35, 43, 47 262

John 6:46 283
John 8:42 263
John 8:56 317
John 8:56, 58 ... 35
John 8:57 317
John 8:58 318
John 10............. 88
John 10:30 204
John 11:25 225
John 12:9-10.. 378
John 12:26 271
John 12:41 .... 189, 233, 378
John 14:1 258, 260
John 14:10...... 289
John 14:17 204
John 14:23 264
John 16:30 232
John 17:3 260
John 17:19 247
John 19:24, 37 369
John 19:34, 37 233
John 19:37 234
John 20:31...... 262
John 21:17 232

Acts

Acts 1:24........ 232
Acts 2:29-31.. 370
Acts 2:34........ 364
Acts 2:36 268
Acts 3:15........ 225
Acts 3:22........ 332
Acts 3:24........ 382
Acts 4:10........ 243
Acts 5:3.......... 258
Acts 5:4.......... 258
Acts 7:31 70
Acts 7:37........ 332
Acts 7:38........ 338

Acts 7:53.......... 42
Acts 10:43 ..... 262, 350
Acts 15:8........ 232
Acts 16:31....... 262
Acts 16:34....... 262
Acts 17:28 228
Acts 20:28..... 213, 245, 380

Romans

Rom 1:3 222
Rom 1:9 264
Rom 1:25 ..... 223, 241
Rom 3:25 244
Rom 4:9........ 146
Rom 4:11 320
Rom 4:19 315
Rom 4:22 146
Rom 8:15....... 272
Rom 9:5 220, 222, 223, 239, 338
Rom 10:4 ..... 277, 350
Rom 10:9 277
Rom 10:11..... 277
Rom 10:13..... 277
Rom 11:34, 36 239
Rom 14:10-11 209

1 Corinthians

1Co 1:24 244
1Co 1:30 210, 245, 375
1Co 2:8 224
1Co 6:2 .. 115, 247
1Co 6:20 381
1Co 8:4 202
1Co 8:6.. 238, 258

1Co 10:1-4 362
1Co 10:4 .. 86, 349
1Co 12:6 243
1Co 15:22 247
1Co 15:45 ..... 248, 302
1Co 15:47 247
1Co 16:22 263

2 Corinthians

2Co 1:20 299
2Co 5:21 244
2Co 6:15-16 .. 344
2Co 13:14 204

Galatians

Gal 1:1............. 93
Gal 1:8-9 264
Gal 3:6 146
Gal 3:8, 16-17 316
Gal 3:16 315
Gal 3:17 316
Gal 3:19 42
Gal 3:20 202

Ephesians

Eph 1:2............. 85
Eph 2:4-5 245
Eph 3:9 238
Eph 4:6 223
Eph 4:8 370
Eph 5:5............. 93
Eph 5:14......... 344
Eph 5:32......... 248
Eph 6:24......... 263

Philippians

Php 2:9-11 210
Php 2:10......... 205

Php 2:10-11 .. 265, 269

Colossians

Col 1:14......... 246
Col 1:15. 237, 266
Col 1:15-17... 235, 236
Col 1:15–18 27
Col 1:16 25
Col 1:17 228, 237, 242
Col 2:2 260
Col 2:3... 232, 373
Col 2:9..... 45, 225
Col 2:17. 338, 350
Col 2:18 92

1 Thessalonians

1Th 4:15, 16 .. 307
1Th 5:23......... 247

2 Thessalonians

2Th 1:7-10..... 272
2Th 2:8......... 216

1 Timothy

1Ti 2:5-6........ 381
1Ti 3:16 213, 258, 301, 338
1Ti 6:14........ 216
1Ti 6:15 224

2 Timothy

2Tim 1:10 216
2Tim 4:1, 8 .. 216

Titus

Tit 1:2............. 205
Tit 2:13.......... 216

Hebrews

Heb 1:2 238
Heb 1:3 ..... 24, 27, 102, 229, 289
Heb 1:4 45
Heb 1:6 281
Heb 1:8 364
Heb 1:10-12... 229
Heb 2:9 268
Heb 2:10 47
Heb 2:11 247, 379
Heb 2:12 369
Heb 3:4 235
Heb 4:12 106
Heb 5:5 354
Heb 6:18 205
Heb 7:1ff........ 312
Heb 7:25 354
Heb 7:26-27 .. 354
Heb 9:14 303
Heb 11:4 304
Heb 11:5 307
Heb 11:6 259
Heb 11:7 309
Heb 11:8-19... 314
Heb 11:22 329
Heb 11:26 ..... 304, 331
Heb 11:32 358
Heb 12:9 258
Heb 12:25 42

James

Jam 1:17... 46, 229
Jam 2:23........ 146

1 Peter

1Pe 1:8........... 263
1Pe 1:10-11.... 359

1Pe 1:18-19....381
1Pe 3:20.145, 309
1Pe 3:19-20....309

2 Peter

2Pe 2:5 309
2Pe 2:6 32
2Pe 2:16 173
2Pe 3:5 27

1 John

1Jn 1:1, 5........153
1Jn 3:4.............245
1Jn 5:7......98, 204
1Jn 5:20..........214

Jude

Jude 4 217
Jude 14-15 307
Jude 25 205

Revelation

Rev 1:4 ......91, 93
Rev 1:7 272
Rev 1:7-8.......234
Rev 1:8 ..210, 227
Rev 1:18 208
Rev 2:23 232
Rev 3:1 93
Rev 4:8 ...93, 233, 378
Rev 5:12 265
Rev 5:6 94
Rev 5:26 225
Rev 6:15-17 ...272
Rev 17:14 224
Rev 19:10 48, 176
Rev 19:13 296
Rev 19:16 224
Rev 22:8, 9 48

Rev 22:9 176, 320
Rev 22:13 ..... 212, 345

Targums

TGen 1 125
TGen 1:1 123
TGen 1:27 ..... 123, 285
TGen 2:8 123
TGen 3:8 285
TGen 3:8-10 ... 123
TGen 3:15 300
TGen 3:22 285
TGen 4:1 301
TGen 4:7 305
TGen 5:24 ..... 123, 306
TGen 6:7 120
TGen 7:16 ..... 123, 145
TGen 8:21 .... 120, 146
TGen 11:8 123
TGen 12:17 124
TGen 15:1 ..... 123, 146
TGen 15:5 146
TGen 15:6 .... 120, 146
TGen 15:7 .... 120, 146
TGen 15:9 120
TGen 15:9ff. .. 146
TGen 15:13 ... 120
TGen 16:13 ... 149
TGen 18:2 124
TGen 19:24 124

TGen 21:20 ... 120, 150
TGen 21:23 120
TGen 21:33 124
TGen 22:8 ..... 124, 148
TGen 22:14 ... 124, 151
TGen 22:16 319
TGen 22:16-17 148
TGen 24:33 124
TGen 26:24, 28 124
TGen 27:28 151
TGen 28:20 152
TGen 28:20-21 .... 152, 285
TGen 30:22 124
TGen 31:3 124
TGen 31:5 151
TGen 35:9 ..... 147, 152
TGen 38:25 124
TGen 39:2-3 .. 120
TGen 46:4 124
TGen 48:10 151
TGen 49:25 ... 124, 147
TGen 50:20 124

TEx 1:21 125
TEx 2:5 125
TEx 3 125
TEx 3:12 121
TEx 3:14 134
TEx 3:14-15 ... 135
TEx 4:12 121, 125
TEx 6:4 135

TEx 6:8 . 125, 146, 149, 150
TEx 12:29 ..... 125, 158
TEx 12:42 ..... 125, 134
TEx 12:43 146
TEx 13:8 125, 158
TEx 13:17 125
TEx 13:18 159
TEx 14:15 159
TEx 14:22 159
TEx 14:24 ..... 159, 163
TEx 14:24, 31 . 126
TEx 14:25 159
TEx 14:32 121
TEx 15:2 121
TEx 15:8 126, 159
TEx 15:10 159
TEx 15:25 ..... 126, 160
TEx 16:8 121, 164
TEx 17:16 164
TEx 18:19 121
TEx 19:3 160
TEx 19:5 126
TEx 19:8 160
TEx 19:9 126, 160
TEx 19:17 ..... 121, 160
TEx 20:1 126, 285
TEx 20:1ff 161
TEx 20:19 161
TEx 20:24 165
TEx 23:20-22 . 126
TEx 25:22 ..... 157, 165, 167
TEx 29:42 ..... 121, 165

TEx 30:36 ..... 121, 157
TEx 30:6121, 165, 167
TEx 31:13, 17 121
TEx 32:13 150
TEx 32:35 169
TEx 33:9 163
TEx 33:9, 11 .. 126
TEx 33:19 126
TEx 33:22 121
TEx 33:23 126
TEx 33:35 126
TEx 34:5 126

TLev 1 126
TLev 8:35 121
TLev 18:30 121
TLev 22:9 121
TLev 23:11 126
TLev 26:11 121
TLev 26:46 166

TNum 7:89 ... 157, 167
TNum 9:8 126
TNum 9:19 121
TNum 9:19, 23 126
TNum10:35 ... 167
TNum 10:35-36 .... 127, 137
TNum 10:36 .. 168
TNum 11:20 . 122, 169, 286
TNum 11:35, 36 136
TNum 12:6 127
TNum 14:9 122
TNum 14:11 .. 122

TNum 14:20 . 127, 170
TNum 14:30 .. 149
TNum 14:41 .. 169
TNum 20:12 .. 122
TNum 20:24 . 121, 122
TNum 21:6 169
TNum 21:6-9 . 127
TNum 22:9 173
TNum 22:18 .. 126
TNum 22:20 .. 173
TNum 22:22 .. 173
TNum 22:31 .. 122
TNum 23 122
TNum 23:4, 16 174
TNum 23:8, 21 168
TNum 25:4 ... 127, 170
TNum 27:16 .. 171

TDt 1:1 .. 127, 159
TDt 1:10 127
TDt 1:26 169
TDt 1:30 122
TDt 1:30, 32 ... 127
TDt 1:32-33 .. 122, 159, 163
TDt 3:2 .. 127, 169
TDt 3:21-22 ... 171
TDt 3:22 122
TDt 4:3 127
TDt 4:7 .. 127, 135
TDt 4:12 127
TDt 4:23-25 ... 127
TDt 4:24 168
TDt 4:33 127, 161
TDt 4:33, 36 .. 122

TDt 4:34 127
TDt 4:36 161
TDt 5 127
TDt 5:23 162
TDt 5:5 .. 122, 161
TDt 6:4 329
TDt 6:13 127
TDt 6:22 127
TDt 8:2-3 122
TDt 9:3 168
TDt 9:23 169
TDt 11:23 127
TDt 12:5 165
TDt 12:5, 11 .. 185
TDt 13:19 122
TDt 15:5 122
TDt 18:16 162
TDt 20:1 122, 158
TDt 21:5 127
TDt 24:18 158
TDt 24:19 168
TDt 26:5 127, 149
TDt 26:14 122
TDt 26:17 166
TDt 26:18 ..... 127, 166
TDt 28 158
TDt 28:1-2 122
TDt 28:15 122
TDt 28:20ff.... 170
TDt 28:45 122
TDt 28:62 122
TDt 28:63 168
TDt 29:1-2 158
TDt 29:22 127
TDt 30:3 170
TDt 30:8, 10 .. 122
TDt 30:9 168
TDt 30:20 122
TDt 31:2-3 171

TDt 31:4........ 171
TDt 31:5........ 171
TDt 31:6........ 171
TDt 31:6, 8.... 122
TDt 31:7 127, 149
TDt 31:7-8 172
TDt 31:23...... 172
TDt 32:36 128,
   170
TDt 32:39 93, 128
TDt 32:49 128
TDt 33:27...... 122
TDt 33:3........ 122
TDt 34:1 128
TDt 34:4 128
TDt 34:5........ 172
TDt 34:5-12... 128
TDt 34:6 135, 147
TDt 34:9........ 173
TDt 34:10...... 157
TDt 34:10-11 135
TDt 34:11...... 158

TJosh 10:14 ... 177
TJosh 23:3 177
TJosh 23:10 ... 177
TJosh 23:13 ... 177

TJdg 6:12-13 . 179
TJdg 6:16....... 178

T2Sam 6:2 137

T1Kg 9 186
T1Kg 9:7 183
T1Kg 19:11-12
   134

T1Ch 13:6 137
T1Ch 29:11 ... 135

T2Chr 32:21 .. 134

TPs 68:11, 18 . 134
TPs 110:5....... 196

TIsa 6:1ff. 188
TIsa 45:17...... 286

TEzek 43:8-9 192

TZech 2:9 193
TZech 2:12 193
TZech 2:13 194
TZech 2:15 194

Apocrypha

1Esd 1:28 113
1Esd 1:47 113
1Esd 1:57 113
1Esd 2:5 107

Tob 5:16 108
Tob 8:6 101

Jdt 5:18 107
Jdt 9:7 106
Jdt 9:8 107
Jdt 16:13-14 ... 101
Jdt 16:14 112

Est 13:15........ 105
Est 13:15-17 . 105

Wis 1:4-7 113
Wis 3:8........... 115
Wis 7:22 103
Wis 7:25 102

Wis 9:1 ... 101, 103
Wis 9:4........... 101
Wis 9:17. 101, 114
Wis 16:12....... 106
Wis 16:8, 12 77
Wis 18:15....... 112
Wis 18:15-16 . 104,
   106
Wis 19:9......... 103

Sir 1:4..... 111, 113
Sir 17:17......... 108
Sir 24:3 102
Sir 24:4 103
Sir 24:8 104
Sir 24:9 111
Sir 24:18 103, 112
Sir 24:23 104
Sir 39:8 114
Sir 45:5 104
Sir 46:5-6 104
Sir 48:24 114
Sir 48:3-5 104
Sir 51:10 103, 114

Eccl 48:22 376

Bar 3:35-37 353
Bar 3:37 .. 115, 374

2Ma 1:25 107
2Ma 2:17 108
2Ma 11:6 109, 115
2Ma 14:35 108
2Ma 15:22-23 . 115
2Ma 15:34, 27 116

Pseudepigrapha

1En 1:9 307

EpJer 6, 7 109

PrAz 36 108

ABOUT THE EDITOR

Doug has pastored the Reformed Baptist Church of Northern Colorado since 2001. He graduated from Bethel College in 1992, majoring in Marketing and minoring in Bible. He was a youth pastor for four years in Denver. He holds the Master of Divinity degree from Denver Seminary (2001).

Doug has served on councils and boards for two Baptist Associations, the current one which he helped found in 2016. The Reformed Baptist Network seeks to glorify God through fellowship and cooperation in fulfilling the Great Commission to the ends of the earth. There are currently 42 churches in this international association of churches.

Doug has co-hosted the radio show Journey's End, the Peeranormal podcast, started the Waters of Creation Publishing Company, owned two small business in Minneapolis, and has appeared on numerous podcasts and radio shows.

Married since 1994, he and Janelle are the proud parents of four beautiful young girls. Born and raised in Colorado, he has climbed all 54 of Colorado's 14,000 ft. mountains and also Mt. Rainier (WA) and Mt. Shasta (CA).

To find out more about any of these things go to:
https://www.dougvandorn.com/

The Church website is
https://rbcnc.com

Books in the Christ In All Scripture Series

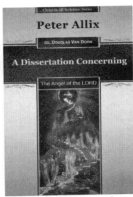

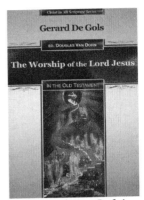

John Owen's treatment is perfect for those wanting to ground their theology of the Angel in the high orthodoxy of the Reformation. The quotations from the Fathers bolster his thesis.

Peter Allix's work is comprehensive and is especially helpful for those familiar with modern scholarship wishing to root their theology in conservative Protestant/Reformed orthodoxy.

Gerard De Gols' study, especially the second half, is imminently practical and would help anyone wanting to learn more about why it matters that Christ is present in the Old Testament.

Owen, Allix, and De Gols together in one volume, minus quotations from the Fathers and Reformers.

The Second Edition of *From the Shadows to the Savior*, it explores even more of the titles given to Christ in the OT than Allix goes into.

Practical sermons are for the further exploration of the fullness of Christ, especially as he is found in the NT.

Other Books by Doug Van Dorn

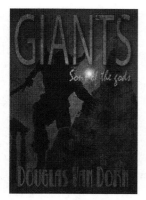

Giants: Sons of the Gods

The bestselling non-fiction book on Genesis 6 and the Nephilim.
150 reviews. 4.5+++ stars on Amazon.

Goliath. You know the story. But why is it in the Bible? Is it just to give us a little moral pick-me-up as we seek to emulate a small shepherd boy who defeated a giant? Have you ever wondered where Goliath came from? Did you know he had brothers, one with 24 fingers and toes? Did you know their ancestry is steeped in unimaginable horror? Genesis 6. The Nephilim. The first few verses of this chapter have long been the speculation of supernatural events that produced demigods and a flood that God used to destroy the whole world. The whole world remembers them. Once upon a time, all Christians knew them. But for many centuries this view was mocked, though it was the only known view at the time of the writing of the New Testament. Today, it is making a resurgence among Bible-believing scholars, and for good reason. The Nephilim were on the earth in those days, and also afterward...

This book delves deep into the dark and ancient recesses of our past to bring you rich treasures long buried. It is a carefully researched, heavily footnoted, and selectively illustrated story of the giants of the Bible. There is more here than meets the eye, much more. Here you will learn the invisible, supernatural storyline of the Bible that is always just beneath the surface, lurking like the spawn of the ancient leviathan. It is a storyline no person can afford to ignore any longer. Unlike other more sensational books on the topic, there is no undue speculation to be found here. The author is a Bible-believing Christian who refuses to use such ideas to tell you the end of the world is drawing nigh. Once you discover the truth about these fantastic creatures, you will come to see the ministry and work of Jesus Christ in a very new and exalting light. Come. Learn the fascinating, sobering, yet true story of real giants who played a significant role in the bible ... and still do so today.

Available in Paperback or Kindle

To order the book go to **https://www.dougvandorn.com/**
or click the picture which will take you to the Amazon page.

The Unseen Realm: Q & A Companion
Edited by Michael Heiser.
Published by Lexham Press.

In *The Unseen Realm*, Dr. Michael S. Heiser unpacked 15 years of research while exploring what the Bible really says about the supernatural world. That book has nearly 900 reviews and a five-star rating. It is a game-changer

Doug helps you further explore *The Unseen Realm* with a fresh perspective and an easy-to-follow format. The book summarizes key concepts and themes from Heiser's book and includes questions aimed at helping you gain a deeper understanding of the biblical author's supernatural worldview.

The format is that of a catechism: A Question followed by the Answer. There are 95 Questions (nod to Martin Luther) divided into 12 Parts:

Part I—God
Part II—The Lesser Gods
Part III—The Sons of God
Part IV—Divine Council
Part V—Sin, Rebellion, and the Fall
Part VI—Rebellion before the flood
Part VII—Rebellion after the flood
Part VIII—The Promise Anticipated
Part IX—The Promise Fulfilled
Part X—The Good News

Available in Paperback or on the Bible-software platform Logos

To order the book go to **https://www.dougvandorn.com/**
or click the picture for the Amazon page or https://www.logos.com/

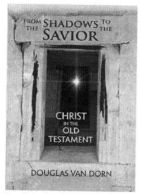

From the Shadows to the Savior:
Christ in the Old Testament

Few subjects are as important--yet ignored or misapplied--as the one addressed in this book. Jesus Christ is the absolute center and focus of the totality of God's word. Many people confess this belief, since Jesus himself taught it (Luke 24:27; John 5:39). Christians have done well to see this on one or two levels, yet truly understanding just how primary he is as an actor—even in the Old Testament—is something few have considered.

In this book, adapted from a series of blog posts for the Decablog, Doug helps us see the light of Christ that emerges from the dark hallways of Scriptures that so many find outdated, unintelligible, and irrelevant for today's Church.

Learn how Christ is found in such things as prophecy, typology, and the law. Then, come in for a deeper study of how the Person himself is actually present, walking, speaking, and acting, beginning in the very first book of the Bible. Learn how words such as "Word," "Name," "Glory," and "Wisdom" are all ideas that the Scripture itself attaches to Christ who in the OT is called The Angel of the LORD. Then see if such ideas don't radically change the way you think about all of God's word in this truly life-changing summary of Christ in the Old Testament.

Chapters:
NT Passages and Reflections
Christ in Prophecy
Christ in Typology
Christ and the Law
Christ: The Angel of the LORD
Christ: The Word of God
Christ: The Name of the LORD
Christ: The Wisdom of God
Christ: The Son of God
Christ: The Glory of God
Christ: The Right Arm of God

Available in Paperback or Kindle

To order the book go to **https://www.dougvandorn.com/**
or click the picture which will take you to the Amazon page.

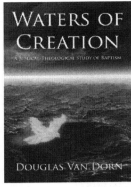

Waters of Creation:
A Biblical-Theological Study of Baptism

This is the one book on baptism that you must read. It was seven years in the making. Doug believes that until a new approach is taken, separations over the meaning, mode, and recipients of baptism will never be bridged.

This new approach traces the roots of baptism deep into the OT Scriptures. When understood properly, we discover that baptism is always the sign that God has used to initiate his people into a new creation. Baptism in the NT is not "new." Rather, it derives its origin from OT predecessors. It has a direct, sacramental counterpart, and it isn't circumcision. It is baptism. When we understand that baptism comes from baptism, especially in its sacramental expression in the priestly covenant, reasons for the NT practice begin to make perfect sense.

Now Baptists have an argument that infant Baptists can finally understand, because we are beginning our argument in the same place. This is an Old Testament covenantal approach to the Baptist position with baptistic conclusions as to the mode and recipients of baptism. That's what happens when we root baptism in baptism rather than circumcision.

Chapters:
The Baptism of Jesus
Baptism and the Sanctuary
Baptism and the Priesthood
Baptism and the Covenant
Implications for Christian Baptism

Available in Paperback or Kindle

To order the book go to **https://www.dougvandorn.com/**
or click the picture which will take you to the Amazon page.

Covenant Theology:
A Reformed Baptist Primer

Covenant theology is often said to be the domain of infant baptists alone. But there really are such things as Reformed Baptists who believe in covenant theology as a basic system for approaching Scripture.

This primer sets out to give the basics of a Reformed Baptist covenant theology and to do so in a way that is understandable to the uninitiated. It was originally a series we did on Sunday nights at our church. It agrees with classical formulations of covenant theology in that there is a Covenant of Redemption, a Covenant of Works, and a Covenant of Grace in the Bible.

Douglas Van Dorn

The book takes a multi-perspective approach to the Covenant of Redemption in that this covenant is the basis for the classic formula that Christ's death is sufficient for all, but efficient for the elect. It sees the Covenant of Works for Adam in a broader context of a covenant made with all of creation, a covenant where laws establish the parameters for creation's existence.

It differs from Paedobaptist covenant theology in that it sees the Covenant of Grace as only properly coming through Jesus Christ. OT gracious covenants are typological of the Covenant of Grace but save people on the basis of the coming work of Christ through faith alone. This is the traditional way Reformed Baptists have articulated the Covenant of Grace.

Finally, it sees an entire covenant in the Old Testament as often (but not always) missing from formulations of covenant theology. In the opinion of the author, this "priestly covenant" is vital to a proper understanding of 1. The continuity of the the practice of baptism from OT to NT, 2. The answer to why we never find infants being baptized in the NT, and 3. A more precise way to parse the legal aspects of the OT economy, thereby helping us understand why the moral law continues today. This volume works from the basic presupposition that continuity in God's word is more basic than discontinuity. In this, it differs from dispensationalism and new covenant theology. The book suggests that this is the greatest strength of covenant theology, which does also recognize discontinuity.

Available in Paperback or Kindle

To order the book go to **https://www.dougvandorn.com/**
or click the picture which will take you to the Amazon page.

Galatians:
A Supernatural Justification

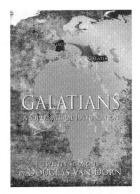

A play on words, the subtitle of this book gives you the two main points it tries to get across. Galatians central message teaches how a person is *justified* before a holy God. This once precious and central teaching of Protestant theology is often misunderstood or relegated the pile of irrelevant, stale doctrine.

Perhaps that is why the Apostle Paul supercharges his teaching with an oft-overlooked side of this letter - the *supernatural* beings who tempt us and teach us to give up the only truth that will save us. Galatian Christians would have been familiar with these supernatural beings; their culture was steeped in it. Thus, they mistake Paul for the messenger-healer god Hermes, and Barnabas for Zeus. Paul's warning: "Even if we or an angel from heaven should preach to you a gospel contrary to the one we preached to you, let him be accursed." This is Paul's fatherly way of showing his children in the faith that the gospel is paramount; it alone is able to save. Such a warning like this can have new power, as people are returning with reckless abandon to the worship of the old gods.

This book is from a series of sermons preached at the Reformed Baptist Church of Northern Colorado in 2011.

Available in Paperback or Kindle

To order the book go to **https://www.dougvandorn.com/** or click the picture which will take you to the Amazon pa

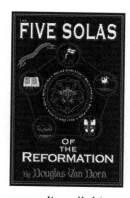

The Five Solas
of the Reformation

The 500th anniversary of the Reformation occurred in 2017. It was October 31, 1517 that Martin Luther nailed his 95 Thesis to the door of the great cathedral at Wittenberg, Germany. He had no idea what that simple act would do. His bold proclamation and challenge to for Rome to reform her ways and beliefs was met with hostility from some and great sympathy from others. Out of this sympathy arose Protestantism, a movement deeply concerned with grounding all things on Holy Scripture, giving glory to God alone, and recovering for that generation the biblical gospel of Jesus Christ. In five chapters, Doug Van Dorn takes us back to these ancient catch-phrases that once moved a continent. Scripture Alone, Grace Alone, Faith Alone, Christ Alone, and To God Be the Glory Alone became the rallying cry of all who longed to see men and women, boys and girls saved and set free from sin, death, and the devil. The end of the book contains four helpful Appendices on songs, Church Fathers on the solas, a bibliography for further research, and a letter from Martin Luther.

Available in Paperback or Kindle

To order the book go to **https://www.dougvandorn.com/**
or click the picture which will take you to the Amazon page.

Made in the USA
San Bernardino, CA
12 July 2020